JOEY'S
LEGACY

SEEKING TRUTH AND INTEGRITY IN VETERINARY MEDICINE

AUTHOR JL ROBB

Energy Concepts Productions books may be ordered through booksellers or by contacting:

Energy Concepts Productions
A Division of Energy Concepts
3328 E Whippoorwill Drive
Duluth, Georgia 30096

ISBN: **9781513678788 Digital**
ISBN: **9781513678795 Hard Cover**
ISBN: **9781513678801 Soft Cover**
Printed in the United States of America

Other Books by JL Robb

The End Part One: And Then The End Will Come

The End Part Two: You Have Been Warned

The End Part Three: Visions and Dreams

The End Part Four: The Disappearance

The End Part Five: The Two Witnesses

The End Part Six: The Third Woe

The End Part Seven: The Ninth of Av

Dedication

This book series is dedicated to our shining star, Joseph Russell Fine, and all of his feline, canine and equine brothers and sisters that met an unexpected fate at the hands of another: veterinarians that committed acts of negligence that resulted in their untimely demise.

May we all see an end to veterinary negligence and the deceitful conduct of some veterinarians in the aftermath.

Joey's Legacy

Seeking Truth And Integrity In Veterinary Medicine

<u>ENDORSEMENT</u>

I cannot believe that it has been a few years since Scott Fine called on me during the very early stages of his founding of Joey's Legacy, and his nonprofit, ground up movement for justice, regarding those "bad actors" Scott refers to, and who are guilty of negligence, malpractice, and/or purposely doctoring and/or altering medical records, in order to hide errors in case workup, case management or clinical judgement. And while I have stated to both grieving clients, and those other professionals involved with Scott's movement, we all are human and make mistakes, and forgiveness is indeed a very important part of the healing process, even in the face of such tragic loss. But when medical professionals go to such extreme measures as to lying, hiding mistakes or altering medical records, then it is my strong view that the tragic passing of these victimized animals does deserve justice. One of the biggest areas of frustrating negligence and malpractice I have seen over many decades of clinical veterinary practice has been the wanton overuse, or inappropriate use of both core and noncore vaccinations in our animal companions. Very often their use provides absolutely no clinical benefit to the animal, and in many cases does both short- and long-term immune system damage. Every medical and veterinary physician has taken an oath on graduation from medical or veterinary school that states, "Above all, do no harm". In my experience, this specific issue is one of the most often overlooked areas of negligence and malpractice in the conventional veterinary profession, especially when administering these vaccinations to chronically ill animals with immune mediated disorders and/or cancers. There is plain and simply no excuse for such practices. In my work with Scott and the grieving clients over the years, I have often found that while the client was pursuing negligence or malpractice for different reasons, that the widespread clinical practice of over vaccination was often the key component in the timeline history of these cases that often triggered or accelerated patient decline. I am proud to be part of Joey's Legacy, both in their quest for accountability of the "bad actors", as well as hopefully working with state legislative bodies in legal reform, relative to characterization of animals as much more than property, in addition to allowing for recovery of more than just property value damage when an animal companion falls victim to negligent or poor medical practice. Ultimately, the goal for all of us in this movement, as well as the entire veterinary profession, should be for all of us to work as hard as we can together, while learning from our errors or mistakes, in providing the most competent and skilled medical care possible. After all, it always should have been about, and hopefully always will be about the health and wellbeing of the animals FIRST.

Michael Dym, VMD.

Dr. Michael Dym is a Presidential Scholar graduate of Cornell University where he earned his Bachelor of Science in Animal Science in 1986.

Dr. Dym received his veterinary degree from the University of Pennsylvania where he was a top graduate. His veterinary degree came from the prestigious University of Pennsylvania where he was a top graduate. Dr. Dym has been treating pets since 1991.

Dr. Dym is one of 250 veterinarians in the United States trained in classical veterinary homeopathy by Richard Pitcairn, DVM, PhD. He is an active member of the Academy of Veterinary Homeopathy and the American Holistic Veterinary Medical Association. He also offers progressive integrative conventional veterinary medicine.

A message from Thomas Nicholl, attorney and veterinarian

I have had the benefit of seeing veterinarian interactions with animals and clients from two different perspectives. The reason for this is that I practiced as a Veterinarian for over 20 years in both the companion animal and equine areas. Then someone I didn't know decided to run a stop sign at about 50 m.p.h. while drunk and try to put his car where mine was. When I came out of hospital about a week later, I was advised to "find something different to do." Therefore, I went to Law School, and have been in practice as an attorney for16 years.

As an attorney, I see a lot of Veterinary malpractice cases (all for the owner of the animal, as all veterinarians are required to carry malpractice insurance, and the respective companies defend them, either by attorneys on staff, or given to a few regularly used outside firms). In SOME cases, there has, indeed, been malpractice – the vet did something below the standard of care which also caused the injury. In ALL cases, the owner is at the very least upset, and perhaps distraught. Even in the cases where there actually was malpractice, a few of these may never progress, but a <u>vast majority</u> of those where there was not malpractice, but the owner is nevertheless (and quite understandably) upset, would not progress if the veterinarian was caring and sympathetic.

Now putting on my Veterinarian hat, I have said, and I know many of my friends have said something similar, "I am sorry about……. I know he/she meant a lot to you. We did everything we could, but unfortunately it just didn't work. Is there anything I can do to help out" Also, when something did go wrong, hopefully not my fault, I would continue to see the animal without charge for that problem, until it was resolved. I'm not making myself to be a saint – I know of many others who do the same. I do know veterinarians who 1) are not perceived to be sympathetic 2) continue to charge full amounts for any conceivable treatment as long as the animal is still alive 3) make a bill dauntingly large (whether intentionally or not), and make a priority of getting paid, sometimes to the detriment of the animal. Although there are some veterinarians who manage well enough on their own, there are their malpractice carriers, who strongly advocate to their client veterinarians 1) admit nothing 2) never apologize 3) never refund any money 4) as soon as you get wind of anything, tell us first, and we will handle it. There is an overwhelming majority of veterinarians who are caring and sympathetic but are also somewhat under the repeated warnings similar to "failure to follow advice may result in us refusing to cover you." I find this a totally unacceptable mandate. Furthermore, some of the adjusters are so obnoxious, any settlement is rendered impossible.

Back to being an attorney. I had one case where the vet. really did mess up, and left the dog on a heating pad, which caused burns so severe that the dog needed many skin grafts.

The veterinarian contacted his malpractice carrier, who I spoke to. When I explained the situation, he said "We are denying the claim because without a skin biopsy, there is no proof that the heating pad caused the burn." I couldn't resist but ask that if the paramedics came to a burning house and pulled out a person in need of treatment, they would not do anything without the results of a biopsy. I had another case where the vet. was a total jerk. However, he was not guilty of malpractice.

Wearing both hats, I see a much greater proliferation of young veterinarians who have a huge student loan debt. (In 1975 there were 13 vet schools in the country – now nearly every state has one, and they usually have over 200 students per year graduating). Because of the plethora of graduates, many of these veterinarians have spent minimal time with an older "mentor," and have set up their own practices. These veterinarians are not like the "old school" vet. many are used to, but instead are younger looking (hey anybody under 40 looks young to me,) are crippled with a vast debt which they must recover to pay both themselves, their loans, and their overhead. As a result, they are stressed, often perceived to be uncaring and money-hungry, and not spending enough time or interacting with patient. Of course., there are some clients who will be dissatisfied regardless of anything.

It's probably hopelessly optimistic, but where possible, it would be helpful to reduce the cost of veterinary education. It is, however, very easy to provide a course (even 1-2 lectures) about client relations. In addition, a letter from the AVMA to the veterinarian insurance carriers explaining to them how difficult their CYA policy makes for good client / veterinarian relationships. You don't have to say, "I'm sorry, I messed up, and as a result your pet died and I'm not going to charge you." But you can say "I'm sorry, I know they meant a lot to you, we did everything we could, but it wasn't enough I know you're upset, but we will take care of the cremation (or something else) as a humanitarian gesture for you. If veterinarians would start to behave like normal people, then I think their previous perception in the public eye can be recovered.

Thomas Nicholl is both an attorney and a Doctor of Veterinary Medicine. He graduated from Veterinary Orlando School in 1975 and has practiced for over 20 years. He also holds a law degree and practices in the Central Florida area. He is a former State of Florida Prosecutor with extensive trial experience and is licensed with the Florida Bar Association as well as being a member of the American Veterinary Medical Association. Dr. Nicholl is originally from Ireland and has resided in the United States since 1975. He enjoys playing golf and has a Black Belt in Martial Arts. His office is located in Orlando, Florida.

FOREWARD

Scott and Debbie Fine
Joey's Legacy

THE FIRST 60 YEARS OF MY LIFE were uneventful with all of my pet companions. All of the veterinarians were caring and compassionate people. Some visits were for vaccinations, some were sick visits, but none were as a result of life-threatening illness or injury. They all lived healthy, happy lives.

It was a different time.

I never experienced, nor heard any others talk about, the subject which is the basis for this book. It was never an issue brought into the public light, as far as I can recall.

The majority of veterinary practitioners today are loving, gentle professionals who entered the profession for the right reasons. They genuinely care about their patients. They want to make sure their patients live happy, healthy lives. They treat their patients like they treat their own loved ones, both human and animal.

There is a minority of veterinary practitioners that choose to follow a different path. Perhaps their practices have been bought by large conglomerates; entities whose bottom line is more important than the proper care of our loved ones. The practitioners, who are now controlled by others, must abide by the demands of their corporate bosses' new policies which often do not consider the welfare of their patients.

Part of this book will contain actual victim stories and photos. Nothing here is enhanced, embellished, or exaggerated for effect. It doesn't have to be. The reality of veterinary malpractice is that it exists. It will always exist because veterinarians are human, just like the rest of us. We accept that. Unexpected things happen to everyone in life. It's part of life.

We want to stop all the lying and deceit these "bad actors" feel is necessary to escape accountability. Ironically, 73% of the members of my Facebook group, Joey's Legacy-VetMal Victims, said that if the practitioner had only been honest with them about the events that led to the death of their pet

companions, they could have eventually found a path to forgiveness, and they wouldn't feel the need for "revenge" by seeking justice through legal action and exposure of the bad actor through social, print and television media. What creates the need for a Joey's Legacy is all of the duplicity and dishonesty these otherwise revered members of a very beloved profession feel compelled to engage in. Maybe one day, there will be a change.
I pray…

JOEY'S LEGACY

It was the summer of 2017 when we lost our shining star, our boy Joey, to whom this book is dedicated. He didn't die as a result of injury or natural causes, like the majority of his sisters and brothers. Joey, our dachshund, was given a drug that was contraindicated for his condition, according to its manufacturer. His condition was unknown at the time because no blood tests were performed to determine organ health. Two days later, we made the impossible decision to put an end to Joey's suffering, and so he was euthanized. We soon learned how many others were lost due to negligence, and so we decided to turn the worst experience of our lives into a place of comfort and solace for other victims of negligence. Joey's Legacy was born.

My vision was to form a non-profit organization that would include veterinary experts and animal law attorneys from around the country. The vets would review medical records and determine if veterinary malpractice occurred. If so, the vet would write an opinion letter that would be forwarded, along with all medical records, to an attorney in the state where the malpractice occurred to pursue legal action.
Simple, right? Not so fast

I contacted a number of vet experts around the country. Most were unwilling to call out their unprincipled colleagues in writing. They contribute to the problem. The "sin of silence". Eventually, I found several vets who liked the idea of a "Joey's Legacy" because they, too, were disgruntled and frustrated with the actions of those practitioners who lacked an ethical and moral compass. They agreed to join our team, on a trial basis. So now I have the first part in place: the vet experts. What about the attorneys?

I contacted a number of animal law attorneys in different states to see what kind of spin they put on my idea. As you might imagine, their responses were similar citing the "pets are property" laws and it wouldn't be economically feasible for them to handle such cases.

Getting nowhere…shot down, over and over again. I wasn't done yet.
One of the victims in our group told me about an attorney that might be interested in what I wanted to do. I contacted her, and she was on board with the idea within a few minutes.

Finally, attorney #1 was on board.

Slowly, we added one attorney after the other and we now have 31 attorneys that can assist members in all 50 states, who work with our 10 veterinary experts to assist our member victims seek justice.

Part of the age-old philosophy of convoluted thinkers like the AVMA and other vet-friendly organizations is trying to convince you that your dog or cat is only worth $100 in court, so suing your vet doesn't make sense. We now know that was part of the indoctrination we all fell for. That's why there were very few attempts to sue veterinarians for negligence. After all, if your potential damages are $100 in court it wouldn't make sense to proceed against a vet.

But Joey's Legacy found a better way in the last three years.

Not only do our attorneys sue for out-of-pocket costs and "replacement value" of your pet companion (still don't know what "replacement value" really means), our attorneys now also may sue for violations of consumer law, deceptive practices and common law fraud . This may include instances like when your veterinarian tells you that there will be someone at the clinic overnight to monitor your pet companion, who just had surgery and......guess what.....nobody will actually be there. Happens more than you know.

Some victims damage awards have since increased substantially from the $100 promised by the veterinary propaganda machine. In fact, some damage awards have reached into the thousands are commonplace. Joey's Legacy has demonstrated, over and over, that if you're a veterinary professional it doesn't pay to lie to one of our members.

THE "GOOD GUYS" IN VETERINARY MEDICINE

All professions have members that are competent at what they do. Let's call them the "good guys". They are ethical, professional, honest, and true. They don't lie, they don't deceive, and they don't play games with their clients. If something goes wrong, they tell the truth. They tell it like it is. They take their medicine, learn from it, and move on. They are professionals in every sense of the word. The same applies to veterinarians. There are 60,000+ veterinarians in small animal practice in the United States. This paragraph applies to most of them. They provide compassionate care for their patients. Pet parents rely on their expertise to ensure a great outcome during a pet visit to the animal hospital. Once in a great while, something unexpected occurs as a result of negligence. Sometimes the vet tech was negligent; perhaps the anesthesia dial was on "5" when it should have been on "2". The patient is overdosed with anesthesia, goes into cardiac arrest, and dies. Nothing done intentionally: just pure negligence. The vet was not present, but he must take the "hit", in most cases, because he is responsible for the actions of his employees. The good guy confronts the pet parent, in what will be a difficult conversation. He/she knows how this situation must be handled: be straightforward, truthful, and transparent no matter how difficult it is. Remorse and contrition must be conveyed in a genuine fashion. Assistance to the pet parent must be offered in the aftermath. The good guy has executed his responsibilities appropriately. The pet parent is now left to deal with grief, despair, shock and presumably anger at the loss of the loved one. If the pet parent decides to take legal action against the vet, the vet must consider it as part of the aftermath that he/she must endure: a relatively small price to pay in light of the emotional turmoil and unnecessary mayhem caused by his animal hospital. However, my experience is that most pet parents in this situation are willing to find a path to forgiveness if the veterinarian was honest about what happened.

THE "BAD ACTORS" AND THEIR PLAYBOOK

Enter the bad actor.

In our group, a bad actor is a veterinarian who is super-motivated by the almighty dollar, someone who is usually a narcissist, is disinterested and insensitive to the needs of his/her clients and their pets and will lie in a heartbeat to protect himself/herself. This is the same misfit that would throw a staff member under the bus to save his/her own ass.

Bad actors are unprincipled misfits. Their depravity knows no bounds. They are trained to admit nothing if they commit negligence. Accountability, responsibility, and liability are words that are non-existent in their vocabularies. They won't think twice about altering medical records, if the pet parent files a complaint with the state board of veterinary medicine, in order to cover up their negligence. Serial offenders, some with a history of disciplinary action that dates back 10 years or more, are sharp enough to begin the process of scrubbing the records right away. The amateurs, those who haven't had an experience with the vet board tend to do nothing, expecting that they are in the clear. Then comes the letter from the vet board, and the race to scrub records begins. Scrubbing records can be done in a variety of ways, like changing lab results to reflect normal values or adding fictitious vital signs to present the appearance of a healthy patient. Just part of their playbook. It is stunning what levels the bad actor will go to in order to protect himself/herself. Nobody is safe, nothing is sacred. The irony of their conduct is that when a death occurs in their care as a result of negligence, they really have little to be concerned about.

Here's why:

1. If the pet parent decides to file a complaint with the vet board, the investigation begins with the vet board sending the veterinarian a letter notifying him/her that the pet parent filed a complaint alleging negligence in the death of their pet companion. The good guy will respond with truth and integrity, sending copies of the deceased's medical records, untouched, unaltered, and appearing as it did after the original vet visit. The good guy responds promptly to any correspondence from the vet board and accepts his punishment. Case closed.

2. The bad actor will typically scrub records after receiving word of the complaint, then respond to the state's request. They contact a defense lawyer, in most cases, to represent them. In reality, they could handle their cases pro-bono since the final order is almost always a joke of a plea deal, constructed well in advance of the final hearing date. For the second and subsequent offenses, while you may think the level of disciplinary action would escalate, in most cases it is the same ineffective discipline as was imposed the first time.

3. Many victims are threatened by the bad actors and their staff, telling them that if they go to the media about what happened, they will be sued. In my experience and opinion, the best defense against being sued is to provide irrefutable facts and pure opinions. Nevertheless, the victims heed the threat and are forced to suffer in silence.

AMERICA'S BOARDS OF VETERINARY MEDICINE-THE ACCOMPLICES THAT DRIVE THE GETAWAY CARS

Let's recap. We have the good guys: veterinarians who entered the profession for the right reasons…NOT for money, but because of a genuine love for animals. These good guys provide great care and compassion for their patients and are truthful and transparent with their clients at all times, regardless of the situation. These are true professionals in every sense of the word. And then, of course, there are the bad actors. If something goes wrong and the patient suffers permanent injury or death, job one is to cover the negligence, deceive the pet parent about what happened, and scrub the medical records to make sure there are no signs of wrongdoing in case the pet caregiver files a complaint with the state veterinary board.

Most complaints are seemingly dismissed by vet boards…statistics show up to 80%. In contrast, Joey's vet team finds malpractice in 70% of the records that are submitted to them by our members.

Why is that?

There is an inherent bias toward forgiveness and leniency by the vet boards toward their "falsely accused" colleagues, so that could explain the massive number dismissals of complaints. A few complaints make it to the probable cause panels of the vet boards, which usually consists of 2-3 board members who screen cases and decide if there is reason to move the case to the next level, which in Florida is the Office of General Counsel. The case then proceeds to a final hearing, although the plea deal outcome is already known. The vet board does have discretion to modify the plea deal and I have seen boards either reduce the recommended sentence or enhance it. First time offenders receive a fine, perhaps a reprimand, continuing education requirements and a period of probation, none of which fazes the average veterinarian:

1. The fine usually isn't much more than an upscale Saturday night out.
2. The reprimand appears on the vet board's public website which most people, even vet mal victims, don't even know exists. It's just

a formal description of what the pet parent writes on Yelp or Google. The difference is they can say whatever they want without fear of reprisal, as opposed to the pet parent who must stick with facts and pure opinions in order to mitigate the risk of being sued for defamation. Of course, any animal hospital that is dumb enough to sue for defamation exposes themselves to a very public lawsuit, which the astute pet parent will exploit to the max by providing all of the tragic details, many of which will not endear the public to the animal hospital. In addition, what pet parent would bring their loved one to a vet that might, one day, sue them?

3. CEUs (continuing education units) are perhaps the most valuable part of the disciplinary action because, as it turns out, education is greatly needed in some cases especially with the vets that have been practicing for 30-40 years who are not up to date on modern veterinary techniques.

4. Probation doesn't impede the vet's ability to generate income. He may practice "under supervision".

Disciplinary action for serial offenders is often the same, or similar, to first time offenders.

Why, you ask?

Think of the vet board members as the drivers of the getaway cars for the bad actors, who commit the negligence and count on the accomplices to help them "escape". Rarely will a veterinarian's license be suspended or revoked. Being that the vet board member is complicit, the act of suspending or revoking a license for something as "insignificant" as negligently causing the death of a pet companion is almost unheard of. They recognize that they can't suspend or revoke on a consistent basis for the same thing because they would be suspending the licenses of dozens of colleagues in their jurisdiction and, you know, that wouldn't do good things for their reputations in the community. However, if you want the reason given to me by one of the consumer advocates on the Florida Board of Veterinary Medicine…this is the official reason: "Who would take care of the dogs and cats if we suspended all of those licenses?"
Spineless cowards.

Even if a pet caregiver proves fraud and deceit to the board, they typically ignore the fact that the bad actor altered medical records to erase the appearance of negligence. Recordkeeping violations by vets, along with practice below the standard of care, are the two most commonly charged violations by the board and the two least deterred by disciplinary action.

The outrageous lack of morals and ethics will continue. The vet boards enact laws to insulate them from legal jeopardy. The veterinary justice system is broken, it's corrupt and is in massive need of reform.

One of the reasons for this book is to educate and enlighten you that vet board exists, the maltreatment of bereaved caregivers is an old story and will sadly continue on and without meaningful, impactful changes I believe this level of injustice will continue. The vet boards allow serial offenders to continue to offend.

It's more than enough to make you vomit.

PREFACE

Dear Bad Actor,

Perhaps you have already heard of *Joey's Legacy*: you may be one of the defendants involved in civil litigation as a result of the groundbreaking work of our animal law team. If you are, you've made mistakes that caused the permanent injury or death of the loved one that lived with our member. You've profoundly impacted a life. The bereaved animal guardian is now overwhelmed with intractable grief, anger and despair caused by your slipshod, "shotgun-style" practice of veterinary medicine. The legal costs that you (your insurance company) incur as a result of your negligence is considered by many bad actors to be just "a cost of doing business", like the electric bill or payroll expenses.

Were your ethics and morals ever respected? If so, what changed you? When did you abandon your professional conduct? Or were you always amoral, devoid of ethics, motivated by the great motivator: the almighty dollar? Was it the influence of a large corporation purchasing your practice, whose primary focus is the bottom line and who has little concern about providing great care for your patients? Do you have a monthly quota to perform 20 ultrasounds or 20 dental cleanings? Maybe you don't have the time to perform these types of procedures yourself, but want to meet such quotas, so you engage your unskilled, untrained office staff to perform veterinary care, many times leading to unexpected, dire consequences.

Did you ever stop to think that providing great care for all your patients would enhance your bottom line, if money is your guiding light, because your satisfied clients would brag about your services to others, who would do the same. Maltreating a patient by engaging unqualified, uneducated staff members invites bad outcomes, and it is your name and reputation that will be sullied by their actions.

Lying about the facts that lead to death is not only unethical and unprincipled, but it also flies in the face of what we all learn as children: that honesty is the best policy. In a recent poll I conducted, 83% of our members declared that if the bad actor involved in the death of their loved one had just been forthcoming about what happened they would not have acted as they did in the aftermath (filing complaints, publicly exposing the bad actor and legal action) and actually would have forgiven practitioner. You alter medical records to try to exonerate yourself. What concerns do you have? Your friends at the Board of Veterinary Medicine will protect you from meaningful disciplinary action. American courts do not provide appropriate justice in veterinary malpractice cases. The nominal settlements, which are typical in these cases, are paid by your insurance company. Even if they increase your malpractice insurance premiums from the average cost of $300 per year by a factor of 10, you can easily absorb the increase by raising your already exorbitant medical fees, which many do. Paying inflated costs for quality veterinary care is one thing; gouging a bereaved pet guardian for euthanasia and cremation costs is outrageous and contemptible. You are no different than retailers that charge $8.00 for a bottle of water when a hurricane approaches, due to short supply. Florida imposes stiff civil penalties for those that gouge the public. As a price gouger, you should be subject to the same treatment.

Are you wondering if I have anything good to say about you? Let not your heart be troubled; here it is:

There is still time to change your shoddy, insensitive behavior. Imagine becoming an ethical professional who is revered by the veterinary community, like the ethical majority of veterinarians in the world: veterinarians who put their patients care first; veterinarians who don't charge for certain services and demonstrate their kindness and consideration for animal guardians and the dire predicaments many find themselves in; veterinarians that cry genuine tears along with the family when the time comes to say good-bye to the family's loved one. Wouldn't you like to join, or rejoin, that highly esteemed, well-regarded part of your industry?

Sadly, most of you will continue your misguided, foolish ways that are motivated by your insatiable greed and sustained by your lack of integrity and conscience.

We don't want to meet you, and you certainly do not want to hear from us. If we hear about you in an unkind way, as a result of alleged mistakes made resulting in permanent injury or death of a beloved family member, rest assured we will investigate and, if warranted, pursue with great vigor and explore any and all legal remedies. Regardless of the outcome, we will become part of your life for a while.

In the past two years, we have assisted over 50 bereaved pet guardians. Our mission and our message continue to be heard all over the world, our membership continues to grow quickly, and with that growth more and more of you will be held accountable for mistakes made. The days of sailing along with no concern about accountability, responsibility and liability will now be replaced with accountability, responsibility and liability.

All we ask is that you treat your patients, our loved ones, with the same dignity and respect that you would hopefully treat your own pet companions, and your human family.

We fight bullies all the time, and we prevail most of the time. Don't be one of those bullies. ABOVE ALL, DO NO HARM. Make $1MM per week if you can, but do it ethically, honestly and professionally, and DO NO HARM.

DO NO HARM

A WORD FROM THE AUTHOR

I first learned of Joey's Legacy last July 2020. I was unaware of the veterinary malpractice issue.

When Scott Fine, the founder of Joey's Legacy, contacted me about his non-profit group, I was in the middle of writing a 3-part trilogy about Abe the Bartender, one of the characters in my series about the last days described by biblical prophets 2000 to 2700 years ago. Abe was the most favorite character. I told Scott I would have to finish the series' first.
I am the proud owner of my sixth Great Dane since 1976. I have had pets my entire life: dogs, cats, rabbits, skunks. My mind started working on me, and Scott was pleasantly persistent.

I have used the same veterinary clinic, Duluth Animal Hospital, since 1985; and they have taken care of all my Great Danes. I have never experienced the loss that the stories in this book series lay out. They are heart-wrenching to say the least, and the tragedy lives on through the poor victims who took their pets to the veterinarian for routine procedures and never saw them alive again. Then the veterinarian doctors the notes and the coverup begins. I am convinced that God made all the animals, domestic and wild, for a purpose; and he classified the animals as domestic and wild in the very first book of the Bible.

On the very same day Noah with his sons, Shem and Ham and Japheth, and Noah's wife and the three wives of his sons entered the ark, they and every wild animal of every kind, and all domestic animals of every kind, and every creeping thing that creeps on the earth, and every bird of every kind—every bird, every winged creature.

Genesis 7:13-14

It was my honor to have a part in Joey's Legacy and this book!
Joey's Legacy-Seeking Truth and Integrity in Veterinary Medicine
www.TheEndtheBook.com

CHAPTER ONE

The world is a dangerous place to live; not because of the people who are evil, but because of the people who don't do anything about it.
                                                            Albert Einstein

A few months ago, a gentleman named George Floyd died in a confrontation with the police in Minneapolis. The police had been called because Mr. Floyd appeared "high on drugs" and was passing counterfeit bills, so it was reported.

Months later, there are still major riots in some of our largest cities, with some metropolitan areas actually commandeered by the rioting anarchists.

Why did this happen?

We hear the answer often: A few bad apples.

Every industry has *a few bad apples,* but city police departments seem to have a few more than other industries; and no one dislikes the bad apples more than the policemen who are good apples. That is the way it is in all industries.

The phrase is first found in the English language in 1340, and the original reads: A rotten apple quickly infects its neighbor.

By the 19th Century, church sermons used a modified version, "As one bad apple spoils the others, so you must show no quarter to sin or sinners."

Actually, the science is sound. Place apples in a group, and when one starts rotting, it quickly infects the others. So can one bad actor taint the entire group? Apparently so.

Studies have been done and a single bad actor does taint the entire group. This is what happened in the George Floyd case; and as a result, dozens of police cars and other vehicles have been burned, buildings have been burned, historical statues have been torn down or defaced, and the beat goes on.

According to a study conducted by premarket.org, a whopping 40% of large police departments are corrupt:

A key strength of our setting is that the average officer writes hundreds of tickets over a several-year period. The high frequency of recorded activity allows us to adapt our empirical approach to estimate the degree of discrimination for each individual officer. Doing so, we find that 40 percent of officers practice discrimination.
While this figure is not the majority of officers, it is hardly a few bad apples.

With all this information available to the public, why do so many bad actors remain in our police departments? How did the FBI end up with so much high-level corruption?

Our police agencies are protected by Police Unions that have great power in expunging the records of the bad apples, and they do. Like the U.S. Congress, full of lawyers who write laws that often enrich and protect other lawyers, the fox is guarding the hen house. And the beat goes on.

Police Unions require that disciplinary records be expunged from a policeman's record, sometimes after only a few months. Even when an abusive policeman is fired, the unions often require that they be hired again. Though police unions decry judges who let criminals out of jail, they do the same thing by protecting the bad actors *from* jail. And then they demand the fired officer get back pay, which we the taxpayer, pay. It is truly a swamp.

What about the bad apples in the medical industry?

In the 1950s, there were few medical malpractice cases, doctors were doctors because of good hearts; and it was not unusual for doctors to make house calls, for $20 or whatever you could afford, maybe a bushel of potatoes. Prior to the 19th century, medical malpractice was unknown to most. You went to the doctor and took your chances, because a lot of things were different then. Doctors were individuals rather than corporate-owned entities.

In the mid-1800s, malpractice suits did increase as doctors tried to repair broken legs rather than amputate. Sometimes the fix left a slightly shortened limb, resulting in a limp, *and* damages. The attorneys achieved income by defending the victim, and the victim began to get the attention of the bad actors and large monetary awards.

As we entered the 1970s, there seemed to suddenly be a plague of narcissism. There was the sexual revolution of the late 1960s, legalized abortion in the 1970s and the corporate takeover of America's hospitals. Good hearts were replaced by the desire to make the big bucks.

According to Johns Hopkins, medical malpractice is the 3rd leading cause of death in the United states, resulting in more than 250,000 deaths per year.

If you are a concert pianist and go to the hospital to have your gangrenous left foot amputated, what if they accidently amputate the left hand? What is your recourse? What is a *fair* settlement? What will your new career be?

Fortunately for we-the-people, malpractice among doctors is nowhere near the 40% of big-city cops.

According to a 2014 report in The New England Journal of Medicine, only 4.8% of doctors account for 50% of malpractice settlement claims. Physicians with 2 or more settlements in 2014: 22.4%.

Human life is certainly a gift from God and should be protected with ultimate care. Negligence, especially negligence that causes loss of life, should have a stiff penalty. Going after the negligent doctor's pocketbook is about your only opportunity.

Most of Americans are pet lovers and look at our pets as a Divine gift also. For whatever reason, God made dogs to love us unconditionally. They live for two reasons: To eat and to please their owner(s). If your house catches fire in the middle of the night, it is unlikely that your cat, rabbit or canary will try to save your life; but it happens every day in the life of dogs.

My personal dealings with veterinarians goes back to 1968. During those 52 years, I have never had an instance of malpractice among the veterinarians who have treated my 5 Great Danes and 3 pet skunks. And the rabbit and chickens. Veterinarians are veterinarians because of their keen, almost obsessive, love of animals. The animal clinic I use for my animal's care, I have been using since 1980. Most veterinarians would never intentionally harm your pet, but sometimes mistakes happen.

In my research into veterinarian malpractice I have read so many sad and tragic cases, heartbreaking cases that were caused by veterinary negligence. A few decades ago, veterinary practices were basically small, mom and pop businesses. Now this is becoming less and less the case as corporations do to the veterinary industry what they did to the hospital industry. They are turning the field into a money machine. Veterinary costs have skyrocketed to the point that many are forgoing the pleasure that pets provide.

The number one emotion I have noticed in all the stories I have read is the anger when the veterinarian lies to them. It happens often, as you will see when you read actual, heart-wrenching stories.

"If the vet had just told me the truth, I would not have sued."

And the beat goes on.

CHAPTER TWO

If having a soul means being able to feel love and loyalty and gratitude, then animals are better off than a lot of humans.

James Herriot

Veterinarians deal with animals daily. Day in and day out, that is what they do; and the large majority do their jobs zealously and professionally.

Their intentions are good, but mistakes do happen. Too much anesthesia, a dropped scalpel severs an intestine, a wrong medication for a cat with kidney disease.

Americans, as a whole, are in love with our four-legged friends, especially dogs and cats. Dogs are unusual among domesticated animals. They are the bearers of unconditional love and seem to exist for one main reason: To please their owner.

According to the American Veterinary Medical Association (AVMA), their data indicates the following (2018):

- Percent of households owning dogs (38.4%), cats (25.4%)
- Number of households owning dogs (48,255,413), cats (31,896,077)
- Average number owned per household: dogs (1.6), cats (1.8)
- Total number in the USA: dogs (76,811,305), cats (58,385,725)

When a dog or cat owner loses their pets at the end of their lives, it is not uncommon to hear them compare the experience to losing a child. The depression suffered is real, long-term and often, intense; but the great joy they bring to your heart and your life makes it worth it. Dogs, after all, are people too.

As an owner of my 6th Great Dane since 1976, I have faced this depressing experience five times. Scarlette died from cancer August 17, 2020; and now we have Princess.

But what if your dog or cat or bird does not die of old age, cancer or CoVid-19? What if your beloved pet does not have the opportunity to bring years of love and happiness to your life, and theirs; because the veterinarian injected your pet with three times the normal anesthesia?

Though rare, anesthesia related deaths happen more than one would expect.

In one article I researched, Cindi, a victim reports in 2012: *My heart is broken and I can't stop crying. Last Thursday my 2-and-a-half-year-old Wheaten Terrier went in for a biopsy and passed away under anesthesia before surgery began.*

In another disgusting case, a family dog went in for surgery and died. The veterinarian told the owner that her dog was so cancer-ridden, she died during surgery. In this case, the owner told the vet that she wanted a necropsy. The veterinarian volunteered to perform the necropsy, but the owner took her dog to another veterinarian. Turns out the dog had no signs of cancer but did have a severed intestine and bled to death. The doctor finally admitted that a scalpel had been dropped into the body cavity.

Twenty years ago, veterinary malpractice was basically a non-issue. The veterinarian would offer a hundred bucks for the dog, and that was it. In the world of settlements, your beloved pet was worth little.

Thanks to organizations like Joey's Legacy, this malpractice injustice is rapidly changing.

Founded in November, 2017, Joey's Legacy has become the malpracticing veterinarian's worst nightmare, as you can see from their web page, JoeysLegacy.org.

The non-profit business was begun by Scott Fine and his wife Debbie, in an effort to comfort and benefit others through the tragedy they suffered when their trusted veterinarian cut a critical corner to save a little time because he thought he knew what was wrong with little Joey, the family dachshund. Since the doctor skipped the lab tests, he did not know that Joey had a kidney disease. As a result, the injection that Joey received was contraindicated for dogs with kidney disease and cost his life. And the happiness of Scott and Debbie

Founded in order to help others to benefit through their personal tragedy, Joey's Legacy has assembled a nationwide team of animal-loving attorneys and some of the top veterinarians in the land. Settlements have grown from $100.00 to settlements in the thousands of dollars. Deservedly so.

Most veterinarians are dedicated to helping animals of any kind, loving their profession more than the almighty dollar. Most is the keyword, here. There are always some bad apples in every group, and crooked veterinarians are not above altering medical records.

The bad apples are the veterinarians that Joey's Legacy pursues, holding them accountable for their malpractice and the grief they bring to so many.

Joey's Legacy is new to me but have done a lot of research on this group. They give the grieving some hope as they pursue the bad actors for retribution via the only way they understand. The pocketbook.

This is a fantastic cause, so if you have a little money lying around and thinking of a good cause to donate to, Joey's Legacy is a non-profit group; and donations are tax-deductible. There are currently more than 1,500 members. Just made a donation myself. I love dogs and cats, and most any animal.

Closing advice: If your veterinarian kills your dog, let someone else do the autopsy.

CHAPTER THREE

A Brief History of Veterinary Medicine

There is no clear record of when veterinary medicine came to be, but it was a long time ago. In Genesis, the very first book of the Bible, there appears to already be a knowledge of genetics, though they did not know what a gene was at that time.

Jacob, however, took fresh-cut branches from poplar, almond and plane trees and made white stripes on them by peeling the bark and exposing the white inner wood of the branches. Then he placed the peeled branches in all the watering troughs, so that they would be directly in front of the flocks when they came to drink. When the flocks were in heat and came to drink, they mated in front of the branches. And they bore young that were streaked or speckled or spotted.

Genesis 30:37-39

The early domestication of animals, believed to have begun 14,000-15,000 years ago, probably resulted in early veterinary care. Man would have quickly learned it was necessary.

Though Europe generally gets credit for the development of veterinary medicine, they only built upon the accomplishments of much more ancient cultures. There is evidence of veterinary practice in ancient Egypt, China, Mesopotamia and India, provided by the physicians of the day.

Veterinarian is an English word meaning anyone who medically services animals. Its origin is Latin, veheri, and was a little more specific than the English definition, referring to anyone providing medical care for any animal that uses a yoke to perform work.

Scholars in the 18th century assumed that Europe was where veterinary medicine originated, but the earliest documented evidence comes from China. There really was no evidence at that time, but archaeology proved otherwise with the discovery of the people of Banpo.

The people of Banpo, like most people during the Neolithic Age, were vegetarians; so they were great farmers. The animals in Banpo Village, located in the Yellow River Valley of China, were found to be domesticated dogs and pigs. Discovered in 1953, the people reigned from 4500-3750 BC.

The villagers had many gods, but Fuxi was known as the domesticator of animals, his particular gift, "the ox-tamer," and clear evidence of domestication was already long established by the time Banpo Village was thriving between 4500-3750 BCE.

Once Fuxi domesticated an animal, he taught mankind how to take care of the animals, including medical care. The first of these documentations of veterinary care in China refer to the care of horses and cattle. The doctors of the time, known as *horse priests,* actually utilized the science of acupuncture to treat colic in horses.

Veterinary medicine with a touch of the divine, was practiced in Mesopotamia by 3000 BC.

Modern-day veterinarians know much more than the discoverers and the early Europeans did about medically caring for animals; and with the advent of pain medications and anesthesia, many animals have been saved... painlessly.

When people have surgery, it is a requirement to talk with the anesthesiologist; because anesthesiology is one of the most dangerous aspects of surgery. To keep us from feeling any pain or discomfort, the anesthesiologist must decipher how much to use in order to get the patient near death but not let him die. Sometimes the anesthesiologist calculates wrongly, and those instances do not turn out well.

When a patient dies or suffers permanent damage for dying at the hands of the anesthesiologist, a medical malpractice usually follows, often with huge monetary awards. The pocketbook is the only way to get a doctor's attention, hoping he will not be so careless in the future. Doctors have malpractice insurance, but it often does not cover the awarded amount. And if the anesthesiologist tries to lie and not take responsibility, making up some answer like the patient died from cancer, the award is usually much higher. Significantly higher.

In the world of veterinary medicine, malpractice was not in the vernacular about 50 years ago. Over the years, the courts have begun to realize that our furbabies are people too.

Thanks to groups like Joey's Legacy and their wonderful membership of victims, top-notch veterinarians and animal-loving attorneys, the veterinary industry is changing.

About time.

CHAPTER FOUR

Pets are people too.

According to *National Geographic*, April 7, 2014, about 90% of owners consider their pets part of the family. More than 80% of us would likely risk our lives for them. Last year, we spent $55 billion on the animals that share our lives.

Dog and cat owners have increased 400% since the 1960s and have now made their way into our justice system. In the last 20 years a lot of laws have passed that consider the "rights" of the pet: The right to be freed from abuse; the right to rescue from natural disasters; the right to legal protection against veterinary malpractice.

An article in *Psychology Today*, October 7, 2015, references a 1980s study by Sandra Barker and Randolph Barker that asked dog owners to complete what is called the Family Life Space Diagram, in which symbols representing family members and dogs are placed within a drawn circle representing one's *life space*.

In nearly 40% of the diagrams, the dog was placed closer to the self than were other family members. Similar studies of pets' placement within a family constellation have similar results: pets are quite often drawn very close to the center—closer even than human family members.

When I was a kid, the dog slept outside in a doghouse or on the porch. Today, over 62% of our pets share our bed. Our pets are now considered part of the family, and we hold great emotional ties to them.

In the world of 2020, a weird world indeed, the constant stress and worry of pandemics, riots, unprecedented hurricanes and fires, our pets offer something that is most difficult to find - unconditional love and dedication. They are here to please.

The American Pet Products Association claims the pet industry has surpassed a whopping $63 billion in spending; and 65% of our households own a pet, which is an increase of 10% from 12 short years ago. These are astonishing numbers that increase every year.

What does this all mean? The average annual cost of owning a pet can be in excess of $2,000, and that is without complications. Additionally, our love affair with our pets is translating into astronomical increases in veterinary spending.

Statistics provided by AVMA, American Veterinary Medical Association, indicate that in 2016 pet owners spent over $44 million dollars taking their animals to the vet. Costs for some procedures rival that of human healthcare.

Common ailments such as joint injuries in dogs can cost around $3,480. Removal of foreign objects ingested can average $1,755. Cancer, which is diagnosed in 12 million pets annually, will set an owner back an average of $2,033. However, if an animal is injured or killed due to veterinarian malpractice, the same animal its owners spent thousands of dollars on for treatment is considered by our judicial system as almost worthless, just a *piece of property.*

We all know the state of medical malpractice in healthcare, but what happens when something goes wrong with the treatment of your beloved pet?

Currently, the majority of courts view pets as personal property and restrict damages to their market value replacement cost, even in the event of proven wrongful death. Until the mid-part of the last century, the term "malpractice" did not even apply to veterinarians (and still does not in some states where the profession is not listed under the malpractice statute).

Recently, however, veterinarians have become subject to state malpractice actions. As the value of animals subject to malpractice actions increases from the traditional "market value" approach, it is expected that the number of malpractice claims will increase. To date, most animal medical malpractice cases are settled outside of court and few have won big settlements or verdicts.

The AVMA does not collect statistics on veterinarian malpractice suits and is against any changes in veterinary malpractice laws.

However, many states are beginning to give recognition to our furbabies as more than a piece of property. As a result, and because of groups like Joey's Legacy, veterinary malpractice awards have jumped from a hundred, insulting bucks to settlements of $5,000 to $139,000. In a recent settlement, the court awarded $39,000 for a companion dog. The veterinarian offered $400.

When looking for a quality, honest veterinarian, do your homework, like you would do if you were having heart surgery. Do not be intimidated by the veterinarian and ask questions.

AVMA PLIT Professional Liability for Veterinarians

When you are accused of professional malpractice, the program will vigorously defend you and pay the costs that you become legally responsible for due to allegations of professional negligence. Coverage automatically extends to veterinary-related activities such as speech making, consulting, clinical instructing, and serving as a member of a licensing or veterinary accreditation board. Limits below are listed as per occurrence / annual aggregate.

II. Summary of Potential Legal Actions

Veterinarians by the nature of their occupation deal with animals on a daily basis and in a variety of contexts. The core of their activities relate to the providing of professional services, which are usually performed to the satisfaction of both the animal and his or her owner. But, invariably some of the interactions do not have the desired outcome. Based upon my research, the veterinarians who have been defendants in lawsuits find themselves confronted with a wide variety of legal claims:

1. **Malpractice.** Discussed in full below.

2. **Res ipsa loquitur.** This is an important alternative cause of action against a veterinarian, as an expert witness is not needed. Some mistakes are so obvious that the average person (the jury) can make an informed judgment without an expert witness.

3. **Administrative Action for Malpractice.** A person may file an action against a veterinarian with the state administrative licensing board that oversees veterinarians.

4. **Negligence.** As discussion below, if the actions in question are not within the realm of malpractice, then there may be legal liability based on common negligence. For example, if a veterinarian was overseeing the loading of a horse into a trailer and did not properly secure the horse, the standard of care is that of negligence.

5. **Gross negligence.** This is the more egregious form of a claim of negligence. If an animal came in for a treatment for fleas, and the veterinarian removed a leg, that would be gross negligence. A claim of gross negligence may support different kinds of damage awards, such as punitive damages or emotional distress for the owner.

6. **Intentional and negligent infliction of emotional distress (on the owner).** This may arise when the actions (against an animal) are intentional and likely to produce a strong reaction in the owner. This is an action in torts which is explained further in the Pet Damages discussion.

7. **Duties of bailee.** When a veterinarian acts as a bailee of an animal (for example when he or she boards pets), then legal liability may arise either out of negligent care of the animal or failure to redeliver the animal to the owner. In one case, an insured veterinarian was bailee of an elephant, who died from poison while in his custody. While his negligence in allowing the animal near poison would normally give rise to liability, the bailor and bailee had signed a release which held the bailee "harmless from any liability in the event of the death of the elephant 'Sparkle.'" A claim based upon a bailment does not require an expert witness and may have the effect of placing the burden of proof upon the veterinarian to explain what happened to the animal.

8. **Violation of a contract obligation.** This may be a useful approach if there is a written contract. However, oral agreements may also constitute a contract. The normal conversation with a veterinarian before rendering services would not constitute an oral contract. A contract claim cannot be based on general statements of reassurance, "I'm sure Fluffy will be better after the operation." Rather, it must be a specific promise to do something or obtain a specific result. In a contracts action, the promise in the contract becomes the standard for conduct, not the general standard of veterinarian care appropriate to the community. There may be a difference in the statute of limitations for filing a contract action (longer) verse tort or malpractice action.

9. **Deceptive trade practices.** However, professional services are often specifically excluded in the statutes that create the cause of action.

10. **Taking.** This may occur when the actions of an agent of the State result in the death of an animal. Only one case has been found to support such a cause of action. It first requires that the veterinarian

be an employee of the State. Secondly, because of some state policy the injury to the animal occurred.

III. Malpractice Distinguished

At common law, and even prior to World War II in the United States, legal claims based upon malpractice did not apply to veterinarians (just doctors and lawyers). The 1936 edition of the legal digest, CJS, has 289 pages of information about animal legal issues but the term "veterinarian" and "malpractice" does not occur anywhere in the material. Since that time, there has been an expansion of the application of the concepts of malpractice to include veterinarians. This has been done by judicial rule and by the adoption of new legislation. In understanding the scope of a claim based on malpractice, it must first be distinguished from an action based upon negligence. An action is properly based in malpractice if the acts or omissions at issue involve matters of medical science or require special skills not ordinarily possessed by lay people. When an injury occurs as a result of something that would be considered within the professional knowledge of the individual who holds him or herself out as a veterinarian, the legal cause of action will be classified as one based in malpractice. Some state law provides help in discerning which issues are professional by listing those actions for which an individual must have a state issued veterinarian license.

When a veterinarian is acting in other than his or her professional capacity, the normal negligence standard is used. For example, if a veterinarian performs surgery on a horse, the surgery shall be judged under malpractice standards, but if a veterinarian is arranging for the transportation of a horse by trailer, the reasonable person standard applies, since the activity is not within the bounds of his professional knowledge or skill. Likewise, if a veterinarian provides boarding facilities for healthy animals, then he or she would be judged under the same negligence standard as would any other bailee of an animal. Sometimes humans are injured in the offices of veterinarian. In one case, an injury to a worker in a human society shelter was found not to support an action in malpractice. As a veterinarian has a professional duty only to his or her animal patients, an action for injury to a human will be based upon negligence not malpractice. In another case, the court held that the disposing of an animal's body was not within professional standards and therefore only an action in negligence might be supported by the facts.

IV. Malpractice Generally

For a plaintiff (animal owner) to recover damages for injury to an animal, in an action based on malpractice, all the following elements must be proven by the plaintiff

(1) The defendant was under a duty of care toward the animal in question. The veterinarian had accepted the responsibility to treat the animal.

(2) The actions or nonactions of the veterinarian did not conform to the professional standard of conduct.

(3) The failure to conform to the professional standard was the proximate cause of the injury or harm at issue.

(4) The injury or harm resulted in damages to the plaintiff (not just the animal in question.

Veterinarians are under no legal duty to treat an ill or injured animal. The decision whether or not to provide a service is an individual decision. A decision to not provide treatment is not malpractice. One case suggests, however, that professional ethics may require some level of attention in emergency situations, but this does not give rise to a legal cause of action. Once the decision to treat an animal is made, the veterinarian has a duty to continue to treat or at least inform the owner of his or her decision to stop treatment of the animal in question.

To lose your beloved pet to malpractice is bad enough; but the veterinary coverup makes it all worse. People make mistakes. Just own up to it.

The following stories are real and most are verified via correspondence, court records, veterinary analyses and legal documentation. Many of these owner-victims will never be the same, and their stories are heart-wrenching.

CHAPTER FIVE

Zach's Story
Maryann and Jon Porter

We are filing a complaint against the Veterinary practice Noah's Ark at 44 Mill Plain Road in Danbury, CT due to negligence in the death of our dog. Please see what occurred below:

We have two dogs-Zeke and Zach. They are 10-year-old Yorkies who we got from a breeder in North Carolina. They are brothers and are inseparable.

A few months ago, we decided to change our vet to Noah's Ark at 44 Mill Plain Road in Danbury, CT, closer to where we live. We brought Zeke and Zach to Dr. Pia Hiekkaranta at Noah's Ark on Thursday May 9th for an exam. She recommended teeth cleaning for both dogs. We both did not feel comfortable getting their teeth cleaned. Dr. Pia Hiekkaranta said it was a larger risk not getting their teeth cleaned as it could lead to heart issues. We made an appointment to bring both of our dogs, Zeke and Zach to Noah's Ark to have their teeth cleaned by Dr. Pia Hiekkaranta on July 5th. The day before, my wife told me she did not want Zeke's teeth cleaned due to his numerous health issues. Although Dr. Pia Hiekkaranta felt it was not a risk, my wife did not feel comfortable doing it. I left a message on Thursday with the office that we would only be bringing Zach in.

I brought Zach into the office at 8:30 am on Friday July 5th. I filled out the form on Zach. I told the person at the desk that we did not want to get Zeke's teeth done due to his illness. I also told her I had put Zeke back on his medicine prescribed by Bethel Vet. Dr. Hiekkaranta had told us at the first visit in May to take Zeke off of the medicine he had been on for 6 years for Chiara Malformation. We had taken him off and he started to have issues with his walking. We put him back on.

Dr. Hiekkaranta called me at 10 am. She was confused what dog she had. She told me she contacted a neurologist this morning and found out the anesthesia she was going to use on Zeke would have put pressure on his brain. The neurologist told her to use a different anesthesia, so she said she was all set. I told her she doesn't have Zeke, she has Zach and if she looked at the form, she would see that.

I called the office at 12:26 to ask how Zach was. The person I spoke to said, "he's so cute and doing fine".

Dr. Pia Hiekkaranta called me at 12:49 and said it looks like he has 14 teeth that might have to come out.

I called the office at 3:59 to see what was happening as we hadn't heard anything. The people that I spoke to put me on hold and came back and said "he's up; you can come and pick him up at 5:00"

At 4:50 I went to the vet's office. I sat in the waiting room for 20 minutes. While I waited, they called two other customers before me. I was then put in a room in the back. I thought I heard Zach barking (he doesn't usually bark) and it sounded like he was in distress. I opened the door to see someone and spoke with an employee in the hall. I asked her if that was Zach and was he alright. She stated, "Yes, he's just coming out of the anesthesia"

I opened the door again as I was concerned, I was hearing Zach. At that point I saw the doctor who said she would be a minute.

In total between the front and back, I waited 40 minutes.

When the doctor came in the room, she started telling me about Zach's teeth. She said he lost 19 teeth and was describing what the teeth looked like. She brought the teeth in and they were bloody. She asked if I wanted to keep them. She described having to cut two of the teeth out. As she continued to talk about his teeth, I asked her, "Is that Zach I hear? He sounds distressed". She then stated there was a problem. The anesthesia was on 2 which was correct. She showed me the log and it showed it on 2 six to seven times. She then said Zach's tongue turned blue and he had no heartbeat. She proceeded to do chest compressions while another person worked on his mouth. She looked at the anesthesia and it was turned up to 5. She said to me "I asked who did this and no one fessed up". She told me I should bring Zach to a hospital "to be monitored". I said to her "What are you talking about? Please bring my dog in! "She brought Zach in and I was beside myself.

Zach's one eye was completely white. His other eye was rolled back in his head. His head was pulled back, his mouth open and he was barking and crying and looked like he was in a constant seizure state. His legs looked all distended. None of his legs could hold him. He was completely non-responsive.

I called my wife and told her we had a big problem and had to bring Zach to the hospital. My wife came to the vet's office and upon seeing me crying and Zach's condition screamed to see the vet. She was absolutely hysterical. The woman at the front desk said to her "You need to bring your dog to the hospital. You can come back and scream at us tomorrow".

My wife drove myself and Zach to the hospital. It took 20 minutes, and it was horrific. The entire time Zach was doing this horrible bark/cry. He appeared to be in distress. He was having a seizure every second. We both talked to him and petted him. We were absolutely terrified. We were both crying but kept saying to each other to stop so he could not hear us. We arrived at the hospital only to find Noah's Ark had not even called them to let them know we were coming. Zach was brought into the back immediately while I explained what had happened. The woman at the desk had to call Noah's Ark to get the details of what had happened and have them fax the information. After 20 minutes, the doctor came out and told us he was in critical condition. She said he had not had oxygen to his brain, so he probably has brain damage. She felt he had had a massive stroke. She told us one of his lungs was collapsed and they were filled up with fluid. She showed us the x-rays of his collapsed lung that was filled with fluid and his swollen brain. She told us they had to give Zach naloxone due to Noah's Ark giving him a painkiller. She said we should go in to see him. I could barely walk and both my wife and I were hysterical. He was in a glass cage lying on his side. He was exactly in the same state as when we saw him at the vet's office. He was in complete distress. He was still making the barking/crying noise and was having constant seizures. I put my hand in the hole in the cage and pet him. He urinated all over himself. We were told by the hospital we should leave him there and they would see how he did. They were not hopeful as to what the outcome would be. We drove home in shock and we were hysterical. One hour after getting home I got a call that he had passed away. The hospital doctor told me Zach started bleeding from his nose and mouth. She said he was defecating blood. She said his whole body just gave up.

No one from Noah's Ark called on Friday. The Medical Director, Dr. Jeffrey Hubsher.

Called on Saturday at 1:00 pm and left a message (we have the voice mail). His message stated he was not there and was not 100% sure what had happened. He heard there was an anesthesia problem and it's going to be thoroughly investigated. He also said he was not the owner and was not in a position to tell us what financial responsibilities he could do. He ended saying sorry for your loss.

Dr. Pia Hiekkaranta called on Saturday at 3:30 and also left a message. She said, "I'm sorry, that is all that I can say".

On Sunday my wife and I spoke to Dr. Hubsher

He said he was so sorry what had happened. He stated he was not there but was told some of what happened. I filled him in on what I knew. I told him what Dr. Pia Hiekkaranta had told me regarding someone changing the anesthesia and no one "fessed up". I also told him they told me at 4:00 to come at 5:00 as he was up and doing well. I explained the entire horrible story.   He stated he would do a full investigation. He said he would get back to us in a few days.

On Thursday July 11th, my wife and I spoke together with Dr. Hubsher
He told us he had done a full investigation, and this is what he found:
He stated "human error caused his death"
He said the anesthesia was turned up to 5 when it should have been on two and "they did not look and did not see it"
Also said "By the time they saw it, Zachary had passed".
Repeated "no one saw it".

He said Dr. Pia Hiekkaranta is "shell shocked" He said when he spoke to her, she said "This has never happened in 30 years and I wasn't prepared".
Also said "I wasn't doing rational things".
Then said, "To make matters worse, Pia should have called you".
He said in his opinion it did not make sense how it was handled after the "human error".

He also said, "She did not make the right decision".
My wife asked Dr:

"What have you done now? How can we feel comfortable that no dog will ever go through what our dog went through?"

This is how he responded:

"Dr. Pia Hiekkaranta is "Positive she won't make the same decision again".
He is: "Putting protocols in place".

He gave some examples:

If anesthesia is put on 5 again, someone will be stationed next to it and call it out.

They are purchasing more monitoring equipment including some kind of stethoscope (we were not clear on what kind he said)
He is talking with the team about protocol going forward in terms of calling the pet's owner when making decisions.
He stated he is talking to both staffs in his two clinics.

My wife said to him she still does not understand why they could make such a mistake and then not call us, call at 4:00 and tell us the dog is fine, and then let me sit in the office for 40 minutes before finally showing me our dog. He said there is no excuse it was wrong. He stated Dr. Pia "wanted to tell us face to face". My wife stated this is not true as Dr. Pia spoke to me about Zach's teeth and did not even tell me there was an issue until after I asked why Zach sounded the way he did. He also stated he believes everyone waited to contact us to see if Zach would "get better".

It is both my wife's and my opinion, our beautiful dog Zach died due to repeated negligence on the part of Noah's Ark and their staff. Negligence from the anesthesia being on more than double what it should have been and no one noticing, to no one calling myself or my wife at the time our dog died on their table. Negligence from no one bringing him to an emergency hospital in their animal transport vans, to telling us at 4:00 we are good to pick him up at 5:00, to not calling us immediately to bring him to the hospital, to me waiting in their waiting room for 40 minutes, to Dr. Pia still not immediately telling me what happened when I did arrive. The negligence goes on from the beginning to the end and Zach lost his life due to it.

Zeke and Zach

CHAPTER SIX

Princess' Story
Heidi Wise

The story of Princess the diminutive 3-lb Pomeranian.

7 years ago, I brought home the most precious little angel named Princess. She was one year old at the time I brought her home. When I picked her up, for the first time, she immediately cuddled in my arms and I knew I had just become the owner of an incredibly sweet and loving dog. Princess was a diminutive 3lb Pomeranian, very dainty and delicate. Her tongue stuck out, just a little bit, because she did not have her front teeth, making her all the more endearing to me and everyone who met her. In addition to her adorable appearance, Princess was the sweetest dog anyone has ever met. She would lay in my arms, or anyone's arms, like a baby. She was so trusting. Everyone who met Princess fell in love with her. She was the kind of dog who was content no matter the situation. She was very easy going; never difficult. She was just an incredibly gentle and loving soul and we went everywhere together. Additionally, Princess did work in tv and film and had been on many tv shows such as The Blacklist and Blue Bloods.
On July 28th of 2017 Princess was having some labored breathing. I rushed her to Blue Pearl Animal hospital, in Paramus, NJ, on the recommendation of my veterinarian, who was closing for the day, so could not see her. Blue Pearl is a chain of emergency animal hospitals that have opened up around the country and are corporate owned by the candy company Mars.

Princess was diagnosed with pneumonia and pulmonary hypertension. Both very serious. The cardiologist ordered two medications to be given immediately, but only one was given and even then not until 5 hours had passed. Subsequent discussions with an expert witness revealed she was also given the highest recommended dose of the medication instead of starting low and titrating up! The expert believed this could have been a contributing factor in her death. The antibiotic was never given at all.

Princess's lungs filled up with fluid and she went into respiratory arrest and died from pneumonia. Blue Pearl gave her back to me with blood all over the front of her and did not even clean her up. This was so horrific and heartbreaking for me to see my precious Princess this way. While the vet techs were performing CPR on Princess the vet techs said some very ugly things to me which only compounded my unbearable pain and grief.

Since the death of my beloved Princess Blue Pearl has refused to give back her special pink blanket with her name embroidered on it. I have picketed Blue Pearl only to have the administrator of Blue Pearl come out and yell at me. Another employee came outside and laughed at me after reading my sign about my dead dog asking Blue Pearl to do the right thing. I found Blue Pearl, their employees, and Dr's. to be extremely callous and inhumane to both my dog and I. I have nightmares about Princess's death now and keep reliving the horror of what happened to her and the callousness with which we were treated. I could barely eat for months.

What can be done to stop callous inhumane, incompetent places like Blue Pearl, who are corporate owned leading to apathy, and worse, towards owners and their pets? Why would they behave in such a callous manner to such a vulnerable precious diminutive, trusting dog, and her owner? How could the medication not have been given immediately per the doctor's orders? How could they allow such a terrible tragedy to happen? How can they not do the right thing, by owners and their beloved companions? Why are all the local vets, and vets all over the country, referring to Blue Pearl? There are over 100 complaints about Blue Pearl, of a similar nature, on various online review sites and more come in with each passing day.

The pain that these pet owners are now experiencing, I believe, could have been mitigated had Blue Pearl and their employees shown kindness and empathy towards them. I just wish our local vets would see our pets when we have an emergency. They used to do that before the big corporate hospitals started opening.

What happened to Princess did not have to happen. She was only **8 years** young and had many years of life ahead of her. My heart will be forever broken and the pain of this tragedy unbearable.

Pet owners need to pressure our legislators to break up these inhumane corporate monopolies that have no place in the caring professions. They have conflicting allegiances, and our pets care will never be their first priority. Their allegiance is to their stockholders.

For the wellbeing of the pets, Coddled Creatures, LLC

CHAPTER SEVEN

Mia's Story
Debra Lombardo

Mia's story should be about a spunky five-pound Yorkie with a huge personality. I should be sharing stories of her quirky ways, sassy attitude and loving spirit; those beautiful memories have been overshadowed by her senseless death and her final moments will forever be etched in my memory. Mia died 6/19/2020, she was 11 years old.

Instead, Mia's story is about broken trust, lies, upselling, greed and negligence.

Mia's story begins with a dental consultation at Long Island Veterinary Specialists (LIVS). Mia had a malformation called Atlanto Occipital Overlap (AOO). I scheduled a consultation with Dr. Catherine Loughin, a board-certified surgeon. She had performed surgery on another dog of mine, and I have read some articles that she co-authored on AOO. Her credentials are impressive, she is a founding member of the Canine Chiari Institute and serves on the board of directors of the Bobby Jones Chiari & Syringomyelia Foundation and is the director of research and education and of general and resident internships and serves as the surgical resident advisor at LIVS.

The consultation was on 5/18/2020. COVID restrictions prevented me from going inside with Mia. I waited in my car for the phone call from Dr. Loughin. We discussed the condition of Mia's teeth and it was determined that Mia would need a dental with extractions. She mentioned that although Mia had a soft palate, she was not concerned about anesthesia, since Mia had previously tolerated it without any issues. I was provided with a treatment plan and an estimate and was told that I could schedule when ready. I was not comfortable with the COVID restrictions that were in place and decided to hold off on the dental. I quickly reviewed the estimate which was the low price of $1,759.00 and the high price of $2,211.50 but did not review the treatment plan or consent until after Mia's death.

On 6/2/2020, two weeks after the dental consultation, Mia had a medical emergency. Mia was struggling to breathe, she had bubbles and mucus coming out of her nostrils. I rushed her to LIVS where she was promptly admitted. Mia was examined by the ER veterinarian who I will call Dr. K. They ran bloodwork, x-rays and an abdominal ultrasound. The diagnostic tests did not determine a definitive cause for Mia's episode. Dr. K suspected that Mia had aspiration pneumonia and although it did not show up on the x-ray, she explained it could take up to 48 hours for aspiration to be evident. She told me that Mia was being treated medically as though she had aspirated and repeating the x-ray was not necessary. The plan was to hospitalize Mia overnight, monitor her condition and provide supportive care. If her condition improved, they would consider discharging her home for continued monitoring. If she continued to exhibit upper respiratory congestion, further evaluation with LIVS surgery department could be considered. The cost for the diagnostic tests and overnight stay was $2,848.00.

The following morning Mia was transferred to the surgery department and into Dr. Loughins care. She called me in the morning and said that Mia did well overnight but had not eaten. She did not want to release Mia until she ate. I told her that Mia was trained to not accept food from strangers and if she looked at Mia's records from past hospitalizations, she would see that Mia never ate while hospitalized. She still wanted Mia stay overnight and did not want to release her until she ate. She also wanted me to consider a CT head-thorax and dental. Mia stayed overnight and although she did not eat, she was released the following day. The cost of the overnight stay was $900.00. Mia was to be monitored at home and it was recommended that Mia return in two weeks for a follow up.

Mia continued to do well at home and on 6/18/2020 I brought her to LIVS for a follow up appointment. COVID restrictions were still in place, Mia was handed over to a vet tech and I was instructed to stay in the car and wait for the doctor to call. The first call I received was from a surgery resident who works with Dr. Loughin. I gave him an update on Mia, telling him that she was doing great at home, but had started coughing the day before. I mentioned to him that I suspected it to be an allergy to a new kibble, more specifically food mites. Mia had severe allergies and she had developed a cough to allergens in the past and records at LIVS should reflect the same.

A few minutes afterwards, I received a call from Dr. Loughin. She didn't mention examining Mia, instead she strongly suggested that Mia have a CT scan so that she can see what was going on in the head and nasal area and if everything looked good, she would proceed with the dental.

I was very hesitant, and in hindsight, I should have went with my gut instinct. I addressed my concerns with Dr. Loughin, specifically I was concerned that it was too soon to put Mia under anesthesia, since she aspirated two weeks prior. She assured me that it was okay and that she highly recommended that we do the test. She told me that Mia's heart and lungs were good, and she would be examined before the procedure. She wanted to do the test the following day and she was willing to keep Mia overnight at no charge. A few minutes later, her assistant came out to my car and provided me with an estimate, credit card approval form and two blank pages that each had a spot for a signature. The cost for this procedure was $3,110.00. I signed the estimate and the credit card form and gave them back to the her. She asked me to sign the other blank pages and without questioning her, I signed them. I am assuming that those pages would later be put in Mia's file and used as a consent.

Mia was still inside the building and COVID restrictions prevented me from going inside to say good-bye and to tell her that I loved her. The vet tech told me not to worry, they would take good care of her and I could call later in the evening to check on her. I never saw Mia alive again.

J.L. Robb

The following morning around 9:30 am, I received a call from a surgery resident. He wanted to let me know that Mia was doing well and due to late night emergencies, Mia's scan was pushed back to later in the day. He told me that I shouldn't worry, no news is good news, and I would receive a call when she was done.

I anxiously awaited for the phone call and at 12:30 Dr. Loughin called and she simply said Mia's heart stopped. I went silent, I heard what she said, but my brain couldn't process her statement. She went on to say that "they" were trying to resuscitate her and she would call me back in 15 minutes.

I didn't wait for her phone call. I headed directly to the hospital and was there within 10 minutes. At that point, I could care less about their COVID restrictions and went directly into the building and requested to speak with Dr. Loughin. I was told that she was doing a procedure and she would be with me when she was done. They allowed me to wait for her in a private room, I called my husband and asked him to come in and wait with me. We waited about 15 minutes. It struck me as odd that she would be performing a procedure 10 minutes after my dog died.

I asked her what happened, and she told me that she didn't know. She said her heart stopped while going through the scan. She tried to comfort me by telling me that "the girl" was holding Mia the entire time and Mia was not alone and CPR was performed immediately. None of this made any sense to me. I pressed her for more specificity, telling her that I needed to understand what happened and I needed closure. She said Mia may have had a bad heart and then rambled on about black specs on Mia's brain and a possible mass in her throat. I asked more questions, then she quickly retracted the statement saying that she wasn't a radiologist and really had no idea what the specs were.

I asked more questions about the timeline of events, the anesthesia and if she was present. She said Mia was only given a small dose of propofol and she personally administered it. As to the timeline, I did not find her answers to be satisfactory and got the feeling that she was not present for Mia's procedure. She told me she would get back to me when she received the radiologists report.

Her assistant came into the room, filled out the paperwork for the disposal of Mia's remains and said that she would adjust the bill, remove the charges for services not performed and I should receive a credit in a couple of days. This struck me as insensitive and the reality hit me, this was just a business transaction that went bad. After the paperwork was completed, Mia's lifeless body was brought to me, so that I could say my final goodbye.

Later in the day, Dr. Loughin called. She received the radiologists report, and it didn't provide any answers as to why Mia's heart stopped. I asked her about the black specs and the mass, and she said the report confirmed it to be air. I wanted an answer, I needed to know what caused her death. I pressed her again and she said it could have been Mia's heart or a reaction to the contrast dye. I asked if Mia's heart was checked before the procedure and she said it was. I then said to her, maybe Mia shouldn't have had the test, it was not medically necessary, and it killed her. Her response was, she was going to die anyway. I was shocked at the response and said maybe she would have died, but not today.

I asked her about doing a necropsy and she said that she did not recommend it and said that I would have to bring my dog's remains to a veterinary college, the closest being Cornell, which is 300 miles away. I still trusted her and believed her and based on her comments, I did not pursue a necropsy. I have since called Cornell and was told that typically the hospital would send the remains.

That day was an emotional rollercoaster. My husband and I were grieving; our dogs and cats sensed our grief; our happy home was filled with sadness. I decided for the sake and well-being of my other pets, I was going to try my best to move forward.

The following day I made the final arrangements for Mia's remains, feeling emotional numbness, it was surreal. I continued on my moving forward mission and called LIVS to get Mia's medical records and a final invoice. I wanted to submit the bill and records to the insurance company and be done with the business side of death.

The weekend had past, and I still did not receive the medical records and final invoice. Typically, in the past, I received records upon request, and this was highly unusual. I emailed Dr. Loughin's assistant and requested the records and invoice again. She told me that she was out that day but would make sure that my request was taken care of. It took several days of emails and phone calls to finally get Mia's records and my credit charge back of $1,234.55. I asked why it took so long to get the records and was told that Dr. Loughin had to approve the records to be released.

I emailed the records and invoice to the insurance company and then placed them in Mia's folder. I didn't want to look at them, I couldn't relive the horror, but I had this nagging feeling telling me that I needed to look at them, not for me, but for Mia.

The first record that I looked at was from 6/19, the day Mia died. It stated that an oral exam was performed and reviewed bloodwork from 6/2. It further stated, after CT scan was done, Mia was in acute cardiopulmonary arrest that was not responsive to CPR. The postmortem study stated, "no cause for cardiopulmonary arrest is identified, no cause for acute coughing is apparent, the lungs appear normal, the nasal cavities are also unremarkable, with no cause for prior nasal discharge, based on CT report and patient history, highly suspicious for heart related incident but cannot rule out fatal reaction to contrast".

After reading this, I had so many questions. Why wasn't a CBC and chemistry done? Why would she rely on bloodwork from 6/2? What patient history made her highly suspicious for a heart related incident? Why did she use contrast dye on a dog with severe and documented allergies?

I reviewed Mia's records from past surgeries and MRI, all performed by different veterinarians from LIVS. They all conducted a CBC and chemistry before putting her under anesthesia and I don't understand why it was not done this time. This prompted me to review records of my other dog, Dr. Loughin preformed a CT scan on him, 2 years prior. Just like Mia, he also did not have blood or chemistry testing prior to the test, sadly he died two weeks after his scan.

As to Mia's heart. An x-ray performed in January 2016 noted that she had mild left atria enlargement, she had another x-ray April 2018 that noted cardiovascular structure normal, Cardiopet proBNP tests were conducted by Idexx on 9/16/2018, 12/29/2018, 8/27/2019 and 1/21/2020 all showed results were within normal limits and clinically significant heart disease is unlikely at this time. Mia's final x-ray on 6/4/2020 showed cardiac silhouette mildly enlarged, mild cardiomegaly maybe artefactual due to lack of full inspiratory effort especially as there are no auscultable abnormal heart sounds. Additionally, Mia was seen monthly, sometimes more by an integrative veterinarian at LIVS, and at no time was Mia treated for a heart condition.

I found it highly suspect that so much emphasis was on Mia's heart. When Dr. Loughin initially called, she said Mia's heart stopped, when I met with her in person, she stated that Mia may have had a bad heart and on our final phone call she said the radiologist report stated that it could have been Mia's heart or the contrast dye, she failed to say fatal reaction to contrast. Why did she detract from the fatal reaction to contrast? Was it because Mia had severe allergies that were well documented? Was it because I was not told that a contrast dye would be administered? Or was it because I was not made aware of any risks associated with contrast dye? I will never know. All I know is Mia didn't need that test and Mia didn't have to die.

I continued to search for answers carefully reviewing Mia's records, starting with the dental consultation. What I found stunned and angered me.

The dental consultation on 5/18/2020: I received an estimate and consent. The consent stated, I have been made aware of the risks associates with anesthesia and surgery, including but not limited to infection, dehiscence, and the need for further therapy, bleeding, suture reaction, and cosmetic changes. All of my questions have been answered to my satisfaction and I have approved the treatment plan.

I received the medical records for the dental consultation after Mia passed. The disclosure and consent on the medical record was different from the treatment plan. The newly revised record stated, "the owner is aware of the risks associated with anesthesia and surgery (infection, dehiscence and possible jaw fracture due to extensive disease and death) and have elected to call to schedule". The medical record added possible jaw fracture due to extensive disease and death.

The medical record for the CT scan and dental dated 6/18/2020, had a disclosure that stated, "the owners are aware of the risks associated with anesthesia and surgery (infection, dehiscence, the need for further therapy, bleeding suture reaction, cardiac and respiratory arrest) and have elected to proceed tomorrow with Dr. Loughin".

The discrepancies were upsetting. The consent on the dental estimate omitted possible jaw fracture and death. Those were two very important risks that I should have been made aware. Were they were added to Mia's record after her death? The medical record for the CT and dental included cardiac and respiratory arrest but omitted possible jaw fracture and death. It didn't make any sense to me, if Mia had a dental only, she was at risk for jaw fracture and death, but if she had a CT and dental, she was no longer at risk for jaw fracture and her the manner of death was predicted to be by cardiac and respiratory arrest.

I believe the medical records were changed after Mia's passing and were specifically tailored to fit a narrative and that narrative was a heart condition.

Mia's medical chart was never updated to reflect her current primary vet, instead it listed a vet that I haven't used in years. When Mia died, Dr. Loughin told me that she would send a report to Mia's primary vet. I informed her that the chart was outdated, and Mia's primary vet was now Dr. Selmer, her co-worker. She looked surprised and, in my opinion, relieved. She told me that she would let Dr. Selmer know of Mia's passing and she would forward her report to him.

I expected to hear from Dr. Selmer, as a professional courtesy. After all, he had been treating Mia since March 2018 and I spent $39,445.26 on her care with him. I received a generic condolence text and that was it.

The events following Mia's death left me searching for answers. I found mixed reviews on google and yelp, four news articles purporting that 2 canines died after having an MRI at LIVS. The articles appeared in the NY Post on 7/8/2019 and 7/31/2019, The City on 7/7/2019 and News 12 Long Island on 8/7/2019. The article in the NY Post stated that the owners of both dogs filed complaints with the Office of Professional Discipline and were pursuing litigation.

I searched the courts for litigation and only found one case. I can only assume that one of the parties opted to settle out of court, while the other party pursued litigation. The case is still pending and is filed in the Supreme Court of New York County, Index No. 15663/2019, Harold Lehr vs. LIVS, Dr. Catherine Loughin etal. This case immediately caught my attention, Catherine Loughin is the veterinarian that performed the CT scan on my dog.

There were allegations in the complaint that were eerily similar to the circumstances I experienced with Dr. Loughlin.

The case has many allegations and those that stood out and were similar to my experience with Dr. Loughin are (1) proposed, recommended and pushed to purchase a procedure (2) did not disclose any other risks associated with the procedure and further stated that it was extremely safe and it was strongly recommended (3) advised that the dog stay overnight (4) the owner was instructed to sign an e-signature pad and was not told his signature could be transferred, applied to and printed on a liability release form (5) recommended a procedure based on a false diagnosis which served no reasonable or appropriate veterinary medical purpose (6) failed to reasonably and appropriately supervise the test (7) it was the culture of LIVS of proposing, recommending and pushing unnecessary, inappropriate and lucrative services to maximize their profits.

I went through the entire case and was surprised to find that it included copies of complaints that were previously sent to Attorney General and to the Office of Professional Discipline by former clients. The complaints revealed horrible stories of negligence, malpractice and loss of life. There was also a letter written by a former LIVS surgery resident addressed to the American College of Veterinary Surgeons, the letter had corroborating statements from veterinarians and former employees revealing a culture of misrepresentations, inaccurate record keeping and altered medical records. After reading this case, I felt that there are many other victims out there. In my opinion, these were not isolated cases but rather casualties of business.

It is also a sad realization, that most victims for whatever reason, do not pursue their case to fullest. I applaud the complainant in this case for his perseverance for justice, his ability to get the media to report his story and being bold enough to fight his case in the Supreme Court of New York. I wish I had read his story last year when it was published, it may have saved Mia's life.

By now I truly believed that Mia was a victim, and her death was preventable. I knew that I should at the very least file a complaint with OPD, but I was hesitant. I was afraid to cut off ties with them, I was familiar with the staff, it is close to my home and mostly, it is convenient for emergency situations. I went on their Facebook page, I needed to read the positive comments from past and present clients, I needed the validation to support my reasoning as to why I shouldn't file a complaint. I read the comments and went through the pictures. Then I saw the most appalling picture, and that was the turning point. The picture was posted on April 2, 2020, it appears to be in an operating room, there is a small dog lying on a surgical table, anesthetized, Dr. Loughin and presumably staff residents ham it up for the picture. The picture made me sick to my stomach. I couldn't help but to put Mia in the place of that dog on the table. Was Mia left unattended while a photo shoot was in session? So many scenarios went through my mind and I couldn't stop thinking about Mia's last moments. It was at that moment that I knew I had to file a complaint, cuties and take the necessary steps to get justice for Mia.

I filed a complaint with the Office of Professional Discipline at the end of June and was interviewed by an investigator in August. It was a lengthy and encouraging interview. The investigator did not give me any false hope and she thoroughly explained the limitations of OPD. I hung up the phone with the feeling that Mia's case was being taken seriously. Whatever the outcome is, Mia isn't coming home. That is the harsh reality.

I have to believe that Mia's death was not in vain and my promise to her is, I will fight every day for innocent pets, and I will use every resource available to me to help combat veterinary negligence and malpractice.

I am attaching links to some newspaper articles.

https://nypost.com/2019/07/31/another-dog-dies-after-mri-at-long-island-vet-owner-claims/

https://www.thecity.nyc/health/2019/7/8/21210958/one-man-s-fight-to-fix-a-failed-veterinarian-discipline-system

http://longisland.news12.com/story/40886856/li-family-blames-plainview-vet-for-death-of-their-dog

Mia

CHAPTER EIGHT

Milly's Story
Corey Dafnis

On Friday March 21, 2014 @ 9:00 am I brought my healthy, happy 5-year-old German Shepherd Milly into the Calumet Animal Clinic to be spayed. Dr. Charles Carter Matthews was her veterinarian. A vet that I had taken all my pets to for over 20 years.

She never minded going to the vet before because she knew there would be other dogs there to play with. But something was different this time. When we got to the door she stopped and wouldn't go in. It took a lot to get her into the clinic. When I finally did, she sat and shook so bad. I got on the floor and held her as tight as I could trying to calm her. I told her over and over she was going to be ok. One of the receptionists came and took Milly's leash. She fought and cried pulling as hard she could to get back to me. Begging me to get her and take her home. The woman told me I had to leave because she was having a hard time getting her in the back. I asked more than once if I could pick her up after her surgery. I was told NO. She had to stay overnight for observation. I asked if someone would be there to check on her through the night. I was told YES. I turned and left in tears. I got in the car. My husband asked why I was so upset. I didn't know. All I knew is something didn't feel right. My hand was on the handle of the car door. I was going to go back in and get her. Sadly, I didn't, and we left. I was told by the veterinarian to call about 4:00 to check on her. I couldn't relax all day. My daughter asked me why I was having such a hard time. My exact words to her were. I just feel like Milly's not going to be coming home. I couldn't wait any longer. I called to check on her @ 3:00 pm. I was told she was doing very well and had been up and walking already. Once again, I asked if I could bring her home. I was told no. How would you feel if something happened to her if you brought her home? I felt guilty and agreed to leave her. They told me to call in the morning @ 10:00 am.

J.L. Robb

I woke early the next morning excited to pick Milly up. It was 9:07 I couldn't wait until 10:00 to call them. I reached for the phone before I could dial it rang. The caller ID said CALUMET ANIMAL CLINIC. My heart sank. I picked up the phone and didn't even give the person on the other end a chance to say anything. I said Dear God please tell nothing happened to my girl. Dr. Matthews responded in a cold and uncaring manner. Yes, she died. She bled to death. She was a hemophiliac. I screamed your lying!! If you knew that, why would you do surgery on her? He then asked me What do you want me to do with her?? I said get her ready. I'm coming to get her. I knew something was terribly wrong. I was going to file a lawsuit. We went to the clinic and the same woman that told me my Milly would be safe and cared for carried her dead body to me. I couldn't believe what I was seeing. I asked for all her medical records. I was told there was none. I told them I wasn't leaving until they gave me her records. We were given a card with nothing on it. I said there has to be more than this. I then told them I wanted all my pet's records. I had another Shepherd at home 7-month-old female Cheyenne that they had just spayed the month before. And I had 2 cats. We were told to take Milly and leave. We were also told to cover her with the dirty yellow blanket that they had her wrapped in so their clients that were in the waiting wouldn't see her. I said absolutely not! I uncovered my girl and my husband, and I walked through the front door. I told everyone there THIS IS WHAT HAPPENS WHEN YOU LEAVE YOUR PET HERE OVERNIGHT.

We took Milly to another veterinarian to have a necropsy done. The necropsy showed the the hemo-clips that were used to clamp off the arteries had come off. But it also showed that the clips were not meant for a dog of Milly's size. More for a smaller animal.

A friend had started a Facebook page called JUSTICE FOR MILLY DAFNIS. Stories started coming in from others that had bad experiences with the clinic and the staff. One story was of a 4-year-old Doberman named Eve that had died a few weeks before Milly. She died the exact same way. Small hemo-clips that had come off and Eve bled to death. I later

44

found out from an inside source that Dr. Matthews was not the one doing surgeries. These stories were documented on court transcripts also. He had trained his receptionists/pet handlers how to do surgeries over 20 Years ago. It was one of them that killed my girl. He did this so that he could see more clients while they operated on family pets.

I filed my lawsuit. This veterinarian and his staff had to be stopped before any other family suffered the loss of their family pet.

I had found out that Dr. Matthews had an expired license to distribute drugs. I went to the police to file a report. They gave me a hard time., kept telling me it was a civil matter. I kept going back. I also brought the woman that lost her 4-year-old Doberman Eve so she could file a police report. Finally, we got the reports written. The DEA was sent to the Calumet Animal Clinic. They confiscated all his drugs.

I hired Anna Morrison-Ricordati with AMR LAWGROUP to take Milly's case. She is one of the Attorney's now with Joey's Legacy. She was amazing. She fought hard for Milly and I. I had also filed a complaint with the IDFPR.

I believe the veterinarian and some of his staff told lie upon lie in court depositions. Almost as if they tried to blame me for Milly's death. I heard that one of the receptionist/ pet handlers that was doing the surgeries had bragged to her best friend how she was trained to do surgeries and had been doing them for years. I believe she also said that she knew that the hemo-clips that were used on Milly were too small. They had a lot of old stock and needed to use it up. It was like Milly's life didn't matter. She mattered to me. I'm devastated. One thing Matthews and his staff taught me is what a broken heart feels like. A heart that will never heal. It's been six years and not day goes by that I don't cry for my girl. I'm not sad for me. I'm sad for her life be taken from her. I've had many pets in my life. Milly was special to me. We had a very close bond. She was my canine soulmate. No one has a right to do this to a family. I trusted her life with people I thought were professionals. I'll never trust like that again.

The Calumet Animal Clinic was closed, and the veterinarian is no longer practicing. One thing is for sure. For the rest of their lives, they will remember a beautiful German Shepherd named Milly.

Milly

CHAPTER NINE

Lord Nelson's Story
Sue Lux

I took my 14-year-old Norwich terrier Nelson to Dr. Dana Hardison, Mclean Animal Hospital in Virginia in May 2020 after he was vomiting and had difficulty eating. After bloodwork and an ultrasound, the ultrasound suspected mild pancreatitis and/or enzymatic process indicating cancer.

I was told by Dr. Hardison that Nelson does not have pancreatitis because bloodwork showed normal levels of amylase and lipase. She gave me medicine to treat cancer at home, while his condition worsened so I hospitalized him a few days later. I was told to wait for the medicine to work.

The hospital immediately diagnosed Nelson with pancreatitis using a simple Spec cpL blood test and ultrasound. Amylase and lipase are poor predictors of pancreatitis and a simple blood test (Snap cPL) would have indicated pancreatitis. Mclean Hospital did not have updated bloodwork in spite of charging me $800 for an inaccurate diagnosis of cancer.

My sweet little Nelson stayed three nights with 24-hour care in the hospital, but his organs shut down because he was not diagnosed properly or given fluids soon enough, which he desperately needed. Mclean Animal Hospital is negligent and incompetent, and my dog passed away due to their (in)adequate lack of care. I am heartbroken and angry. He was like my baby and I miss him every day.

CHAPTER TEN

Danny's and Dominic's Story
Ron

Here is the story of my 2 dogs dying 21 days apart last June 2019. It's a long read so be patient. It should be a warning to many other pet owners. This is the story of my 2 Cavachon lil buddies Danny 10 ½ and Dominic 5. I just lost Dominic yesterday, Saturday, please read.

DEAR Bayer: Makers of Seresto flea & tick collar

I am writing this letter telling you at Bayer my experience with your Seresto collars. I bought 4 collars for my 4 dogs on 5/6/19 at the Abington animal hospital in Abington Ma. I have a female 13 1/2 yr. old Cocker spaniel, a male 2 yr. old Golden doodle, & 2 male Cavachons 10 1/2 & 5 yrs. old. On Thursday 6/6/19 @ 3am my 5 yr. old Cavachon Dominic had a seizure, we immediately took the collar off him along with the Danny our other Cavachon & had our son at home take the collars off our other 2 dogs. Dominic vomited pooped & had muscle weakness during the night. he seemed to bounce back some the next day. Later that same day 6/6/19 at 4:15 pm my 10 1/2 yr. old Cavachon Danny had a seizure. We took him to the Country Veterinary clinic in carver ma near my seasonal camper in carver. There he was examined They did blood work & checked him out & couldn't find & issue other than hi sugar & phosphorus levels. They said try feeding both dogs boiled chicken & rice or boiled hamburger & rice or pasta. later that night Dominic had another episode where he fell over & vomited & pooped all over our campers deck. He was lethargic all day on Friday 6/7/19, He would not eat anything. The 10 1/2 yr. old Danny was lethargic early in the day he perked up in the midafternoon & ate chicken & pasta while Dominic remained lethargic.

On the morning of Saturday 6/8/19 my 10 1/2 yr. old Danny had another seizure with coughing. He was laying down in our camper kitchen floor as we patted him to bring him out of it. Suddenly his legs started to stiffen & started wrenching back & forth towards each other as he died at my feet. We brought Danny's body back to the vet at the Country Vet clinic that morning when they opened. The Dr took him in the back room to do an autopsy after they closed at noon. We came back at 11am with Dominic who remained lethargic & still was not eating. he did blood work & iv fluids to hydrate him. Dominic's blood work showed hi phosphorus levels like Danny's, but his blood sugar was normal compared to Danny.he thought Danny's hi sugar was caused by the seizure. Dr Simpson's autopsy did not show any abnormalities of any of Danny's organs kidneys liver, lungs, stomach. He had some thickening of the arteries around his heart which may have caused the cough he had along with the hi pollen this spring. Dr Simpson still could not find a reason for all that had happened to our cavachons & the seizures that they had 15 hours apart from each other.

My dogs are always with us they got into nothing that might cause these problems whatsoever. We looked up the ingredients of the Seresto collars especially the HIGHLY TOXIC pesticides used by the name IMIDACLOPRID & FLUMETHRIN. We found that every symptom both our little dogs had can be caused by this pesticide that you use in these collars. the only thing we did different with our dogs is to get them these Seresto collars. Now my Danny is dead & as I write this on 6/17/19. My Dominic has showed some improvement but is still far from the active & playful dog he was before his seizure on 6/6/19. We took Dominic back to the vet on Monday 6/10/19 where he received more iv fluids & shots of prednisone & an anti-nausea to help his appetite out. he also gave us pills of both meds to give him for 5 days. The vet gave Dominic as he went 5 days without eating but just drinking some special dog food. On Wednesday 6/13/19 Dominic finally ate some without us feeding him. His back legs were still weak where we had to carry him down to go the bathroom. On Thursday 6/13/19 he finally went down then back up the stairs on his own, the same on Friday 6/14/19. By the end of Friday & after a few short walks his back legs were still weak trying to stand. He finally moved his bowels on Friday 6/14/19 2 times. On Saturday 6/15/19 his birthday at around 5:10

pm he kind of rolled over & couldn't get up. My wife picked him up, but he seems just dead tired. He has been eating a little better each day but has continued to vomit on occasion. Dominic is at best 1/2 of what he was before his 1st seizure on 6/6/19 @ 3AM. I'm just hoping there's no neurological damage IMIDACLOPRID can cause. The vet told us he could not rule out the collars from causing these symptoms in our beloved pets Danny & Dominic. My regular vet of the Abington animal hospital where we bought the collars. He basically said it's like hitting the lottery it's possible the collars may have caused it. both vets said what are the odds of 2 dogs 1 month after putting these collars on them having seizures 15 hours apart from each other.

My wife & I truly believe your collar killed my precious dog Danny& has almost caused Dominic to die twice on 6/8/19 & 6/9/19. We have spent $285 for the 4 collars we bought our dogs that wore them for 1 month to the day 5/6/19 – 6/6/19. We believe it killed 1 dog & another is still fighting the effects of them as I write this letter on 6/17/19. Then throw in my vet bills treating 2 dogs & getting another 1 checked out its over $1,500. I will tell you this now I will tell every pet owner I know in person & others on social media what I truly believe what your Seresto flea & tick collar did to our beloved family pets. I'm also sending with this letter my $15 rebate for each of the collars I purchased for my 4 dogs. Wow isn't that nice, a big $60 back for my poor dead Danny & possibly another dog dying down the road or never being his playful energetic self again.

Thank you for a horrible 2 weeks. This is the letter I sent to Bayer earlier last week along with my rebate mail in for the collars. I can't wait to hear from them if they even do.

As of yesterday, 6/29/19 Dominic passed away after not eating for the last 5 days on his own. My wife & I were actually force feeding him by spoon he was throwing it up meds & food then the water. He got an anti-nausea shot on 6/27/19 by the vet along with pills for the same. He just got worse & worse till he passed. Now he's back with Danny in doggie heaven as he's also been grief stricken from Danny's passing 3 weeks ago to the day. Dom Dom as we called him was the black & white dog. these were my best dogs ever Danny got me thru 10 surgeries over a 9-year period with Dom Dom also there for a few. these cavachons are the most loving & happy dogs I have ever had & now they're gone over a chemical collar that can kill your dog by the pesticides in them. I truly believe it killed them both & feel the need to warn all you pet owners.

The vet called me with what he found on Doms autopsy on 7/1/19. He said all Doms organs showed no problems whatsoever. Even his stomach throughout all his vomiting the last 3 weeks & his loss of appetite which was a complete loss the last 6 days. When we brought Dom to him on Thursday 6/27/19 he gave him an anti-nausea shot & some pills for that & see if he would try eating. If that didn't work, he said you may have to go to an animal hospital & maybe have a scope to see what his stomach problem is. So, when I asked would a scope have done or found anything, he said no his stomach was fine. He said he took specimen samples from liver & other organs to be sent out to a lab. He also talked to Bayer the maker of the Seresto collars. They say the collars don't do this, but they will pick up the cost of the lab work. Isn't that so nice of them. I truly believe their product killed my beloved dogs. God forbid this get out & slow down their profits on the collars that I believe can kill pets across the country. It's all about profit over pet health. The vet again told me he can't rule out the collars he just doesn't understand how a healthy 5-year-old like Dominic died when he shouldn't be dead now. I've looked online & found many hundreds of pets & their owners going thru the exact thing we went thru.

This is the letter I sent to Bayer after my 2nd dog Dominic died on 6/29/19.

Danny & Dominic   Danny & Dominic

CHAPTER ELEVEN

Chyna's Story
Brigid and Nicholas Balesterri

For Chyna

Our beloved Chyna was born on July 1, 2005 and we welcomed her into our family in September 2005 which consisted of myself, my husband and our 2 other dogs at that time who were Humboldt an English Mastiff and Kane a Basset Hound and would later become a sister to Shayna a Great Dane in 2007 and Darcie a chewennie in 2012. Chyna also had love from her cousins who were 7 other dogs along with aunts, uncles and grandparents who loved her so much. Chyna was a funny, loveable, comedic dog who loved to go for car rides, walks and loved to play with everyone and just loved life and had much more life to live but her life was cut short due to the negligence of a vet. Dr. Alan Krause from Faithful Companion Veterinary Services in Lady Lake Florida was found guilty in a case that involved another dog Tebow. Tebows story was first posted in The Villages News of The Villages Florida in January 2019 with an updated story regarding Tebows case in February 2020 explaing the discipline that was handed down to the vet from The Department of Business and Professional Regulations which included probation, fines and continuing education. Our dog Chyna was given a medication metronidazole and was dead 5 days later. She was also prescribed a combination of carprofen and prednisone in September 2018 by the vet for a herniated disc. Based upon my research prescribing the combination of carprofen and prednisone causes death in dogs and I believe is considered malpractice by many veterinarians. Pet parents need to know that these medications are dangerous and I believe they are prescribed too freely by veterinarians. This is Chyna's story.

Our dog Chyna was having diarrhea for a couple of days and we were trying to control the diarrhea with a bland diet of chicken and rice like we were instructed many times to do with our pets before if they had diarrhea. We started to see blood in her stool the morning of January 8th, 2019. We called the vet's office and brought her in that day. The vet did some bloodwork on Chyna and also took a stool sample from her because she would poop in the vets office from being nervous. We were given the medication Metronidazole and a pro biotic and they gave Chyna an injection which included B12, penicillin and centriane. We asked the vet if there were any side effects from the medications and we were told no just an increase of water intake because of the dehydration from the diarrhea. So we paid our bill and left and started her on the medication that day. On January 9, 2019 Chyna was still having diarrhea and we gave her the metronidazole and the pro biotic with her carprofen which she took for a herniated disk she had in September 2018 which the vet had also done bloodwork at that visit which also showed her liver enzymes elevated which he wasn't worried about. We continued giving her chicken and rice which she ate very little of and also was drinking alot of water and panting. Her stool was mushy but not watery that night. I recieved an email from the vet asking how Chyna was and to let us know that her stool sample came back negative for parasites and told us her bloodwork showed elevated liver enzymes again just like at her September 2018 visit which he told us goes along with liver problems and pancreatitis which he never tested her for. I called and left a message for the vet to call back because we wanted to know if it was ok to still give her the carprofen. The vet emailed me back and said to stop it because it can cause diarrhea. So we did. On January 10, 2019 Chyna was having a hard time walking, she was eating chicken and rice and was lethargic. She continued to drink a lot of water and was still panting. Her urine was also dark and her poop was mushy in the morning and was back to diarrhea by the evening. On January 11, 2019 we gave Chyna the carprofen again because she was having a hard time walking which the vet was made aware of, she was still having diarrhea and her urine was still dark and she was still lethargic and panting. We continued giving her chicken and rice which she was eating very little of. She was still drinking alot of water and we gave her some cranberry juice mixed with her water which she also drank very little of. She started making grunting noises when she would eat or drink anything. I called the vet's office and spoke to his assistant at the office to let her know how Chyna was doing and what she was going through and the assistant told me to give the medication a chance to work and if there is no change by Monday to bring Chyna in. On January 12, 2019 Chyna's urine was still dark, she was still having diarrhea, still lethargic, still panting and drinking water and ate very little of chicken and rice and she also had a small piece of a plain cookie which she ate. She was still grunting when she ate or drank anything and this is when her labored breathing started. Sunday morning January 13, 2019 Chyna was still acting the same and she also threw up. I sent the vet an email explaing what was going on with Chyna thinking he would check his messages on the weekend. I also called the emergency vet and told them what was going on with Chyna and they told me to bring her in. My husband was at work that morning so my brother in law picked me up with Chyna and as we were driving to the emergency vet she was having a hard time keeping her head up and her breathing was getting less and less. As I was holding her head in my hands I was looking at her and talking to her telling her to hold on. We pulled up in front of the emergency vet and Chyna passed away. We then took Chyna back home and layed her on her bed in our living room so her loved ones could come and spend time with her and pay their respects before she was cremated. And the vet never answered my email until later that evening when Chyna was gone. I have read that metronidazole is toxic to animals. I have also read that if your pet has any liver problems or pancreatitis or if they have any elevation in liver enzymes they should not be given metronidazole. I had also read that carprofen should never be given with prednisone which Chyna was given at her September 2018 visit to the vet. As I have read, NSAIDS should not be used in conjunction with corticosteroid hormones such as prednisone, dexamethasone, etc. and to allow at least one week between prednisone and carprofen. Based upon my research if carprofen is used concurrently with phenobarbital, it is especially important that appropriate liver monitoring be performed and Chyna's never were monitored. It is my understanding that Carprofen should not be given to dogs with preexisting liver or kidney disease. Bloodwork from Chyna's September 2018 visit to the vet showed elevation in her liver enzymes and she was put on carprofen and continued to be prescribed carprofen until December 2018 with no additional testing done. Bloodwork from Chyna's January 2019 visit to the vet also showed elevation in her liver enzymes again, a low platelet count and a low white blood cell count and knowing this the vet prescribed Chyna metronidazole which is another drug that should not be given to a animal with elevated liver enzymes or underlying liver disease. I truly believe this is considered malpractice and that our dog is gone because of this. We have pictures and videos of Chyna before all of this started happening to her and pictures and videos of her during the last 6 days of her life after she started the metronidazole. My husband and I went in to talk to the vet on January 14, 2019 the day after Chyna passed away and the vet told us not to email him on the weekends because he doesnt check his emails and that is what the emergency vet is there for. As we were talking to the vet, I kept questioning him on metronidazole which he didn't like and how I had read that metronidazole isn't even approved by the FDA. The vet then told us that the FDA gives veterinarians the right to "extra or off lable" medications that are used for humans to use on animals which I dont agree with at all. By doing that I believe they are putting our animals lives at risk. I believe every medication that we give our pets should be and needs to be approved by the FDA. After a long conversation the vet asked us what he could do for us and we said we want our money refunded back to us. He had refunded our money from the office visit on January 8, 2019 without hesitation which in my opinion shows guilt. The vet also kept insisting that we continue to keep him as our vet and how he just wants to be our friend and how he doesnt want to receive papers from a lawyer saying that he's being sued 3 months down the line, which in my opinion is another sign of guilt. We left with our money refunded and our dogs records and proceeded to find a new veterinarian. I believe every medication for animals should have side effect lables on them which they don't and I believe it should be mandatory for all veterinarians to warn us of all potential side effects to medications and have pamphlets on the medications to hand out to us "pet parents" because not everyone has internet access, this way we can be given the option if we want our pet on a medication or not. I feel that because we trusted the vet and everything he would tell us, we were robbed of that and never given that option because if we were we would have never given Chyna the metronidazole and I believe she would still be here with us. I have contacted 72 lawyers and they all said they don't do any malpractice cases on animals because the turn out isn't great and the state of Florida looks at animals as a piece of property not a family member which I find disturbing and disgusting. I've sent paperwork to the State of Florida Department of Business and Professional Regulations and was later told her case was closed due to no probable cause found. In my opinion the department protects their vets for all of the bad that is done to our animals and that needs to change. Even though we were not successful with the Department of Business and Professional Regulations I will not stop trying to be successful in other areas to get justice for Chyna. I have started a group on Facebook called "Justice for Chyna our beloved basset hound" for all to join and follow her story. Chyna's life was taken too soon from her and we are not done and never will be done fighting for our beloved Chyna. I have also reported what happened to her to Pfizer who is the manufacturer of metronidazole and the FDA and have been told the only thing they can do is make note of it and add it to the side effects which is disappointing. We are our pets voices. So please help us in getting Chyna's story and her fight out there so this doesn't happen to anyone else's pet. We love and miss you smurchles!

Chyna

CHAPTER TWELVE

Marvin's Story
Judy Santerre

Marvin is a little black mixed breed dog who appears to be a pug body with a terrier head that appears as if it was stuck on by mistake.

He weighs about 16 pounds. I adopted him from the San Marcos (Texas) Animal Shelter in June of 2018 after seeing his pleading little face on their website. Marvin was heartworm positive and had received the first treatment by the shelter. He was at least stage 3 because he was still very ill. Marvin also had emotional issues from his past. He was starved for attention and hated being alone. Because of his heartworm treatment, I had closed him into a bedroom one day to keep him from playing with my other dog. He chewed a dog-sized hole in the door and escaped. He also had an eating disorder and ate everything. He was cleaning out the cat box and eating bird seed and horse pellets out of the bags in my utility room in addition to his dog food. On our walks (off-lead on my small property), he would eat anything he managed to find.

After two months, Marvin looked like a dog balloon. Marvin proved himself to be an invaluable and loving addition to my little family. I had rescued a little dog on the side of the road who was missing her eyes. Zoey had been brutally and criminally abused but is now treated like a princess. Marvin became her protector. He did this by running in front of her and turning her so she couldn't run into anything. If she fell behind, he would race back and walk with her. Marvin adored Zoey and stayed with her every minute of the day unless he was with me. I entered Marvin and his "chewing through a door story" to Dog of the Day along with photos of the damaged door and of Marvin in a Superman cape because he had become our hero. He was featured shortly afterward and drew many wonderful comments from his Dog of the Day fans.

Marvin was severely burned as a result of veterinary malpractice during a teeth cleaning. The following is my recounting of the events. I am not naming this veterinarian for reasons I won't go into. On November 7, 2018, I took Marvin, then in continuing treatment for heartworms, for removal of a suspected tumor in his perianal area. When I dropped Marvin off on the morning of November 7, 2018, my expectation was only the tumor would be excised. I had told them by phone that I didn't want Marvin to have a teeth cleaning. He's a young dog, his teeth are fine, and I didn't want him under the anesthesia for longer than necessary because he's still recovering from heartworms and had been very ill.

Marvin had nearly died from complications of heartworm treatment. That he was still coughing indicated to me he was not sufficiently recovered. I had phoned on November 6, 2018, the day before the scheduled surgery, to report Marvin was coughing and I was concerned about proceeding safely. The clinic phoned back to tell me Dr. X said he was sure he could handle the issue without problems. When I arrived as scheduled, a staff person presented me with a choice of a $900 estimate with the teeth cleaning and tumor removal or nearly $1,100 for just the tumor removal. She explained there was a special, so it was cheaper to do the teeth cleaning than not to do it. She also wanted me to sign a paper saying it was okay for them to pull teeth. I refused to do that, but I reluctantly went along with the teeth cleaning.

I had never before been presented with this kind of bait and switch tactic. For the first time, Marvin was reluctant to be left at the veterinary clinic. I should have listened to him and the vague unease I was feeling, but this veterinarian had earned my trust and that reassured me and caused me to proceed.

When I picked Marvin up that evening, he was subdued but wagged his tail to see me. I assumed all had gone well, as was reported by the clinic. When I got home with Marvin, he wouldn't eat anything, and he's normally a ravenous eater. I noticed some sort of cream on Marvin's side and I didn't know what it was. No one at the clinic had mentioned the cream.

Marvin was unusually quiet that evening and just slept. By the next morning, something was obviously wrong. He was whimpering in pain and again would not eat. He was especially sensitive on one side. He cried if I tried to pick him up.

I had a meeting at the office I absolutely could not miss, so I went to the office and phoned the clinic. I spoke with Dr. X and he told me he thought Marvin would improve later that day, so we agreed to wait until that afternoon. The plan was that I would leave work early to give me time to check Marvin while I still had time to get him to the clinic.

When I arrived home early that afternoon, Marvin was in more pain and had developed blisters along his side. I immediately drove him to the clinic. Dr. X shaved Marvin's side near his abdomen where the blisters were appearing. Under the shaved hair, there was a striking burn pattern, which included a perfect curve. Dr. X immediately covered the area with a white cream before I thought to take a photo. I'm sure Dr. X recognized it immediately for what it was, but he told me to check the electrical outlets at my home because he thought Marvin had put his paw in an electric outlet. The outlets in my home are fine, and Marvin had been too lethargic and in pain to be moving around much between the time I brought him home the evening before and the following morning when he was very clearly injured. Dr. X showed no surprise at the burns and I believe he lied about the cause to cover up what he had done.

The largest of Marvin's burns included a very clear perfect half curve. His burns were only along his right side, clearly indicating he was burned while lying down. The burns were on his rib cage, his hind feet, his hip, and his sheath, obviously the parts of his body in contact with the heat source. What is particularly disturbing, the pattern of Marvin's burns reflects his upper body was not burned, indicating his upper body was elevated off the heated pad or table that burned him. It appears his burns occurred during the teeth cleaning and not afterward. Since the burns on his hips had melted his hair into all layers of his skin, I felt there must have been a smell, burning flesh, which should have been noticeable to anyone nearby.

How could this happen? Why wasn't I told? Dr. X told me to get some T-shirts and keep him in T-shirts. I was given silver sulfadiazine cream to put on his burns. It is obvious to me the cream I had noticed on Marvin the night before was this same silver sulfadiazine used to treat burns. I was not given pain medication for Marvin for burns Dr. X knew were very painful. I drove from there to a pet store to get doggy T-shirts. Marvin was in so much pain, he didn't want to go in. He just lay in the car, suffering. It hit me in the parking lot of that store, after leaving the clinic, that Marvin had been burned at the clinic, and Dr. X was lying about it.

I was so upset I backed into a pole leaving the store. The burns obviously occurred at the clinic. Had Marvin not had a teeth cleaning, I do not believe he would have been burned. Excising the tumor would have taken minutes, leaving no time to burn him. I was frantically worried about Marvin. There was no way to know how deep the burns were and whether they would prove fatal. I read burns can worsen for up to a month.

Marvin suffered horribly through that weekend, but I was afraid to take him to any veterinarian. Following the gross veterinary malpractice death of my horse, Harvey, and now this, I have lost all respect for them, but on Monday, November 12, 2018, I had to take Marvin to a different clinic for treatment. His burns were looking worse, getting redder and starting to slough off large patches of skin.

The new veterinarian at first tried to cover up for her guilty colleague because she knew immediately how Marvin had been burned, but I refused to go along with her proposal and demanded his burns be treated. Marvin was given pain medication, antibiotics, and silver sulfadiazine cream. Marvin continued to scream with the pain of his burns whenever I had to move him to change his shirts. He ate very little and I anxiously watched and waited to see if his bladder was working (it was) and his bowel was working (it wasn't).

On Thursday, eight days after his injury, Marvin took a turn for the worse, becoming very lethargic and unwilling to eat or engage with me or my other dogs. Fearing the worst, I took Marvin back to the new clinic where he was diagnosed with dehydration, a sign of more serious injury. They kept him on IV hydration that day and I picked him up that evening, refusing to allow him to stay overnight. When I got him home, I took him outside and observed his first bowel movement. That was my first hope he might survive.

Over the following ten days (days eight to eighteen), his burns slowly began to heal. It took a month for the patches of hair burned into his skin over his hip area to peel away with the hair and skin, leaving white scars. He bears scars across his side and his foot as well as his hip. He also has mental scars. I can take him in the car with me, but wherever I go he will not get out of the car until I am home. He is now deathly afraid of veterinarians, and he wasn't before. He understands who hurt him. On March 2, 2019, I mailed a certified demand letter to the veterinarian and I received the green cards stamped March 5, 2019, the same day I had walked over and filed my complaint with the Texas Board of Veterinary Medical Examiners (TBVME) in Austin.

I had little hope for justice when filing the complaint because I had already been through this process concerning the killing of my horse. Based upon my opinion and my previous experience. I figured filing a complaint with the TBVME would be worthless, but I feel victims must complain and make their voices heard for there to be any change. Our legislators must know how prevalent veterinary malpractice and negligence is before they will take action to prevent their voters from being harmed. Eight days later, on March 13, 2019, I received a phone call from an attorney stating he represented the veterinarian. I thought this was odd because I expected to be contacted by the insurance company. I still have the notes I took from that phone call written on a yellow legal pad: "[attorney's name], - w/d [withdraw] my complaint, - no social media cover, - blackout all of it & they'll pay." I remember thinking this attorney spoke as if he was reading from a script, he had read hundreds of times before. I responded I would have to think about it. I refused to withdraw my complaint or sign a non-disparagement agreement.

In Texas, that means paying the veterinarian's legal fees if he decides you violated that agreement and sues you. I sent that attorney a signed version of what I would agree to, but it was never signed by the veterinarian, and I was never paid anything. I revoked it months later. As for the complaint, I was never advised of the timeline pursuant to Texas Administrative Code 575.28(b), nor were the regulations provided in the TBVME Complaint Procedures adhered to, in my opinion. I do not believe Periodic notices required under Texas Occupations Code 801.204(c) were never sent, nor was I provided a timeline as required in Texas Occupations Code 801.206. I was fully unaware the TBVME dismissed my case until the day after the board meeting in which the Board voted to dismiss it. The cause for the dismissal was not reported in the October 21, 2019 case closure letter (sent after case dismissal), which should have been reported in accordance with Section 801.208(c). I filed an open records request for more information regarding the reviewer's determination that the original case be dismissed for no violation, and I was surprised to be told the TBVME would be seeking a decision from the Office of the Attorney General.

It is concerning the burning of a small dog on one side of his body, clearly burn injuries that occurred while the dog was laying down and unconscious, is deemed insufficient evidence. A conscious dog being burned would have immediately moved away from the source of heat, but Marvin did not move to save himself from injury which clearly indicates he was not conscious.

Since Marvin slept in my bed the night of the teeth cleaning, and I am not burned, I asked the reviewing veterinarian in my appeal letter by what alternate method he/she believes my dog was burned. Marvin was unwell the evening of the teeth cleaning and in pain the following morning. The burns were clearly visible during the veterinary office visit that afternoon, less than 24 hours after I had picked him up. Pursuant to TBVME Rule 575.281, I requested re-opening of the investigation of Case CP19-192 involving the severe burns to my little dog, Marvin. This is the TBVME appeal process. The TBVME has never bothered to respond. My experiences with the TBVME are replicated by numerous victims I have spoken with. We are treated with contempt, as if our pets don't matter, and we are only nuisances. Our pets are the reason they have a job and a thriving industry. The pain and suffering Marvin endured in connection with this ordeal, and the emotional distress I experienced exacerbated the trauma I am still suffering following the brutal gross veterinary malpractice death of my horse, Harvey. No one who has gone through the loss of their beloved pet by gross veterinary malpractice recovers. It is a very distinct torture. In my opinion, the TBVME is not functioning as a State agency, but as a union office for the veterinary industry. The public only suffers more harm when they realize the State is protecting the abusers of their pets instead of holding veterinarians accountable for the harm they cause. It seems to me that with deregulation in the 1980's, our consumer protections were stripped away.

The Texas Deceptive Trade Practices Act (DTPA) was passed in 1973 and veterinarians were originally subject to it. That changed in 1987 when a bunch of new amendments to the Texas Veterinary Act were passed (SB 1497, 70th Legislature), including an exemption for veterinarians. Unlike doctors, the exemption for veterinarians covers their negligence and their malpractice. Veterinarians can do no wrong. The DTPA provided important protections for Texas consumers, allowing treble damages, recovery of attorneys' fees, and damages for emotional distress. All should be available to pet owners and were prior to 1987.

As a result of lost consumer protections, veterinarians are now the leading cause of companion animal deaths, medical errors by doctors are now the third leading cause of death for people, and people are protesting in our streets against police brutality because police unions are protecting bad cops who have harmed or killed citizens.

Who pays for the settlements to victims injured or killed by police? City and county taxpayers, and since city budgets are declining, city managers and county commissioners must be able to remove dangerous officers to protect citizens and budgets.

I believe we badly need our consumer protections reinstated.

We need a return to accountability for bad actors who harm the public and our pets.

Marvin

 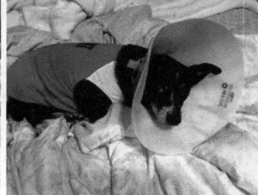

CHAPTER THIRTEEN

Zois Story
Christine Zois

Heartbreak at the Head Butt Hotel
North Myrtle Beach, South Carolina

It's understood that pet ownership, will eventually result in the inevitable heartache and suffering that we all experience, with the loss of a cherished furry family member. Our family's pets, Murphy, Kukla, and Mittens, lived well into their and my teens back in the 1970's when the local country NJ vet, on that rare occasion, they were needed, to oversee their care. Murphy, our canine mutt, was always given table scraps, while his feline counterpart Mittens, a complete freak for black olives, could smell them from the other side of the house, and came running for his share. Vet visits didn't happen very often back then, they weren't necessary, and vaccinations were minimal at best. But that was then, and things have since taken a dramatic change for the worse for companion animals.

My Mom being the responsible and consummate pet owner throughout the 80's, followed her vet's advice, feeding Hill's Science Diet and like clockwork when that postcard reminder arrived, "updating" her cats' "Pure-Vax" rabies vaccinations they "needed". Her Persian Simby and Turkish Angora Punky became my prized possessions in 2009 after her passing, a reminder of her legacy and love for not only them, but all sentient beings who ventured into her NJ yard, a mini outdoor nurturing preserve. In 2012, we packed up, leaving the cold winters and moving south to North Myrtle Beach, SC. Our new residence, two years later, would become known as the Head Butt Hotel, the main location and feline residence for our charitable non-profit organization. And so, commenced the rabbit hole journey, welcoming us to the indoctrination of veterinary care in Horry County, and the statewide misrepresentation of the South Carolina rabies statute. After five "Pure Vax" rabies vaccinations, Punky, never made it to see his 8th birthday. Simby lived merely one year after our arrival, before the "house built for our furry friends" even received our 501c3 status in November 2014.

It's one thing, when individual pet owners are faced with the unfortunate and unexpected loss of their beloved family member due to veterinary mal-practice. One would be led to believe, this to be an isolated consequence, a case of misfortunate consequence. But we have come to realize, that veterinary mal-practice and incompetence, is not only widespread, but rampant; a common and regular occurrence, easily camouflaged, given the general lack of veterinary experience most pet owners have. The allopathic approach of Dr. Whitecoats from a pharmaceutical perspective, is a direct result of the veterinary school training they receive. We've sadly learned the hard way, to now explore, search, and attempt to identify, the causes of the effects of the "dis-ease", that impact the health of each individual feline who joins us here; many times often a result of inappropriate nutrition, excessive or improper use of pharmaceuticals, and regularly, vaccination overdoses breaking down their immune systems from the early stages of their lives. How these fundamental factors, could be so overwhelmingly overlooked consistently by every vet we've worked with to date, is simply incomprehensible and deplorable. The lack of proper breed specific nutrition combined with irresponsibly administered vaccinations in the absence of affordable titer testing, has now become the focus of our mission; not only to prevent the onset of disease and the inflammatory process, but in an attempt to recover and restore the health of pets whose pet owners are within our reach. The idea that veterinarians would incorporate an appropriate food as medicine approach into their practices, to educate pet owners, is evidently an unrealistic and hopeless expectation. Is the evolution of the felines even taught in vet school, the fact that cats are a species of obligate carnivores? To date, not one allopathic vet we've worked with, has offered an intelligent explanation with regard to the omnivore-herbivore regimes they push, those expensive commercial "prescription brands" commonly sold in veterinary practices; never willing or able to provide information about what those "prescriptive" ingredients, corn, corn gluten meal, brewer's rice, soy bean oil, barley, oats, peas and other starches actually do, and how they are able to make felines "healthy". We give thanks to the veterinary practitioners who choose to specialize in integrated, holistic, and/or homeopathy, sparkles of light and hope, given the financially motivated world of profiteering inundating the veterinary industry. We rely on and have a great respect for diagnostics, the countless tools and information they provide, but to identify courses of action needed to restore the health of a pet in need, with an integrated approach.

When a new resident arrives to the Head Butt Hotel, the first thing we do, (besides deworming, bathing, and deflea-ing), is to transition them over to proper food; precisely what we did with the two skeletal senior Persians Daisy and Princess, who joined us in February 2020. The Iam's 33% corn meal, brewers rice, and barley kibble hit the trash bin upon their arrival North Carolina. They ate us out of house and home their first two months here, starving and nutritionally deprived for their entire lives. Only under extreme and life-threatening conditions, would we immediately schedule CBC blood panels with new arrivals. We often hold off several weeks, to provide them with a baseline recovery period of proper nutrition and supplements, to compensate for the effects of the neglect, mal-nourishment, flea induced anemia, and wormy conditions they are faced with.

At the time of a new resident's initial wellness exam and bloodwork, we also do a rabies titer test, and send off a vial of spun blood to Kansas State Veterinary Lab, via the Protect the Pets website. For $55.00, this is a small price to pay, prior to ever consenting to a blindly administered rabies vaccination in the state of South Carolina. We learned harsh lessons too late. Avoidable vaccination overdoses which resulted in illnesses and untimely deaths of countless residents, were major factors during our first years after receiving our non-profit status. The financial burden we incurred, aside from so many lives lost, as a result of so many unexpected and avoidable cancer cases. Those shelter animals' lives we thought we were saving from humane euthanasia, were actually becoming part of the national cancer rate statistics, new annual cases being diagnosed in pets, now close to being double the number of shelter euthanasia rates of animals nationwide. Quite a testimony with regard to the direction the world of veterinary medicine has taken, and nothing to be proud of.

The untimely deaths of my Mom's cats Simby and Punky, was the start of the bittersweet destiny that led us here to begin with. South Carolina is the singular state whose rabies statute verbiage calls for rabies vaccinations at an unspecified frequency, to maintain continuous rabies protection. Titer testing, the medical industry standard a blood test for humans, no different for pets, to measure antibodies which provide and confirm levels of immunity protection.

Footnote **South Carolina Code of Laws, Title 47 Animals, Livestock and Poultry Chapter 5, Section 47-5-60: A pet owner must have his pet inoculated against rabies at a frequency to provide continuous protection of the pet from rabies using a vaccine approved by the department and licensed by the United States Department of Agriculture.** The rabies inoculation for pets must be administered by a licensed veterinarian or someone under a licensed veterinarian's direct supervision, as defined in Section 40-69-20. Evidence of rabies inoculation is a certificate signed by a licensed veterinarian. The rabies vaccination certificate forms may be provided by the licensed veterinarian or by the department or its designee. The veterinarian may stamp or write his name and address on the certificate. The certificate must include information recommended by the National Association of

State Public Health Veterinarians. The licensed veterinarian administering or supervising the administration of the vaccine shall provide one copy of the certificate to the owner of the pet and must retain one copy in his files for not less than three years. With the issuance of the certificate, the licensed veterinarian shall furnish a serially numbered metal license tag bearing the same number and year as the certificate with the name and telephone number of the veterinarian, veterinary hospital, or practice. The metal license tag at all times must be attached to a collar or harness worn by the pet for which the certificate and tag have been issued. Annually before February first, the veterinarian shall report to the department the number of animals inoculated against rabies during the preceding year. The department, in conjunction with licensed veterinarians, shall promote annual rabies clinics. The fee for rabies inoculation at these clinics may not exceed ten dollars, including the cost of the vaccine, and this charge must be paid by the pet owner. Fees collected by veterinarians at these clinics are their compensation.

HISTORY: 1962 Code Section 6-125; 1952 Code Section 6-125; 1950 (46) 2406; 1969 (56) 803; 1992 Act No. 517, Section 1, eff September 2, 1992; 2002 Act No. 343, Section 1, eff July 3, 2002; 2010 Act No. 173, Section 1, eff upon approval (became law without the Governor's signature on May 20, 2010).

This statute, being so commonly mispresented to pet owners by the majority of veterinarians in South Carolina, has become an extreme frustration for our non-profit. Although vets would never blindly consent to vaccinating themselves a second time unnecessarily, they do so willingly to unsuspecting and misinformed pet owners, placing their priority in proper perspective. Pets in South Carolina, should theoretically be the healthiest nationwide; while maintaining public safety and compliancy with the statute, and without compromising the health of companion animals with unnecessary vaccinations. Given the 50% cancer rates, and multitudes of other illnesses as a result of unnecessary vaccination overdoses, the financial benevolence speaks for itself. Our destiny leading us to Dr. John Robb was not coincidental, and we are proud to be South Carolina's premiere "Protect the Pets" rescue organization. We mandate responsible vaccination protocols and titer testing thru his PTP website with Kansas State Veterinary Lab, and will forever continue to support Doc, his Protect the Pets movement and oath to "Do No Harm", leading by example, as every vet should be doing.

Over the last 6 years, many shelter felines whose lives we "saved" from humane euthanasia, ultimately never came close to realizing the current national average lifespan of 12 years old for companion animals. As shelter pet survivors, they were, and continue to be "gifted" with the final freedom send off, that unavoidable rabies vaccine, "healthy" or not. Irrespective of the fact that the vaccine manufacturer's labels clearly state "only to be administered to healthy animals", few shelters vets respect this, and even fewer private practice veterinarians, who continuously disregard the oath they took. Our non-profit can only selectively save the lives of unsterilized shelter animals, after suffering the consequences emotionally and financially of Riley Finn's liver cancer (Greenville SC), Vince's cancer of the spleen (Gwinnett, Ga), both Baby (Marlboro County SC) and Biscuit's Squamous Cell Cancers (Rowan County NC), and Maggie's carcinomatosis (Bladen County, NC). Not to mention the countless seniors whose lives were saved, barely living a year after receiving their final toxic send off. And with so many pet owners being bamboozled into vaccinating pets unnecessarily via the post card due date methodology, it's not surprising that few, are even aware what is printed on the vaccine labels to begin with.

A number of our Head Butt Hotel residents are five cats (Feline Immunodeficiency Virus) which like felv (Feline Leukemia) exempts them from any further vaccinations, according to the vaccine manufacturer, "only to be administered to healthy animals". Brings to mind our 5 yr. old fiv+ female, Coopie, who on November 26, 2019, had a vet appointment with Dr. H, in need of a depo-medrol injection for her stomatitis condition. Her entire vet file was furnished, including her KSVL titer bloodwork results reflecting the state required minimum of 0.50 level: confirming continuous protection from her first and only rabies vaccination administered in 2014 when she was spayed. Dr. H, had already seen a handful of our cats earlier that month, neuters, fecal exams, CBC and titer bloodwork (including KSVL titer blood draws for both Cheddar and Pops). On this particular day, upon arrival, he decided he would not be examining fiv+ Coopie unless her rabies vaccine was directly "updated", stating that he did not recognize Kanas State Veterinary Lab titers, and that he would never subject himself nor any of his staff to a second rabies vaccination themselves, being too dangerous. Hence, the insistence that his clients update their pet's rabies vaccinations every three years. Perhaps he forgot his responsibility to first examine a pet, to determine the pet's eligibility health wise for a subsequent vaccination; refusing to acknowledge immune compromised Coopie's current KVSL titer, which reflected compliancy under the SC rabies statute, from her original "1 year" rabies vaccination administered 5 years prior. Needless to say, Dr.H was merely one of many Dr. Whitecoats we've parted ways with over the years. After receiving copies of our patient charts, his erroneously handwritten notes, confusing orange adult Pops, with orange kitten Redd (the one in fact with coccidia), the following commentary was posted on a page entitled "Coopie":

11-26-29 Cat was scheduled for physical – I did not do physical because client "does not believe in vaccines" especially in an "immune suppressed" FIV cat.

I explained that I require annual or tri-annual vaccine.
Dr. H, we have one commentary to you - live up to the oath you took to do no harm, you are a grave threat, endangering the health and wellbeing of your clients' pets.

Continuing along, Dr. D works at another veterinary facility we recently parted ways with. As much as they willingly accommodated many of our cats' titer blood draws done at the time of their wellness exams and CBC bloodwork, it's evidently a matter whether pet owners are knowledgeable and aware of the statute. Our subsequent adopter's 14-year-old cat's insulin prescription was held hostage, until the pet-owner agreed and consented to update her cat's rabies vaccination blindly, without even a mention of a titer. The woman, unaware of the SC rabies statute being mispresented, or the duration of immunity protection one vaccine in fact provides, was once forced to vaccinate an unhealthy pet, this time her diabetic cat in exchange for the insulin. Prior to allowing her to adopt our Willie, we furnished her with the nutritional guidance she required, in an effort to stabilize and attempt to reverse her sugar baby's condition; information that vet Dr. D, for years was to unable to provide. Simply eliminating the inappropriate carbs, that "prescription" diet they continue to sell and make money on, would have resulted in a favorable effect many years sooner. But we know, maintaining pets in perpetual states of disease, is far more profitable. After removing the carbs from her cat's diet, we are happy to report that her cat remains in remission, healthier than ever in her golden feline years, and our Willie now, is enjoying having a loving family of his own.

Dr. T, the owner of the practice where Dr. D is employed, furnished us with Patterson's patient chart, prior to returning him to the NY rescue who sent him to us to resolve his "ibs/ibd" condition. Upon reviewing her veterinary commentary noted on his chart, our differences with regard to nutrition and vaccinations were clearly evident. We were more than happy to accommodate Dr. T's request: "Owner doesn't like fluoroquinolones, hills/royal canin-very particular client. Per Dr T: prefer not to work with this cat-rescue person. 7/10/2020". Adios, we were more than happy to accommodate her, along with an extensive letter recommending her entire staff, brush up on their Continuing Education Units and so, once again, another local veterinary practice bit the dust. And to think, they offer $1200 quotes for dental interventions in the absence of digital x-rays! But as usual, unsuspecting pet owners, unknowingly would and will ultimately learn the hard way, as we did, patronizing a facility for dental interventions, which are illegal in some states in the absence of digital x-rays.

From 2015 to 2018, those $300 dentals we had done on many of our cats in Loris, turned out to be one of the most detrimental mistakes we could have ever made. Never having a cavity personally, the lesson and importance of digital x-rays with extractions was realized at the expense of victims who didn't deserve the fates they were subjected to. Thanks to Dr. J, countless of our cats suffered and died unmerciful deaths, the result of her inferior dental skills. She practiced three times on Grey alone who remains her last surviving victim in our care, and extreme health issues to impact his quality of life, because of her. Her other victims included Mallomar, Abner, and Bullet, not to mention Clark Gable, barely 5 years old, who slowly wasted away, unable to eat. Her recommended to see our oncologist in Charleston, 2 ½ hours away, ruled out any "suspicions of cancer". But it was not long after Clark Gable's untimely death, that the retained roots and tooth fragments left behind, were identified as the culprit for Grey. He underwent a 4th periodontal intervention in January 2019, to remove the debris Dr. J left behind the first three times. But being fiv+, the damage has been done as a result of her incompetence, we are currently focusing on providing him quality of life for his extreme stomatitis condition using the Assisi Loop and Cold laser until which time we may be in a position to proceed attempt the last and very expensive option being of Stem Cell Therapy. But never fear, Dr.J continues with her dentals in the absence of x-rays, continues pushing vaccinations with no regard for our South Carolina Rabies Statute; vaccinating according to the blindly administered due date post card method, juicing up all the ill, crippled, and aged pets, and then providing them with affordable euthanasia, when their suffering culminates, to a point of irreversibly failing health; justifying in her mind and providing a humane service to end their lives of the suffering that she's in fact, caused.

And as usual, always pushing to update a "1 yr. or 3 yr. rabies vax" rather than checking with affordable titers. Thankfully, we are happy to provide our KVSL titer results acknowledging continuous protection, every opportunity we have, just as we do with Cheddar's some 8 years after from that 1-year rabies vaccine he was administered in Cobb County Georgia, back in 2012.

We were initially thrilled to be introduced to a vet facility in Wilmington, competent to handle the necessary periodontal dental work that Dr. J's victims required, extracting the retained roots and fragments left behind. Unfortunately, that wound up being a short-lived situation also, after the unnecessary and untimely death of our young kitten Artie, with a very close call for Cheddar, as well.

Dr. W, the owner of that practice, minus a degree in oncology, blatantly misdiagnosed Cheddar as having intestinal lymphoma. She arguably insisted upon the accuracy of the VDI-CK Cancer Marker blood test, she requested be done last August, 2019, scheduling him to begin her "big guns" chemo-therapy protocol the subsequent Monday based on the results of the bloodwork panel. Never thinking to rule out any of the other inflammatory bowel diseases, never even suggesting a second opinion and biopsy with our established Charleston oncologist. Several days later, a visit to CVRC it was $1500 well spent to receive a negative lymphoma diagnosis with 100% accuracy based on Colorado State biopsies. Had Dr. W thought to rule out other possibilities, prior to her lymphoma diagnosis, that $40, five-minute pancreatitis snap test that revealed a positive case of pancreatitis, his true diagnosis. Yet Dr. W, never wavered from her misdiagnosis, and adhered to her assertation that her cancer marker bloodwork was in fact more accurate than Colorado State biopsies. Cheddar is alive and well today, his "lymphoma" diagnosis properly treated, averting a close call that could have likely taken his life.

Unfortunately, 14-month-old Artie, wasn't as lucky and died within three months, mid-June, as a result of the short fallings of Dr. W's and her team. Suspecting a kidney infection, she was prescribed Veraflox, the fluoroquinolone classification of antibiotics we have come to avoid using for our cats. Artie was administered this antibiotic, (without an informed consent) for a urinary tract infection she didn't have. When the Veraflox antibiotic began to compromise her kidneys over the next weeks, she wound up hospitalized twice for several days; administered a combination of Sodium Chloride iv fluids with Aluminum Hydroxy. Aluminum hydroxy properly compounded at a pharmacy, is commonly used as a binder, to help lower the phosphorus levels in cats affected with kidney failure. But, in their efforts to scrimp and save money on cats remaining under their care in their facility, the Aluminum Hydroxy they ordered from Carolina Biologics, a product never meant for use in animals nor humans outside a laboratory environment. This resulted in Artie's spiral downward while hospitalized there, resulting in a complete onset of kidney and liver failure, Unable to account for her organ failure, they recommended she be taken to NC State, already past the point of no return. And frighteningly enough, it's very likely, they continue to cause fatal injuries and untimely deaths to other cats, with the continued use of this product, as pet owners, would never know otherwise.

Nor would we want to be remiss in mentioning the Royal Canin hypoallergenic "prescription" brand food they returned, quietly swept under the carpet with no mention of being recalled by the manufacturer. The remaining open bags of bad food, continued to be used for hospitalized cats in their care, never a word mentioned to clients who had purchased it. The ill stricken retail client's cats, were treated on a case by case basis, the result of the food, never identified as the cause.

Starting off the new year in January, Patterson, who we mentioned earlier, was an fiv+ guy who joined us from NY, after receiving a diagnosis of ibd according to their big apple vet. Accompanied by a bag of high carb food, we were optimistic we could help resolve his diarrhea issues. Six months later, we properly had his "ibd" misdiagnosis by the NY vet, identified as three mycoplasmas, haemofelis, hemominutum, and turicens; definitively diagnosed thru the pcr blood test panel we requested Dr. T's facility proceed with in July. Patterson's since back in NY, health restored after completing his Doxycycline treatment successfully, still in search of his forever home. Sadly, our longtime residents Smokey, and fiv+ Abner, and Lt. Dan, all lost their lives as a result of this mycoplasma contamination, all faced with sudden and acute onsets of anemia, misdiagnosed in the emergency rooms, resulting in their untimely passings. Fiv+ Woody, a fourth cat, definitively diagnosed with the mycoplasma as well, continues to live his days out with us at this time, while we provide him with hospice care and quality of life and comfort, in the only home he's ever know in his short five-year-old life: irreversible end stage kidney failure, diminishing red blood cell counts sliding weekly with transfusions ineffective. All thanks to the standard cliché phrase, "ibd/ibs", by vets who don't have the ability to identify the cause of this unfortunate effect.

Did Dayna's 6-year-old cat Stormy need to wind up in liver failure, as a result of the nutritional choices she unknowingly made, backing up his entire gastro-intestinal system, causing irreversible inflammatory issues that enemas, fluids, emergency room treatment was unable to resolve? Did Buddy really need to die, suffering a year-long battle with nonstop gushing diarrhea, his vet claimed was cancer, offering nothing more than Tylan when Crypto could have been, easily diagnosed and treated? Or how about our other friend in Illinois, whose 12-year-old Siamese fed Meow Mix her entire life, recovered from liver disease, only to die two days later from a cardiac infraction. Did our fiv+ Camy need to be wrongly administered Atopica leading to his death and how many pet owners would even know this is not a pharmaceutical that should be administered to fiv+ cats?

Was Metronidazole really the proper antibiotic choice for Cooper, a young Bengal kitten stricken with diarrhea, ultimately resulting in continuous seizures further exasperated by the 1-year rabies vaccine he was administered at the time he was neutered? Even worse, after suffering two grand mal episodes, what ethical vet could ever administer a second unnecessary rabies vaccine (in the absence of a titer), to Cooper, now a two-year-old unhealthy cat, who returned for a subsequent follow up exam and bloodwork the same week he same week he suffered these seizures?

Not much different a case with our 9-year-old Husky Sanford, the vet in Columbia, continued to administer rabies vaccinations in the absence of titers, until he arrived to the point of uncontrollable seizures. Of course, the vet did not have any knowledge with regard to detoxing or reversing the effects of the poisonous neurotoxins injected into yet another victim of veterinary malpractice. Humane euthanasia, not even the courtesy phone call was extended, to return him to our rescue, where we would have attempted to counteract and detoxify the effects of the vaccines thru homeopathy and integrated approaches.

And then we are remined of Sangria, a Siamese beauty who 6 weeks after being adopted out, was euthanized by a Calhoun Georgia vet, claiming she had cancer. Again, we were never even given the opportunity to have her returned, not advised prior, when in fact, that one nickel sized "hotspot" at the base of her tail, had been previously and properly diagnosed, merely requiring an extended regimen of prednisolone; the effects of a hoarding and unhealthy circumstances she was subjected to, prior to being rescued and her life "saved".

Is perpetuating a lack of proper nutrition and vaccinating pets, until they reach their maximum saturation point of ill health and or a cancer diagnosis, the underlying objective? And then to maximize on the strategic plan financially, to treat the pet who will succumb long before ever reaching its natural lifespan, only to subsequently move onto the next victim and start over again? Should ultrasounds really done to identify "inflammation" before ruling out the countless bacterial possibilities that a Flea Tick Born or GI Panel could identify for diarrhea onsets, treating the symptoms rather than addressing the proper cause?

We refuse to support or patronize any of this craziness further. This behavior is rampant nationwide manifesting in one form, or another, not only here in Horry County and South Carolina. And it always begins with the same question when a pet owner or rescuer calls for an appointment, "Is your pet up to date on vaccines"? Imagine how much safer the nation would be for companion animals, if vets were legally obliged to vaccinate themselves, at the same frequency and dosage as they inflict on our pets?

We are grateful for the opportunity to relate some of these unfortunate stories here and reflect on the lessons their lives enabled us to sickeningly realize. Despite the financial and mental challenges, we will continue to oversee the care of every individual feline who joins us at the Head Butt Hotel, with the objective of treating them as if they were our only pet. We will continue to counsel others who contact us, to educate, support, and set an example in our effort to establish higher standards of care and quality of life for the few we are able to help; to advocate for the return of veterinary morality and ethics, to safeguard pets from the widespread veterinary indifference and incompetence that

exists today, for vets to place their health as the priority, while upholding their oath, to "Do No Harm". This is the promise we will keep, here at the Head Butt Hotel in North Myrtle Beach, South Carolina. And we thank everyone involved with Joey's Legacy, for their relentless efforts and contributions, to make the world a better place, for those who rely on us to be their voices.

Heartbreak at the Head Butt Hotel

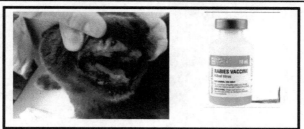

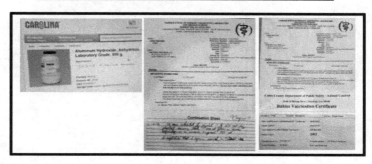

CHAPTER FOURTEEN

Kyle's Story
David Anderson and Debbie Cartwright (UK)

To the Directors (Avril Marriott and Nicola Williams),

Kyle

I am writing with regard to the death of our beloved dog Kyle whom we believe you so hastily discharged on Saturday 28/12/19 and died a mere 15 hours later when he collapsed suddenly at home. Both my husband and I believe that he was discharged far too soon and that there were many areas within his treatment delivered by you which were negligent, unprofessional and ultimately contributed to his early death.

24th and 25th December 2019
To recap details Kyle had been very well up until he vomited once on 24/12/19 – this occurred in the evening (undigested food) and then he had a few further episodes of similar on Christmas day. He was otherwise well in himself just off his food which led us to believe he may have had an upset stomach / stomach bug.

26th December 2019
The next day (Boxing Day) Kyle was still vomiting to the point where he was drinking large amounts and then throwing the entire quantity back up. His behaviour was also different whereby we noted that he just wanted to be alone, taking himself away to hide underneath our back garden hedge.

27th December 2019
At 1.30 am Kyle was restless and struggling to settle down for the night but did not appear to be in any pain. I was concerned that due to his previous

vomiting and inability to even keep fluids down that he may be starting to become dehydrated so decided to phone our on call / emergency vet telephone number. Nicola answered to which I explained everything which had been occurring with Kyle and my concerns. She asked if the problem could wait until 8.30 the next morning. but I explained if I was concerned now then surely it would possibly be even worse a further 7 hours later. She asked us to bring Kyle to the practice for 2am where she then examined him and decided to admit him for IV fluids / antiemetics / analgesia and investigatory blood tests. She did at this point ask us if Kyle would be likely to rip his IV out as there would be no-one permanently on site to monitor him. I asked if they were not expected to sleep-over if on call as they did advertise 24/7 care but apparently not. There was no discussion regarding the option of transfer to an alternate facility.

Nicola rang us at 10am 28/12/19 and explained that earlier bloods taken on Kyle's admission had been deranged suggesting a diagnosis of acute pancreatitis She also expressed her initial concerns regarding his poor kidney function, but then stated that further blood tests repeated that same morning had shown an improvement after iv fluids. She explained that they would keep Kyle overnight as he was yet to pass any urine and was not eating.

We were advised to ring at 5pm for an update but decided that we would call in at 12 noon to see if we could see him. We were told this was not possible as he was in a room shared with other dogs that were recovering from surgery and would need to make an appointment. We accepted this and returned at 3.30pm to a pre arranged appointment and were informed that Kyle had still not passed any urine despite being led outside regularly. So we asked if we could try with him - Kyle walked outside with difficulty / his undercarriage supported by my husband in a sling that the practice had been using and he managed to pass urine well / a good amount. He was returned to his cage and kept in overnight as planned.

28th December 2019

We rang at 9am for a further update to find that there had then been a changeover in vet cover from Nicola to Avril. Avril informed us that Kyle had improved and was drinking well on his own, his bloods were back to normal but he was just not eating. She stated that some dogs just won't eat in the surgery and felt that he would possibly "eat better at home" so she would discharge him and we were to collect him at 11.15am. We were overjoyed that he was getting better / improving and was well enough to come home. There was at no time any mention of "him not being fixed as she put it, or the words "guarded prognosis" which she later recorded in Kyle's records.

On collection of Kyle we were taken into a room first and handed a "large" bag of medication informing us that Kyle would not need any medication until 5pm when he would be due further pain relief and antibiotics as any given in surgery would then be wearing off". I had to enquire as to what medication she was giving him and to run through each as they were not going to be explained. I expressed my concerns that she had prescribed him Tramadol which he had not tolerated in the past. I explained that following 2 stifle orthopaedic surgeries he was given Tramadol and on both occasions he was highly distressed to the point where it was difficult to tell whether he was in actual pain or having other / euphoric side effects of the drug. I therefore stopped giving him the Tramadol at that time and Kyle had been absolutely fine thereafter. Avril did not seem to want to hear this and replied that Kyle had already been given it in the surgery and he had been fine – in other words that is what I'm giving so get on with it. I am however unable to see any log of this within his records and it would appear that he was being kept comfortable with im or iv drugs right up until discharge - as well as on constant iv fluids. In a letter dated 06/01/20 Avril tries to explain herself by stating that I had mentioned Kyle's previous Tramadol use but that I was unsure of the dosage or what side effects he had shown! There was really no concern shown whatsoever as to whether Kyle would actually be comfortable at home without im / iv drugs, or if he would even be able to take any oral medication at all. My husband even had to request an antiemetic be added as a "just in case" medications for the weekend should

Kyle need it. Avril later explains in a letter that she wanted to see how Kyle was after antiemetics given in surgery had worn off and that we were to ring if he then started vomiting again. There was no mention of this at all – she just looked inconvenienced and went off to look for said medication taking approximately 10 minutes before returning.

Avril however did inform us that if Kyle was "worse again" we could ring, plus if he still wasn't eating he would likely need to be readmitted after the weekend / Monday am). She then left to get Kyle from the room he was being kept in so we followed to watch for him. She was gone for some time and finally appeared with him coaxing him down the corridor / obviously struggling with walking. We thought that due to his illness that he was bound to be weaker and likely stiff from being kept in a small cage / space for some time so expected that this would gradually improve. Whilst my husband put Kyle in the car, Avril asked how I was going to make payment. I explained that Kyle was insured to which she questioned "with whom". I told her that he was insured with Equine & Livestock to which I met the reply – "oh we always struggle to get money from them!

Kyle drank very little at home and would not eat at all. He was given his tramadol and antibiotics at 5pm as he was becoming a bit restless and we thought it was likely due to his medication wearing off. He continued to be restless but not crying until approximately 8pm when he settled. This restlessness could have now been due to the Tramadol or discomfort – as Avril was informed but did not listen – it would be difficult to tell. At 11.45pm Kyle suddenly became extremely agitated and crying and passed urine on the mat where he had been asleep by the doors to the garden. We helped raise him and led him into the garden when his front legs seemed to give way and he lay unable to get up with his tongue "lolling" from 1 side of his mouth. His eyes were scared and he appeared in shock so I immediately rang the vets at the then time of 12.30am. (Kyle was not left "in a collapsed state at home by his owners for hours" as Avril later documented).

29th December 2019

Avril answered the phone - she sounded confused and it was difficult to understand her as her speech seemed slurred. I realized this may be from waking her out of a sound sleep at that time but was concerned when even as events progressed over the course of Kyle's readmission, this did not change. We were advised to take Kyle to the surgery for 1am where my husband carried him in and placed him on the examination table. Avril stated that Kyle had poor pulses and that it was difficult to hear his heart and she suspected something else underlying was going on. My husband was asked to carry Kyle along the corridor to the cage he had occupied earlier where an iv could be restarted. As forementioned it was difficult to understand Avril as her speech was still slurred to the point that I felt I had to question whether she had been drinking alcohol. She strongly denied this. There were exchanges of words between my husband, myself and Avril relating to Kyles inappropriate early discharge, however we left not wanting to delay any care that Kyle now urgently needed. Avril stated that she needed to perform an urgent ultrasound scan to see what the problem was. A form was forced at me to sign stating – you will need to sign a consent form before you go.

My husband answered the phone at 2am where Avril explained that Kyle had likely had "a leak or a bleed of some description? peritonitis and needed emergency surgery". She explained that she could either perform the surgery at Witham View now or transfer him elsewhere but as the referral centre was 2 hours away it was unlikely that he would survive the journey. My husband spoke to me and we agreed that the only option was life-saving surgery now and advised Avril to proceed.

At 3.37 am the phone rang and my husband was informed that Kyle had not made it to surgery as he had "arrested". He was told that they had managed to bring him back but arrested a 2nd time and then died. Did we want to come and see him?

We attended the surgery at 4am and were met at the door by Avril and a veterinary nurse – we were shown to a room and left alone with Kyle.

On exiting there was a further heated discussion regarding Kyle's inappropriate discharge. I was at 1 point told by the nurse - that "I was upset, to go away and think about things". I was also told that "as I am a Nurse Practitioner, I should have known better and should expect that these things can happen". There was absolutely no caring, compassion or empathy in either the attitudes of Avril or the nurse. They were argumentative and ignorant to our pain and loss.

We attended an appointment to discuss matters with Nicola as was pre-arranged and relayed our complaints / concerns. My husband mentioned that he did not understand why it had taken so long for Kyle to get down to surgery and Nicola asked us if we would like Avril to ring us to discuss further. We declined due to her previous poor attitude.

We then received a long letter the following day from Avril stating how she was acting in Kyle's best interests, and felt that everything she had done was satisfactory. She gave us a very graphic / upsetting, step by step, cold-hearted medical account of her actions taken up to and including Kyle's death including CPR / resuscitation.

Our main complaints with the care Kyle received are inappropriate early discharge / inability to grasp the severity of the condition with lack of regard for potential complications.

Kyle was admitted for a period of 33hours in total. The research we have done shows that dogs with acute canine pancreatitis need close / vigilant observation / monitoring and advanced care, and require admission for a minimum stay of 3 to 4 days and in some cases much longer. The research also adds that the condition can be extremely painful which Nicola did confirm to us.

Your surgery was due to close for the remainder of the weekend at 12 noon on the day Kyle was discharged. Had Kyle been kept in, it would have meant that someone would have regularly needed to attend to check on his condition, change iv fluids, and administer any medication over this period of time. It would appear that Avril decided that it would be easier for her "duty weekend cover" to actually send Kyle home. She struggled to get Kyle up and out of his cage due to the length of time it took and we had to encourage him to walk down the corridor to us. We were also led to believe that Kyle was actually drinking well on his own but were later told by Nicola that the reason Avril had been so long in getting Kyle from his cage was that she was having to disconnect his drip! Avril appeared reluctant to grasp the severity of Kyle's condition or that there was the possibility of early complications occurring.

If you, as a surgery advertising 24/7 care were aware that you could not provide this - why were we then not offered the option of transferring Kyle to a veterinary hospital who would provide it - especially whilst Kyle's condition was relatively stable or as you said "fit for discharge?"

At no point was an ultrasound performed or even mentioned from admission through to his discharge until his collapse and symptoms / signs becoming life threatening – this may have detected other / co-existing problems / diagnosis or early warning signs of potential complications (pancreatic abscess formation, hemorrhage, necrosis or the start of peritonitis).

Avril was likely awoken by our phone call at 1am and she was very difficult to understand which can be expected – however I was concerned when her speech was continued to be slurred later at the surgery and throughout events. My husband thought it was possible that she had a cold as she was carrying tissues and wiping her nose.

Avril indicated within Kyle's medical records that he had been "in a collapsed state for hours" prior to ringing her which is untrue. She was actually called seconds after he collapsed. She also mentioned "screaming" which we really have no idea what this is about or where this has come from.

Nicola printed Kyle's medical records for us and none of this information was documented at that time but was added later and then sent via email through to us. All of the new information clearly now indicating exact times were not logged contemporaneously within his records and can only have been added at a later time.

At no point did Avril have a discussion with us about pancreatitis being potentially fatal. This and several other entries in Kyle's records appear to have been manufactured to make it look as though she had given full, reasonable, accurate advice and care. Other areas seem to be manufactured to defer the blame on to us as owners.

We were never given the option to transfer Kyle to a veterinary hospital as documented at any point until his condition became an emergency. Even then we were informed that he would likely not survive the journey.

I am finally told, very patronizingly in Avrils letter that "with hindsight things may have been done differently" and that "we must be careful not to use the benefit of hindsight when reflecting on a case". Well to make a point "the case" happens to have a name – Kyle, who was once a beautiful, breathing, living friend. Plus I must also disagree in the fact that hindsight is a vital part in reflection as how else do we learn from our errors? or determine what should have been done differently to prevent it happening again?

We do understand that Kyle may have died even with the very best of care but he did not have to die in the way Avril had orchestrated it – without any consideration for Kyle, ourselves as owners or the possibility of complications. I also have to say that I have never met people who are so cold and without a shred of compassion in a highly paid for supposedly caring service. We have always had Kyle insured and informed you numerous times that cost was never an issue – we would always find a way to pay if necessary – this brings us to your fees.

We signed a consent form at the height of duress when our dog was readmitted in a shocked / collapsed state. There was no discussion – just a handing over of a piece of paper to be signed which is not what I would understand as "informed consent". I have no doubt that treatment was given to try and revive Kyle who was by then dying, however what I am concerned about was how he was basically "thrown out" of your surgery / inappropriate early discharge so he would not need any care over the weekend. I believe that it is within your profession to constantly endeavour to ensure the health and welfare of animals committed to your care. In my opinion, Avril did not undertake this duty of care. Nothing will ever bring Kyle back, however I hope by these actions that no other pets or their owners have to suffer in the way Kyle or ourselves have.

CHAPTER FIFTEEN

Trixie's Story
Toni Moore

My dog, Trixie, a Yorkshire Terrier, died, in my opinion, due to Veterinary negligence. This is her story.

The events in my story took place over two days, the 1st & 2nd of September 2019, two days which rocked my life, and broke my heart. Trixie was my world and I loved her so much. She was only 6 years old when she died and was the center of my very being. Trixie was a very loving and happy dog, she always made me smile and I was just so happy to be with her. She loved her toys and was a little bit crazy, but she was my baby, and I was her human.

She did not deserve to suffer in the way that she did before she died, and if the vet, to whom I entrusted her wellbeing, had carried out his duties correctly (in the way that he said he would) then maybe she would still be with me today.

When I first got Trixie, she was so small, and was prone to picking up small ailments, which subsequently changed to her becoming increasingly ill as time went by. I was unaware when I first got her, that she was from a puppy farm. Unbeknown to me, on the day that I collected her, she was already sick with kennel cough and other health problems, which became apparent later on. She was very unwell for around 6 weeks and I didn't think she was going to make it through, but she did, and this was largely due to the fact that, at that time, she was registered with a different veterinary practice, and received an extremely good quality of care. She was such a fighter, and from then on, we had such a special bond together.

All her life I just tried to protect her and make sure she was ok. Through the years she was diagnosed with patella luxation (kneecap dislocation), skin allergies, a collapsing trachea and stomach problems. This worried me a lot but every day I tried so hard to make sure she was ok and had everything she needed.

I would just like to mention that I only registered Trixie at the veterinary practice that this story relates to around 6 months prior to her death. This particular vet was recommended as a specialist in orthopedic surgery, and my decision was influenced by Trixie's probable need for surgery on her patella luxation in the near future.

Trixie became unwell during the morning of the 1st September 2019, when she went on to the garden to do her usual toileting, and I became genuinely concerned for her welfare. I noticed that there was a lot of blood in her stool so I called the vet immediately, who told me he would call me back to arrange a time to go to the surgery to collect some pro-biotics. He called me around 3 hours later, requesting me to go the surgery in 15 minutes. He said that I had no need to take Trixie with me for a consultation as it was nothing to worry about. When I arrived at the surgery, I showed him a photo of Trixie's bloody stool, and he reassured me that it was normal and that she would be fine. I then returned home and gave Trixie some of the pro-biotics. Later in the day she started with very bloody diarrhea and sickness. I called the vet again who told me to take her to the surgery to be examined. We arrived at the surgery and Trixie was not her usual self, she was noticeably quiet. The vet checked her over and told me she had a bug and that she would be fine in 2-3 days and assured me that no other dogs had been known to die from this condition. I also expressed concerns about her not sleeping properly for the previous two days, and that she kept stretching, which was diagnosed as stomach-ache, so an anti-sickness injection was also administered. Anti-biotics were also prescribed for us to administer at home.

When we returned home, I tried to give her the anti-biotics, but she would not allow me to do so. She continued to be sick around every 10 minutes, and the bloody diarrhea got a lot worse. I became increasingly worried and called the vet again. She had, by now, also developed breathing problems and I was advised that, as she suffered from a collapsing trachea (an ongoing problem) that the sick was aggravating her larynx, and that she would be fine, again advising me to 'let her ride it out'. He did not ask me to attend the surgery with Trixie again, his advice at this point was given over the telephone. I told him that Trixie could not settle, and he told me to leave her to it.

Around 2 hours later, she was still in a bad way, and her breathing seemed to be getting worse, and blood was coming from her back passage, even when she was laid down. I called the vet again, and by this time I was extremely upset and worried about Trixie. I told him what was happening to her and he had an attitude with me on the phone, as though he was annoyed with me calling him. He said "I told you before she will be fine in 2-3 days and another visit to the surgery will achieve nothing, you just need to leave her to ride it out".

During the night, and the early hours of the morning, Trixie was becoming very weak and lifeless, she was still struggling to breathe, and she was still having lots of bloody diarrhea and sickness. We took photos and a video of what was happening to Trixie during this time, in order to show the vet how she was suffering. Around 5am on the 2nd September I called the vet again. I told him Trixie needed to be seen urgently and that she was in an extremely bad way. He agreed to meet us at the surgery in around 20 minutes. During the car journey to the surgery Trixie did not move at all, she was so weak she could not even lift her head up. We arrived at the surgery and followed the vet inside (it was out of hours and the surgery was closed). I put Trixie on the examination table for the vet to check her over and he said that she seemed a lot worse than when he had examined her the previous day, and he listened to her chest and said he suspected she had fluid in her lungs (which he later denied saying, following her death). He said he was going to keep her in for observation, and to give her an injection of Synulox for her lungs and treatment for her sickness and diarrhea and assured me that she would be home that evening or the following morning. I left Trixie with him in the hope that he would look after her and try to help her. I went home and waited anxiously for a call from him, which came at around 8.30 am, and he told me Trixie had suffered a cardiac arrest and sadly died. I cannot even begin to explain how this made me feel, and my whole world fell apart at that moment. He told me that he had left Trixie unattended for around 40 minutes whilst he went home to tend to his own dogs, and also added that he didn't give her any treatment before he left her, so basically we had entrusted Trixie to his care and he just put her in a cage and went home. She was left to suffer and was all alone.

I just could not understand why this had happened and I feel that I deserve some answers to the questions going around in my head.

As he was very well aware of her medical history, why was he not more attentive to my concerns?

Again, knowing her medical history, why did he assume that it was a virus and that she would 'ride it out', knowing full well that she did not enjoy the best of health and was prone to other problems –(documented in her medical records)- which would probably make her less able to do so than a stronger, fitter dog?

Why would he consider it safe for her to be left alone in his surgery for even a minute, let alone 40 minutes, if she were showing extreme signs of distress?

That same morning, about an hour later, I called the surgery to ask why the events had unfolded as they did. His reply was ''I don't know''. He then went on to explain that he had left her alone, unattended, for 40 mins, and then, the practice nurse came into the surgery, to begin her shift, and that is when Trixie went into cardiac arrest.

The next day I went to his surgery, to question him face-to-face, as to why this had happened. I asked him why he did not give her any treatment and why he had left her alone. He replied that she seemed fine whilst he was with her which I consider to be untrue and deceitful and he asked me what would I have wanted him to have done, to which I replied "I don't know as I'm not a vet, but you should have helped her and not left her alone."

With everything that happened to Trixie and the fact that she was left alone suffering I am struggling to cope with it all. She meant everything to me, and I will forever feel guilty that I put my trust in this vet and that Trixie died because he did not do what he was supposed to do. I did not get to say goodbye to her, I thought she would be coming home, as that is what he told me. He told me she would be fine and that I should not worry about her. I wish I had taken Trixie to a different vet as I believe she would still be here with me now if I did. The vet didn't seem to care, and he had been getting annoyed with me keep ringing him. I tried so many times to tell him how bad she was, but he just had an attitude with me, and I felt like he was just trying to brush me off. He has lied and made me so upset. If he had seen Trixie the evening prior to her death when I told him she was struggling to breathe and she was having really bad bloody diarrhea and sickness then she probably wouldn't have got as bad as she did to go into cardiac arrest.

A few relevant points leading up to these events follow. On the morning of Friday, 30th August 2019, I took Trixie to the vet's surgery as I was concerned about lumps on her skin, and the itching it was causing. During this consultation, the vet stated that Trixie had a flare-up of a pre-existing skin inflammation, and he prescribed her 1mg of Prednisolone, to be given once daily.

Following the examination, the vet then proceeded to give Trixie some doggie treats, and when I pointed out that she had previously been diagnosed with an allergy to anything, including treats, that may contain duck, he replied ''oh, ok''. He did feed her a quantity of these treats, which I thought was excessive, given her size. He also commented that she was ''greedy'' as she was hardly even chewing them, just swallowing them as fast as she could, but he continued to give them to her. I later checked with the manufacturer of the treats, who confirmed that they may well have contained some duck derivatives.

When her sickness and diarrhea started over the weekend, and I took her into the vet's surgery for treatment, I kept mentioning about the treats that he had given her, and if they could somehow be connected to the symptoms she was showing, but his reply was that ''no, it's nothing to do with the treats, it's just a bug going around''. He was aware, at this point, that Trixie had been placed on a strict diet, and that I was only able to feed her certain foods.

If he was aware of this from the notes sent to him by our previous veterinary practice, then he should have known that she was prone to both skin inflammation flare-ups, and gastro-intestinal upsets, and that treats could easily have given her an upset stomach.

My follow-up question to this is why were all of my concerns dismissed out of hand regarding the cause(s) of Trixie's sickness and diarrhea. When I further asked if the treats could possibly be a factor in her sickness, the vet promptly replied ''no'', appearing not to give it a second thought. The vet sent Trixie's body to a local university for a necropsy, which confirmed that she had died of acute hemorrhagic gastroenteritis, in itself non-contagious, and also proof that fluid was present in her lungs. Finally, given the circumstances as they were, I ask myself why he himself was funding all costs relating to tests and the necropsy, as this is surely not standard practice? As I am led to understand, all such costs are usually borne by the pet's owner.

The university later released Trixie's body for cremation, which was a very harrowing time for me. I had not seen her since the morning of her admittance to the vet's care, and, following her death, I was unable to bring myself to see her, as I was in such emotional turmoil, and never really had the chance to say goodbye to my baby.

Following on from events leading up to the death of Trixie, I decided to make a formal complaint, to the RCVS, the governing body of veterinary surgeons in the UK.

This complaint was referred to the CEG, (Case Examination Group), and, following their findings, resulted in a referral for a more detailed investigation by a committee known as the PIC (Preliminary Investigation Committee), which consists of both veterinary professionals, and non-professionals also.

During the initial stages of the case examination carried out by the CEG, statements were provided by both myself, and the veterinary practice (including the surgery staff). The statements given by the practice were found to contain discrepancies and contradictions, which were picked up by the CEG, and resulted in the complaint being forwarded to the PIC, an example being that the vet wrote to me and said he did not give Trixie IV fluids as this can aggravate fluid in the lungs but later denied saying that he suspected fluid in Trixie's lungs.

The PIC duly considered the case and basically dismissed it out of hand. The letter I received from them regarding their decision made exceedingly difficult reading for me. They seemingly ignored a statement given by my mother and ignored the video evidence of Trixie's suffering. They appeared to condone his actions, using phrases such as ''with hindsight'' and ''it would have been preferable to have seen Trixie earlier'', but, at the end of the day, they came down firmly on his side, leaving me with no further options to continue my complaint. This group is self-regulating, not answerable to a higher authority, such as an ombudsman, and their criteria for misconduct or incompetency is set so high as to be virtually impossible to overcome by any complaint.

I feel so let down by the RCVS, and my opinion is that they have sought to protect one of their own, and the whole complaints procedure was just a whitewash.

I have, however, raised my concerns about the way that my complaint was handled, with my local MP. He took on board my concerns and has been in contact with the RCVS. Unfortunately, he received similar responses to the one's that I received and has now exhausted his avenues of investigation.

When I could bring myself to return to the surgery to collect Trixie's blanket, lead, and harness, I was informed that her blanket had been destroyed, the reason given being that it was both heavily soiled and contaminated. Yet I was told that I could have some cuttings of her hair. If the blanket was considered unsafe for return, then whatever it was allegedly contaminated with must also have been present in her body hair. In my heart, I believe that the vet thought that if he returned her blanket to me in that condition, then maybe I would have some concerns, or suspicions, about why it came to be like that, if she was, as he claimed, ''under observation''. According to his statement to the RCVS he observed her for an hour, seeing nothing untoward, yet, when he left her alone for 40mins, this is the time frame in which she deteriorated so badly that she eventually died, and contaminated her blanket so heavily that it was deemed unreturnable. By not returning it, I can only deduce that he considered it to be contagious, yet he had told me prior to her death that she only ''had a bug'' and that no dog had ever died from it. If this is the case then he had no valid reason to retain, and destroy, the blanket without my consent, as it should not have posed a threat to anyone or anything else. My little dog was obviously left to suffer alone in her own vomit, blood, and mess, and this is why he refused to return it to me.

Following her cremation, my mum and I decided to have her ashes incorporated into two rings, so that we would have a lasting reminder of her, and which we both wear each and every day. Trixie and I should have had many more years together, we were so happy in each other's company, but this was denied us by the incompetency of one person, for which I will never, ever forgive him.

R.I.P Trixie, we will miss you always xxxxxxxxxxxxxx

<u>Trixie</u>

CHAPTER SIXTEEN

Raymond's Story
Lannie Anderson

Raymond – January 17, 2009 – September 26, 2020

Raymond – July 5, 2020

Raymond – September 26, 2020

On June 29, 2020, on the advice of our veterinarian, we started our 11 year old shih tzu, Raymond, on Apoquel to help with what we thought was a simple seasonal allergy, to help with his itching. The seasonal allergy had been deemed an "environmental" allergy. Apoquel is designed to block the sensation of itching. Our veterinarian told us the drug was safe. We stopped it about a month later when we noticed it gave him diarrhea.

It all happened so fast. He went downhill so fast. He was full of life and happy, just itchy. Then he started to scratch constantly. Unable to sleep he would spend hours compulsively scratching/rubbing. We would wake up in the morning to find clumps of his hair and his little body covered in bald spots where he had rubbed/scratched off his hair. Lumps appeared on his head and body. His quality of life decreased drastically. He was so uncomfortable he couldn't lay down in the last week or two, as his stomach was covered in sores where he had opened the skin from scratching and rubbing.

J.L. Robb

On September 26, 2020, we made the difficult decision to put Raymond down because we didn't want to see him suffer anymore. When the vet tech went to put in the catheter, they remarked "wow, his blood is so thin. His body was definitely trying to fight something".

In a matter of less than three months, something took hold of him and he couldn't fight it off. We believe this was caused by the immune suppression properties of Apoquel. We are devastated.

CHAPTER SEVENTEEN

Taro's Story
Marie and Chip Watkins

IT DID NOT HAVE TO HAPPEN
11/5/2011 – 8/21/2020

Our beloved precious Taro went into the vet for what was supposed to be the final stages of an ear infection that had been clearing up. I remember the night before, when Taro opened her chewy treat box, grabbed her favorite bone and dashed into the backyard, a bundle of joy. We actually saved her other two toys to celebrate the healing of her ear infection planned for the following night after her vet appointment and what we believed would be a joyous occasion. Instead, it all led to her shocking and tragic death. I should have trusted my instinct. The vet prescribed sedatives and I dreaded giving them to Taro. The vet wanted me to give more and more to Taro. I relented and gave her the full dose prior to Taros last visit. Taro was noticeably more sedated than our previous visits. I trusted the vet with Taro's life. A trust that would soon be devastatingly broken. Everything seemed to start going wrong. I called the vet tech from the car on the way over to Taros appointment, trying not to panic, but very afraid that Taro was over-sedated. The vet tech seemed less than concerned. When we arrived, Taro managed to unsteadily walk the few steps to the door of the clinic. I was unable to accompany her any further due to the pandemic restrictions. I waited for what seemed like an eternity in the parking lot until the vet called me to give me the glorious news that Taro's ear infection was finally gone. I was elated. However, the vet also mentioned that Taro seemed "really out of it." I asked the vet to do Taro's Annual Exam to ensure everything else was alright with our beloved girl.

All I could think about was sharing the good news with my husband and looking forward to the celebration later that night.

Again, the vet noted that Taro seems really sedated, and when I express concern, she says not to worry. The next thing I know is Taro is being carried out to my car, the same Taro who entered the facility of her own accord, is now being carried out. She is placed on the backseat of my car. While waiting for the vet to call me, Taro face-plants onto the floor of the car while her body remains partially on the backseat. She was nonresponsive and lacked any control over herself.

Panicking, I looked up and saw a vet tech delivering a small dog to another customer's care and with heart pounding, yelled, "Emergency! I have an emergency over here!" The vet tech came over and repositioned Taro back onto the seat and said, "Everything is going to be fine." I tried to calm myself down.

Then Dr. Eva Armfield calls me to discuss billing, and suddenly Taro face-plants again, unresponsive, and I desperately yell out to the doctor that Taro is slumped over again, non-responsive and we need help. A vet tech arrives at our car and again repositions Taro back onto the seat. I know my dog and all my instincts were screaming inside that Taro needs medical attention. Yet the vet didn't even take the time to re-check her, nor come outside herself to look, instead sending a vet tech out assuring me that Taro was fine. Taro wasn't fine. Taro would never be fine again. Two more calls were made to Dr. Eva Armfield, before even leaving her parking lot telling her Taro is in trouble. Dr. Eva Armfield kept saying Taro will be fine and to go home. I wanted to trust Taro would be OK. Still scared, I drove home slowly, keeping a watchful eye on Taro. As soon as we arrived home, Taro threw up in the car. I literally had to slide my Taro onto a small rug and drag her several feet, sliding her into the garage where she stayed, staring into space, for about two-hours. Still gravely concerned, I called the vet again who said Taro would be just fine. Let the medication wear off was her answer. She recommended that I give her a Pepcid AC. I could hardly believe what they said, and let her know that Taro wasn't even showing interest in her favorite cheese or bacon. Just listless. I told the vet she must not realize what is happening with Taro. Yet, she assured me that Taro would be just fine.

I watched with extreme anguish as Taro tried desperately in vain to lift her body up off the floor. Trying over and over and over again, not even an inch, until she collapsed down again realizing the hopeless futility. Yet, I believed the vet. I wanted to believe the vet, that Taro would be alright, despite my inner instincts telling me that all was not right. I stayed next to her, praying for her, and showering her with as much love as I could muster. Eventually Taro was able to get herself up and took a few steps outside where she threw up, evacuated her bowels and drank a little water. I was so hopeful that she was on the road to recovery, but it couldn't have been further from the truth.

I frantically called the vet again and her advice was not to let Taro drink a lot of water. I couldn't fathom that advice, then, she added that she would wait for me with stomach medicine. I told her Taro was non-responsive and her legs were cold. Something was terribly wrong.

The vet assured me Taro was going to be fine and to call her in the morning. I trusted her yet again against my motherly intuition, however, we would not wait until morning. Not for our beloved Taro.

I knew my husband Chip would be home soon. They were inseparable as he was Taro's world. I thought Taro's excitement would help in her recovery and energy. When Chip finally arrived, Taro had barely enough energy to wag her tail. That was all. I knew it was dire. We brought the car as close as we could to Taro, and as I laid down blankets for her ride to the Emergency room. With her last bit of strength, I turned to see Taro up on her feet, struggling, as she slowly walked to the car. She so loved Chip and didn't want him to drive off without her as he started the car. It was heartbreaking, but gave us hope yet once again, that Taro would somehow be alright.

J.L. Robb

We drove to the animal hospital and arrived in the dark. Staff rushed out at the curb and shined a light into Taro's eyes, stating she was stable and not an emergency. They said they were very busy but would call us in when they could.

To our astonishment, Taro got out of the car of her own accord, urinated, barked and walked around a little. It gave us even more hope. After almost three hours of waiting, and Taro hopefully recovering, we decided to bring her home to allow her to rest as Taro seemed tired. I stayed with her in her bed, at the foot of our bed, for hours with my hand on her pulse. She seemed to be alright.

The next morning, Taro was still in bed which wasn't unusual for her. However, after getting dressed and walking out of the bathroom some ten minutes later, I saw Taro walk from her bed, but her hind legs didn't look right. She collapsed and her laborious rapid breathing started and seemed worse after each passing minute.

Chip picked Taro up and carried her to the car while I frantically called the hospital and told them we had an emergency and were rushing Taro in. I was yelling at Chip to hurry as I felt every second counted as we raced to the hospital. Her head rested on my lap. Deep down I felt the end was near but tried to reassure Taro, my baby, to hold on, despite my own worst fears. She looked up at me with her beautiful sorrowful eyes, they were so dilated. I rested her head back down, stroked her and told her to hold on, we were almost there, as I fought back my own tears. Each time I professed my love for her and reassured her, she would look up at me with those soulful eyes. The last time she tried to lift her head, I pet her and told her to rest. Little did I know that this would be the last time we gazed into each others eyes. Arriving at the Emergency room, they took Taro in on a stretcher. All I could do was pray and cry. I called the Patchogue Animal Hospital on Long Island, New York, to tell her vet Dr. Eva Armfield to have her records sent over immediately to help save her life. It was futile as the tech said the vet

108

was not in until 11:00am. I pleaded, in my darkest hour, that my precious
Taro was fighting for her life.

It was then that I saw the ER doctor emerge and speak with Chip. I will
never forget the horror in Chip's face, forever now etched in my mind, as
he turned and desperately yelled out to me, "She's gone! She's gone! She's
gone!"
Tears burst forth in absolute disbelief and shock, like a nightmare that I
couldn't wake from. We both collapsed to the floor sobbing, pounding the
ground, in such shock. Not Taro. Not our precious beloved Taro. No No
No!!!
Taking up the invitation to view her, and seeing her lifeless body was even
more difficult as Chip and I stood over her, showering her with
kisses and caresses as tears cascaded down our faces onto her. I still
couldn't believe she was gone. Forever.

Ultimately, the ER doctor came to see us, we were in shock, he strongly
recommended to not have a Necropsy, and the overall feeling seemingly
was a lack of empathy and compassion when we truly needed it the most.
None of this had to have happened. Taro did not have to die. Taro's vet
finally returned my emergency call and tearful plea some eight hours later,
to apologize. I was numb. Weak and alone. I just listened. She said Taro
could have had a heart-based tumor or her ear infection could have traveled
to her blood, the ear infection that had already been healed. When we asked
about Taro's white blood count, the vet said it had been perfect. So how
could there have been a blood infection? It didn't add up. I told her my
husband would be calling her back. Something didn't sit well deep within
my motherly visceral instincts.
Our lives changed forever that day. Taro was my baby. My companion. My
life. We were inseparable and life seems empty for us both now that she is
gone.

What was supposed to be a simple ear check led to the inexplicable death
of our family member.

The next morning, we called the Emergency Room Atlantic Coast
Veterinary Hospital to try to have a necropsy performed even though we
were discouraged the night before. We were told it was too late. We wanted
Taro's medical records, but Patchogue Animal Hospital referred us to their
Attorney in order to get the medical records. The next thing I know is we
receive a "cease-and-desist" letter from her attorney regarding our posts on
Social Media.

Chip had been calling Dr. Eva Armfield for a week with no success, and
then finally Dr. Eva Armfield called Chip, a week later, and complains
about social media posts. No compassion for the loss of Taro, but more
worried about the "buzz" on social media.
With all of the unanswered questions, we had a VMD examine Taro's
medical records who informed us that Taro's Vet prescribed 600mg of
Gabapentin and 300mg of Trazodone twelve hours apart. I had reluctantly
given Taro the full dose on the last visit, based upon trusting the vet, as she
insisted.

The VMD that reviewed Taros medical records concluded that Taro's Vet
had inadequate medical records. We were charged for her annual visit but
no mention of her cardiovascular system or heart was ever mentioned. No
SOAP notes were evidenced, a current standard, which is a complete
assessment of body systems.

The sedatives could trigger a state of low blood pressure and if Taro did
have a heart-based tumor, the sedatives could have taken her over the edge,
or, sometimes these bleeds can be an innocent bleed that may never happen
again. From the first signs of distress, someone should have listened to her
heart and diagnosed any issues. An x-ray or ultrasound could have revealed
excess fluid, which could have been removed which would have likely
brought significant relief and can have a good prognosis. The ER could
have listened to her heart to determine the seriousness of her condition.
Lastly, Taro had been administered a Leptospirosis vaccine by her Vet, the
timing here is inappropriate we believe. In combination with all the

sedatives she had been given for her ear infection treatment, ear and skin allergies, which were not in remission, may have exacerbated her decline as well. A possible complication of events. Taro had four ear re-checks over the course of six weeks, in addition to the sedatives and Leptospirosis, Taro was also administered Claro medication for her ear two times, a cytopoint injection two times, all of which was questioned why does she need all this. I trusted the vet.

So many questions, so many "what-if" this or that. But answers would never bring Taro back. In my opinion Taro could have been saved if either Dr. Armfield or the ER at any time had taken the time to check her vitals.
I first met Taro after Chip and I were married. Taro was four years old already. I moved back to New York to discover Chip had a dog. We quickly became a family.

I learned that Chip's daughter acquired Taro from a man in Brooklyn who had taken Taro from her own mother at only three weeks of age. Chip's daughter became Taro's mother, bottle feeding her and caring for her. Chip decided to care for Taro when Chip's daughter ended up moving to a small apartment, thinking that one day Taro would return to her. Taro's bond with Chip grew as he took her to work with him for about two-years. He shared about how Taro greeted everyone at the shop and the affection was mutual as Taro embedded herself in the hearts of so many.

People would bring their children to introduce them to Taro as well. She was that loved.

Now Taro entered my life. I was now a novice dog owner. I had to ask Chip how to walk her. After two more days of accompanying Chip to work, I asked Chip to leave her home with me.

I sat her down and looked her in her beautiful soulful eyes and had a heart-to-heart with her. I told her I would love her and care for her and we would get to know each other's hearts. That was truly the beginning of a most precious relationship. Taro became my everything. We spent quality time together, as I taught her tricks and we played together, and weather permitting, we would go out on grand adventures together. We enjoyed life and learned from each other. Chip, Taro and I lived a most beautiful existence.

Chip so loved Taro and she loved him. He would do anything for her to make her happy, including the best medical care and food, and found the most trusted dog sitter when we couldn't take Taro with us on trips. Chip, Taro and I exchanged hearts and affection and she always showed us her unconditional love. She was always animated and excited to see Chip arrive home each day racing to greet him with tail frantically wagging, jumping up to kiss his face. She even waited by the front door for hours in anticipation of his imminent arrival. She laid next to Chip each and every night on the couch, with one eye on me so she would know when I was headed towards the fridge. She was our beloved family member.

All was shattered so quickly with devastation and the hole left in our family, in our hearts, casting a shadow and pallor over our happiness in this life. The sorrow is unbearable at times, even today.

Taro didn't have to die. All we have left, is her precious loving memories, of a beautiful dog who gave her love away to all, so genuinely and unconditionally, is to ensure she did not die in vain. That those who choose a career and a responsibility for caring for our beloved dogs uphold their sacred oath to "do no harm."

**Rest in Love Dear Taro. We love you. Always have. Always will…
Mama and Dada**

Taro

CHAPTER EIGHTEEN

Emma's Story
Jenny Bellandi
EMMA'S LOSS BY MISGUIDED CHOICES

I hope in telling my experience with my own dog that it will get many of you thinking why our beautiful pets are now the sickest they have ever been in history. Skin issues, autoimmune diseases, and cancers are very common occurrences affecting our companion animals. Why are veterinary hospitals reporting the highest reason for appointments is an itchy dog? Why when a dog is seen for skin issues it is never mentioned that this ailment is the first sign of a weak immune system? Why is it not told to clients the things that may have caused the immune system to weaken in the first place? If they did state that, they would ultimately need to admit all they were taught in veterinary school like vaccines, monthly chemical filled preventatives, as well as processed kibble are the leading precursors to weakening the body's ability to maintain strength and vitality. Although my writing will alarm you its sole intention is to shed light on the dark reality to how our pets are being treated medically due to ignorance or driven by profit.

I have been an animal lover all my life. So much, that to help them I studied small animal science and received an Associates degree in 1996 from The University of New Hampshire. I am the girl that saves the turtles on the side of the road and will stop to help any stray that I come upon. I have done years of rescue, helping many animals including dogs and cats, that had been unwanted and abused. My experience with veterinarians was always a positive experience. I never thought I'd find myself in a position where I would begin to question the veterinary field as a whole. I always had immense respect and trust in all veterinarians and the protocols in which they were taught in veterinary school. I believed they had my pets best interest at heart and I did not need to question the medical care given by them. It never occurred to me to research any information they gave me. They went to school and by all common sense would know more than I ever could. That is what I believed until Emma came into our lives and changed everything.

On July 18, 2015 my husband and I received a phone call from a rescue we have volunteered with for years. We were asked to do a wellness check on a female English Setter in upstate South Carolina. The foster home was not returning calls and the rescue was extremely concerned. We left our home immediately to go check on this dogs welfare. When we arrived, I knocked on the door and a woman came to the door, she was very nice, however we quickly realized she was likely a hoarder. Her porch was full from top to bottom with odds and ends. Her front door was open so we were able to see the inside of the home as well, which was also extremely cluttered. We introduced ourselves and told her why we were there. The woman said she would bring the dog outside. As the woman came out a large amount of cats followed her. The little dog at her side had no hair and was covered in fleas. Her eyes were swollen and inflamed. Her nails were so long they were curling over into her pads. Her ears were so swollen they looked like elephant ears. I told her as a representative of the rescue I was taking her and we would be taking her to a veterinarian.

On the drive home we were thinking of a new name for her for a new beginning. My husband thought about it and quickly named her Emma. I did contact animal control that following Monday morning. They did ultimately visit the women's home, but I was not legally authorized to be told any specifics of the outcome. The only information I could gain was that she did have a set time frame to seek medical attention and find homes for many of the animals in her possession. If she did not meet this time frame the city would come in and take them all. I unfortunately do not know if she complied or what the final ruling was.

I contacted a vet I trusted, who was a long distance from my home, so she could have a wellness visit. Emma was seen by this vet and put on prednisone to hopefully aid in healing her skin. At the time I did not realize adding an immunosuppressant drug to an already weak immune system is not a wise choice, which I will discuss later. Regardless, she took the drug for several days and then stopped eating, she began having black tarry like stools and vomiting. We went back to the vet who confirmed she likely had an ulcer we didn't initially know about and the prednisone opened it up. We stopped the drug and prescribed medications to soothe and heal her ulcer. We trusted in good time she would heal with good nutrients and care. As weeks went by the diarrhea and vomiting did clear up, but her skin was not improving as I had hoped. I decided to bring her to a more local veterinary hospital called Wateree Animal Hospital in Elgin South Carolina. Emma did not like to ride for any long distance so it seemed like the better choice for her overall. I recall her being seen a couple times before we ultimately saw Dr. Jennifer Varilek. It was at that appointment that Apoquel was finally mentioned to me as an option to supposedly heal Emma's skin issues. I did question the drug, but I was told it was safe and had no known issues. It did seem like a miracle drug, within a few days her skin began to finally clear up and in time her hair finally grew in. For approximately 1 year and 8 months I continued to refill the prescription of Apoquel per the vets suggestion to keep her on it for life. I never thought to research the drug, I simply trusted the veterinarian.

During the time frame Emma took Apoquel she suffered from recurring ear infections, urinary tract infections, diarrhea, even skin itching. I researched later and found vomiting and diarrhea were common side effects of Apoquel, including skin issues, the very thing the drug was suppose to stop. She would need to go back to Wateree Animal Hospital several times for these ailments. She saw different vets there, including the owner of Wateree Animal Hospital Dr Eric Rundlett. The vets failed to connect the dots when Emma started having these common side effects. I have looked at Emma's records numerous times, it was very common practice for this veterinary practice to prescribe medications to clear up these issues and then still refill the apoquel at the same time. They never told me Apoquel may have been the reason for any of it. I did have a couple instances where I began to question the vets decisions. Dr. Rundlett prescribed the drug Rymidal to Emma at one point for her arthritis. Within days of beginning the drug Emma lost her appetite, began pacing, drinking more and urinating more. I researched the side effects of Rymidal and became extremely alarmed to learn she was exhibiting all of them. I immediately called Dr. Rundlett who told me these issues were not from the Rymidal. He said he prescribes the drug a lot and his own dogs are on it and all are doing fine. I still did not feel right administrating this drug to her after our conversation so I immediately stopped it. Within a couple days Emma returned to normal, but it did take several more days for her to begin eating on her own again. That was my first time deeply questioning any vet. In my opinion it is extremely ignorant to think what may work for some dogs with no noticeable side effects would not cause any issues in another dog. Had I not stopped the drug it is reasonable to think the drug could of taken her life. In doing more research on Rymidal I found it has indeed killed dogs and necropsy has proved it. There are cases against Pfizer, the manufacturers of this drug, for dogs lives lost after taking it

As many months moved forward and Emma continued to take Apoquel, she once again was seen at Wateree Animal Hospital for pacing, lethargy, and twitches. At this vet visit they did a urine test, which showed negative, and they also suspected focal seizures. I decided at this time to stop the Apoquel, it was just a strong feeling I had and I declined any refills moving forward. A couple weeks later she was not eating, vomiting, and had diarrhea again. I decided at that time to take her back to the vet who was a further distance from my home. I had already began deeply questioning the decisions of Wateree Animal Hospital and I thought it best I go back to the veterinarian that I had a better relationship with. I knew the long riding distance would be tough on Emma, but I felt it was necessary to see this particular vet for her overall well being. At her visit, the vet prescribed some medications to help with her suspected GI issue and he also aspirated a tumor she had near her mammary gland. Within a few days I got the call every pet parent dreads, the aspirate confirmed she had mast cell cancer. Mast cell cancer releases an abundance of histamines and these histamines are notorious for causing ulcers. Where Emma already had an ulcer when we got her, it certainly exasperated things.

My primary education to fight her cancer was with chemotherapy and drugs. My background is veterinary assisting and unfortunately I also had personal experience with my past dogs who had to fight cancer. I knew Emma would never be able to handle these common protocols, she was just too frail. I began researching the natural options, such as fighting cancer through a real food diet that are free of processed nutrients, sugars and carbs. I began to understand 80% of the immune system is within the gut and its vital to whole body health to keep that strong.

In all my research on different natural options, I FINALLY decided to actually look up Apoquel on the internet, knowing it was the only drug Emma had taken long term. I remember being horrified to learn that Apoquel is classified as an immunosuppressant drug, something the vets not once mentioned to me. It is my opinion Apoquel shut off Emma's immune system and left her body open to disease. Its suspected to awaken preexisting cancers and is also suspected in a variety of other ailments including bone marrow issues. It's suggested that blood work prior to starting Apoquel should be done and periodically as well. However the veterinarians never mentioned any of these things to me. It's also suggested by Zoetis to wash your hands after touching Apoquel, that also was not conveyed to me. It seems too many veterinarians tell their clients not to believe everything they read on the internet. I concur with that assessment pertaining to the inaccurate promotion of things like flea preventions, processed food, or cover up drugs that do not get to the source of the problem. Our televisions are riddled with commercials telling us to trust these products to support health in our beloved animals. They play on our emotions to love and care for them. Research past your vets and the marketing campaigns and know what you're administrating to your pet. If we all feed real food and avoid chemicals we will gain a healthier dog/cat, thereby needing a vet much less often, if at all. It would appear by fearing us away from researching they can assure their annual profit margins. How would a healthy dog make any profit for a veterinarian?. If we all fed real food to our pets and not processed food, the kibble companies would certainly suffer monetarily. If we have overall healthy pets that do not need to see a veterinarian as often, we also have no drugs being prescribed. If that happens the pharmaceutical companies lose money as well. It's my belief all this is well planned for profit, and seemingly even established as soon as the vets enter veterinary school.

I learned that Apoquel works by interrupting the JAK (Janus kinase) receptors, which are the pathway for the immune system, there are essentially 3 receptors. These JAKS are also what signals the dog to itch. Simply put, Apoquel works by interrupting those receptors, primarily 1 and 3. The JAKS role in the body is vital. They are responsible for things like detecting cancer cells and killing them, they assure red and white blood cells are formed, and they also regulate inflammatory responses. JAK's regulate the production of blood cells in bone marrow by signaling the cells to divide and grow. Unfortunately, by suppressing the dogs itch in this manner it also suppresses the immune system and leaves the body wide open for infection and disease to develop.

I found it ironic to learn Emma's cancer could be fought much the same way that would also heal a dog's itchy skin. I learned that when the immune system is struggling the skin is usually the first to show signs of that struggle. I went on to learn the kibble she was eating was feeding disease and inflammation. Disease thrives on sugars and carbs, which is what kibble is. Kibble is all processed, essentially, it's like humans eating junk food every day for life and expecting our bodies to thrive. Any healthy ingredients added is heated extremely high in order to form kibble and that kills off all the nutrients. Kibble is dead food. It's highly heated which kills nutrients and its full of harmful fillers like BHA/BHT, a chemical preservative that is also used in cosmetics, rubber and petroleum products. The FDA regulations still allow it as a fat preservative saying its generally safe. It is often contaminated with mold that grows and produces carcinogens, also known as aflatoxins. Kibble offers no usable nutrients to properly heal the body and ultimately keeps us going back to a veterinarian when health issues arise. Many of the ingredients, as mentioned, will actually make the skin issues worse, including the abundance of sugar in kibble. The lack of nutrients will suppress your dog's immune system, feed such things as cancer, and the organs will begin to fail. For the ones saying right now, "well kibble is working for my dog", synthetics are used to achieve a desired result and they are very tough on the body, no real healing is happening, it's simply a cover up. Prescription kibble diets are also not prescription at all. If a consumer looks at the ingredients there is nothing different in them from any other kibble to warrant a prescription. In my opinion it's a wonderful scam for profit.

Emma was unfortunately fed kibble the entire time she took Apoquel. I did her absolutely no favors by not maintaining natural health for her. Her body came to me struggling, and while I thought I was helping her, I was actually continuing to allow her body to struggle. So not only was she getting no real nutrients to support her body to heal, but unknowingly to me the drug Apoquel was, in my opinion, also shutting off her immune system. It was certainly a recipe for disaster for my little girl.

Emma's issues were an eye opener for me. It was heartbreaking to feel I possibly brought on her cancer with my lack of education. Since Emma took the drug the FDA I believe did put pressure on Zoetis to state the warnings of the drug, such things as it is awakening preexisting cancers and possibly causing infections in their leaflets, inserts, and now their commercials. However, the commercials now use a cute talking dog for their marketing campaign. The side effects they mention are the common side effects of vomiting and diarrhea. Nowhere in the commercial does it mention the drug being classified by the FDA as an immunosuppressant drug. They end the commercial by saying Apoquel is your dog's best friend. How can a drug that shuts off a vital system in the body be your dog's best friend? I blame the vet too; we are supposed to trust them, and we are not taught to question them. They are the ones with years of education and are supposed to warn us if our pets could be in harms way. Had these vets told me Apoquel is an immunosuppressant drug I would never have given it to Emma. However, I certainly didn't expect the vet to teach me how to heal her without cover up drugs either. Veterinarians are taught only kibble and drugs in school. Unless they further studied holistically, they know very little of anything else. I would suggest always seeking a holistic veterinarian who believes in real food, titers, natural repellents for insects, and drugs as a last alternative. A homeopathic veterinarian can help as well. (To find a holistic vet visit www.ahvma.org)

Many don't understand the vaccines also do harm with their destructive ingredients like heavy metals that can last in the body for a lifetime with one shot. So, every time another vaccine is given, when they are already protected, its truly like trying to charge a battery when its already charged. The body is then damaged whether you see it right away or not. Many health issues are suspected from vaccines. Over vaccinating confuses the immune system and it is why titering is so very important. A titer is a laboratory test that measures the presence and amount of antibodies in the blood. A titer may be used to prove immunity to disease. A blood sample is taken and tested. If the test shows any number at all, that individual dog has immunity. It means their body can recognize the disease and build antibodies for it. I highly recommended everyone to learn from Dr John Robb, he established Protect The Pets and is fighting for our animals health in making states and veterinarians see the importance of titering for antibodies instead of vaccinating (Www.protectthepets.com). Many dogs can build immunity naturally even if they never had a vaccine, it is why it's so vital to always do a titer before vaccinating any dog. Also, per the vaccine company guideline, vaccines should only be done in healthy pets ONLY. Many dogs with skin issues are still irresponsibly vaccinated by their veterinarian. Skin issues would also fall under the category of an unhealthy dog just as cancer would.

As far as the chemical monthly preventatives we are pressured to give every 30 days, many have a history in causing everything from neurological issues to death. There are many Facebook groups with thousands of grieving pet owners who also trusted their vets and gave these preventatives. Many incidents are not reported because, in my experience, the vet usually says it wasn't the preventative and likely something else. Natural repellents work if you are diligent in their proper use. Such things, as for example, Dr Bens, amber collars, essential oils (be sure you are using them correctly and that they are safe for your dog or cat). Products like Dr Ben's and diatomaceous earth can also be used in your yard, as well as certain plants planted in the yard to repel, such as lavender or marigolds for example. I find it interesting that we humans use repellants to avoid insects. We are not taking monthly preventatives every 30 days, especially with neurotoxins in them to avoid the human spread diseases from these insects. So why do we fall for this for our precious pets? No true healing can happen with all these chemicals being thrown at our dogs, along with poor food, none of which have the probability to support a strong immune system for years to come. Insects hate a healthy host, so keep the immune system strong and it will naturally help repel parasites.

Convincing fear mongering is done to build profit as well and that is why it is even more important to look past the vet's information and research things for yourself. From my observation, the vet schools are bought by the big kibble companies and the pharmaceutical companies. So guess what aspiring vets, who go into vet school wanting to help our pets are learning? They are taught processed kibble is healthier than real food, they are taught to over vaccinate, they are taught to give the animal chemicals to avoid insects, instead of repelling like we do for our own bodies. Then when the body starts to show stress from all this constant abuse they are taught to cover it all up with drugs, which further weakens that already struggling system. All these things are taught to be done in the name of true health. This is not what true health is and is the reason why we have seen an increase in unhealthy pets. Again, we have seen skin issues become a very common problem being presented in veterinary practices.

Most often leaky gut mimics allergy symptoms. Leaky gut is when gaps in the intestinal walls allow bacteria and toxins to pass into the bloodstream and triggers the body's immune response. It weakens the microbiome, which is made up of trillions of microorganisms that live in the intestinal tract that are involved in functions critical to your pet's health and well-being. The bacteria helps digest food, regulate the immune system, and protect against other bacteria that causes disease. They produce vitamins like B12, thiamine, and riboflavin, including Vitamin K needed for blood coagulation. Vets do not discuss leaky gut; I believe if they did discuss it, they would have to admit all they do in the name of health probably caused it by weakening the microbiome. We have also seen a huge increase of disease in very young dogs. None of these ailments are coincidental as the vet was taught to believe in school. To me, it seems like vets are essentially taught how to keep income flowing in for profit for the major kibble companies, pharmaceutical companies, as well as themselves.

I was successful in slowing Emma's cancer by feeding her real foods, probiotics, and supporting her already damaged microbiome. I avoided all chemicals and Emma lived for almost a year past the two-month expected time frame had she followed the typical veterinary protocols. She was sadly sent to heaven July 28, 2018 and we suspected in the end she might have had a brain tumor. She would run in circles and get lost in the house, eventually she could no longer stand or walk. She started having seizures as well, and we began CBD oil, which kept her seizures away. We were able to fulfill a bucket list we made for her that included a trip to the ocean. She was the sweetest soul and I wish so much I could go back to the day we got her so I could take all I know now and do better, not just for her, but all my past pets. I would have fed her real fresh food, given probiotics, avoided drugs and supported her body that way. There is never a guarantee our pets will not get sick. However, we can do the best we can to fight against the possibility and not contribute to it.

It is all that experience and research that led me to start my Facebook group. It is named Bringing Awareness To The Link Between Apoquel And Cancer In Dogs. I wanted to bring awareness to others about Apoquel and save others the same heartache and loss. My group teaches the possible dangers in using Apoquel and other cover up drugs like Cytopoint (which has some alarming side effects of its own). We teach proper nutrition and how to support the immune system to achieve true healing without harmful drugs.

One of the main points I stress in my group is the importance of becoming your own researchers. If your vet is prescribing anything, look it up yourself, do not take one person's word for it. In my opinion, Dr. Eric Rundlett is the type of vet who doesn't look at his patients as an individual. I am willing to bet many vets rarely do any research and listen solely to their pharmaceutical reps who are taught to make the sale. I blame Dr Jennifer Varilek for starting the Apoquel with no warnings, but I blame Dr. Rundlett more as he saw Emma moving forward and he owns that hospital. It didn't stop with his failure in telling me Apoquel is an immunosuppressant drug. He also failed to tell me that Emma's ailments could in fact be directly linked to Apoquel's side effects, including his failure to connect the side effects of Rymidal that she experienced when he prescribed it. It was also his anger that made me lose all respect for him. He had at one point tried to prescribe Emma Clindamycin for a urinary tract infection and I questioned it. I went to the CVS pharmacy on a Friday to pick up the prescription. I realized it came with 6 pages of side effects and I immediately called his office and told the receptionist my concern and to please have him call me. The warnings of the drug were alarming, but I also worried as it said to take no dairy while on the drug. Emma was on a real food diet that also consisted of raw goat's milk. Raw goats milk is extremely healthy for dogs, especially dogs fighting cancer (we teach more about this in my Facebook group). Dr. Rundlett and I finally spoke on the phone. He said he would never prescribe something to my dog if he thought it would harm her. (Yet he gave her Apoquel and Rymidal and failed to link her side effects to the drugs). He continued to inform me that he could no longer see my pets because I didn't trust him. He told me that he wasn't happy I was seeing more than one vet as well (noting the vet I saw for Emma whom I liked that was a further distance from my home). I was upset by his attitude, but it was almost 5pm on a Friday night and I was concerned about her not having a medication for the weekend, as her other vet was not in his office and she was uncomfortable. I remained as calm as possible and said could you please call her in something else so she would not suffer through weekend with no relief. I then informed him that the warnings of the drug stated it should not be taken with dairy. I told him how Emma was on raw goats milk to keep nutrients into her. He quickly changed his attitude and told me that if that's the case he would call in something else. That is a fine example of a vet not knowing his client and an arrogant vet as well. Why couldn't Emma have two vets? Why was that so bad for two perspectives to assure Emma gets the best treatments? Why couldn't I express concerns for a drug I was about to give my dog? I assume I bruised his ego, and he wasn't very experienced in being called out when he is wrong, which in my personal experience with him, was quite often.

There are so many natural options that truly do work in place of drugs. Cats claw, colloidal silver, D- mannose, and dandelion are some of the replacements for drugs, including for a UTI. I wish I had known this long ago. Unless it's a life-threatening emergency there is always time to take a deep breath and educate yourself on all options. In my experience Apoquel comes with a big price tag in hopes of a quick fix, which is only human, we all hope for the quick fix. It may solve the itch, but that's even temporary as Apoquel usually stops working. Its highly likely by giving Apoquel much more sinister issues are coming. The worry of fighting the cancer Emma had was so much more difficult to battle than it would have been to just properly support her microbiome initially with diet and detox to heal her skin. It is never worth interrupting a dog's immune system when diet, detox, education, and some patience can solve the issue and create a healthy body overall. Anything else is simply a cover up and a poor example of what TRUE health is. Many say quality of life is why they choose a drug like Apoquel, those are the people believing processed kibble and continued chemical intake is what really heals. Support the microbiome and you'll heal your dog.

I have also heard vets say well everything has a side effect. While that's true, not everything is an immunosuppressant drug and natural options usually come with a lot less serious side effects than we see with pharmaceuticals. Unfortunately, many vets are handing Apoquel out like candy ignorantly telling their clients its perfectly safe. They are prescribing it even if a dog is being seen for an ear infection, something the drug was not intended for. Many times, issues are not being reported because nobody thinks of Apoquel as the possible cause, that is true of many drugs. The adverse reports for Apoquel grow every year at an alarming rate and we do have those reports in the files of my group. Why are these vets so misinformed? Why is it when a dog is diagnosed with cancer the majority of oncologists state to stop the Apoquel immediately, evidently there's a reason. Why is this information I discovered in my research rarely being disclosed to the client at the time the drug is prescribed? I also had a member recently join whose dog was put on Apoquel at 4 months old. The drug company specifically states no dog is to be given the drug under 1 year old. So, I just can't understand how vets don't know this if they are allowed to prescribe it by law. Why are vets out there prescribing it and saying it's perfectly safe? Also, if a 4-month-old puppy is already having skin issues it might be worth a look at what has already been done to weaken their bodies at such a young age. Keep in mind, even in these young pups, by supporting the microbiome from the beginning it can also help battle against environmental issues and genetics.

To conclude, I like to think of my group as a place for pet parents to go to stop wasting more time and money in making their dog healthy. Many members who have come into my group to learn have been successful in healing their pets bodies without drugs. Many members who have healed their dogs say they have been with their vets for years, they loved and trusted them, and couldn't understand why they weren't informed by their vets of everything my group teaches. My answer is always one word, profit! In my opinion, the vets schools teach the aspiring veterinarians how to build profit for the kibble companies and the pharmaceutical companies. Once veterinarians graduate they make profit for all entities involved, including themselves as previously mentioned above. They are the ones winning while our pets and ourselves are left struggling. Feeding real food and avoiding chemicals will support the body and limit any veterinary visits. Who would lose if all the dogs were healthy? I recently heard of someone attending a veterinary seminar. It was brought up that vaccines didn't need to be given so frequently and that annual vaccines are not as necessary as previously thought. When that was said sighs were heard in the room. That is because part of the annual profit for clinics is clients coming in for vaccines. The very vaccine that if the dog was titered for would likely be found to be unnecessary.

My group is in memory of beautiful Emma. She was an angel sent to teach me and pass the information I have learned onto all of you. If you only remember one thing in this then remember to always ask questions and then go research for yourself so you can make a well-informed decision for your pet. There are so many successful natural alternatives to many ailments that support the microbiome and do not tear it down. There is a lot of misinformation keeping many of you scared, spending money, and running in circles to heal your pet.

To all those who have lost a pet, and like myself, just weren't aware of a better path. What I try to remind myself is we do the best we can with the knowledge we have at the time, we are only human. I feel these animals are angels sent to teach us so we can help others. If you asked them if it was enough, they would say yes it was. For them it's just about love, and in our journey to try to do the best thing we know how in the moment, we are indeed loving them. We take what they teach us and we continue to do better moving forward. If someone is warning you about any of the things mentioned here, please listen to them. Research past your traditional minded veterinarian, for the sake of your precious animals life. Be patient while healing occurs, detoxing the body can take several months depending on the amount of damage that has been done to it. Many will see a worsening of symptoms because dogs detox through their skin.

For those interested in joining my group and want to learn more about natural health and nutrition for your pet, please find my group on Facebook at Bringing Awareness to The Link Between Apoquel And Cancer In Dogs, or feel free to message me on Facebook under the name Jenny Bellandi. You can also find us on MEWE or email me at jenny.bellandi@yahoo.com

I am not a veterinarian and I do not claim to diagnosis or treat any animal. What I am doing is sharing my many years of experience of more natural alternatives that are healthier than the usual methods sold to us by too many traditional veterinarians. Often these vets offer only cover ups that keep many going back to them due to more problems, or worse possible death of our pets. Sadly, too often this is done due to ignorance or solely for profit.

Play with the angels our precious Emma Lou.
We Love you sweet girl, always.

Emma

CHAPTER NINETEEN

Maddie's Story
Marsha Pazos

This is my story about our Maddie (Maddie girl) as we called her. Maddie was born on June 6, 2011

We picked Maddie up in August, only six months after we had lost our Peaches Beignet who lived a long and beautiful life 16 years 1 month and 23 days.

This case is really about two bad actors as Scott calls them.

On December 8th, 2017, our vet who replaced the vet we loved that retired in early 2017, gave Maddie 42 Apoquel pills. Maddie used to lick her feet till they were raw. On January 19, 2018 I took Maddie back for a checkup and the vet gave me an additional 40 Apoquel pills. We boarded our girls with our groomer/boarder that January and when we picked them up, after giving Maddie these pills per my instructions, she begged me not to give Maddie these pills. I asked her why and she said they had not done enough research on this drug so please stop giving it to Maddie. She said it was being given by the vets as the new fix all drug. I decided to ask one other person the lady I dealt with where I bought all my girls' food and special items. Carol told me she wouldn't give that drug to her pets so that was it. I came home and threw the pills in the garbage. These two prescriptions cost was $94.08 for 42 pills and $89.60 for 40 pills, a total of $183.68. When I went back on May 8, 2018 for the same issue with Maddie, again the vet wanted to give me Apoquel and I said no. She said well there is nothing else I can do. With that I paid the office visit and left. She didn't even offer an allergy test which at this time I didn't even know they did. I went home and called a friend of mine to ask where she took her two dogs. She told me and we made an appointment for the vet who, I believe, would eventually cause Maddie's demise.

On May 17, 2018 we had our first visit with the new vet, Dr. Maya Chapman at Midbay Veterinarian Hospital, Niceville, FL. At that first meeting I told her why we had left the previous vet because all she wanted to do was put Maddie on Apoquel and I was not giving Maddie Apoquel NO APOQUEL!!!!!!!

At that meeting she asked if Maddie had ever been tested for allergies, I said I didn't know you could do that. So, we ordered an allergy test at $337.50 and when we left that visit, I had hope. But unbeknownst to me she gave Maddie a Cytopoint injection that very day. But not once did Dr. Maya Chapman tell us that the shot was made by the same company that makes Apoquel and for the same thing to help stop dogs from itching from allergies. Maddie received five of those shots and the last one would be the one given to her with a rabies vaccine on October 16, 2018. The girl behind the desk said Maddie is due for her Cytopoint injection. Still not knowing what this drug was or that it was made by Zotis who makes Apoquel, I then asked the girl who was taking Maddie in the back to get her rabies vaccine should we separate these two shots. The girl stated "Oh no there won't be any issues."

This is where all the problems Maddie went through began.

Twelve days later October 28, 2018 we left to head to Charlotte North Carolina to spend Halloween with our Daughter and her family. She has three little ones than 7, 5 and 1, plus her two dogs and our Gracie. Maddie was not interested in eating, and that lasted until we left on November 3, 2018. Only small amounts could I get her to eat. Once we got home, I thought she would get back to her normal self and routine. But that didn't happen, so I called the vet and made an appointment to bring her in. Monday November 13, 2018 that would begin the next two and a half months of vet office visits. On November 28, 2018, just two weeks after the first visit I believe Maddie's immune system was attacking her immune system. And we went weekly to the vet's office for blood work and medications.

When Maddie had a bout with pancreatitis on Sunday January 27, 2019, we brought her in on Monday January 28, 2019 and were informed that Maddie was now diabetic, and she was put on more medication and insulin and had to be feed by syringe because she wasn't eating at all. Dr. Maya Chapman didn't work on Fridays so she asked us to bring Maddie in on Thursday January 31, 2019 so she could check her. We did and were told Maddie's kidneys were shutting down. Dr. Maya Chapman said she didn't know what else to do to bring her back in the morning and she would give Maddie a blood transfusion. We arrived at 7am and picked her up at 1pm and rushed her to Auburn Veterinary Hospital arriving at 5pm. Maddie was there for 12 days, 5 in ICU. We got to bring her home on February 12, 2019 four and a half pounds lighter and very weak. But they saved her. It took two months to get Maddie's weight back to where it was when we first got her there. Then nine months and thirteen days later, November 25, 2019 we would lose Maddie to being paralyzed on her hind legs. Everything Maddie went through was caused by the rabies vaccine. The vet Dr. Maya Chapman admitted that to me during a meeting I requested on December 30, 2019. I came out and asked her after looking over Maddie's file could she have been so sick because of these two injections she received on October 16, 2018. Her exact words where it wasn't the Cytopoint injection if ANYTHING it was the rabies vaccine. Dr. Maya Chapman never told us what she had just admitted to me or my husband in 13 months why Maddie was so sick not until I asked her.

Two months prior to Maddie getting these two shots together she had her teeth cleaned and her blood work was perfect and when I pointed that out to her in that meeting her response was well things can change in two months. Really!!!

In my opinion when Maddie got those two shots, the rabies vaccine and the Cytopoint injection on October 16, 2018 she was given a death sentence that no amount of money we spent would be able save her. From November 13, 2018 till November 25, 2019 not including the cost of those two injections, the Rabies and Cytopoint, the day we had to let Maddie go and rest in peace we spent $11,863.85.

So, Maddie had two bad actors that, I believe, ultimately caused her short, beautiful life to end. She was only 8 years and 5 months old, and I miss her dearly.

Yes because of so much research I have done since Maddie is gone, I have learned that a Titer test is what we need to request so our pets do not have to be over vaccinated. A Titer test proves the antibodies they still have in their systems. And the groups I have joined like Joey's Legacy or Protect The Pets with Dr. Robb and even BRINGING AWARENESS TO THE LINK BETWEEN APOQUEL AND CANCER IN DOGS, with many others I am learning why our pets are so sick with allergies and arthritis why we must stop trusting a Vet and learn to ask questions about medication and things they do that can cause harm to our pets. The Veterinary Profession isn't respected like it used to be years ago. We are our pet's voices and its time we speak up and start to ask questions about their care and stop blindly trusting the vet who went to school and took an Oath TO DO NO HARM. I OWED THIS TO MADDIE BUT I DIDN'T KNOW, NOW I DO FOR GRACIE WHO TURNS 7 ON APRIL 8TH, 2020.

Maddie's Mom and Dad missing her dearly, Marsha and Paul Pazos

Maddie Girl

CHAPTER TWENTY

Rafa's Story
Phillip Jones

Dr. XXX has been treating my afghan hound Rafa since 2014. In March 2015, Rafa was given a rabies vaccine, which caused a very strong negative reaction. From March 2016 to March 2018, Rafa had a 23% weight gain and went from 80 pounds to 98 pounds, which is seriously obese for an afghan hound. I expressed concern over Rafa's weight gain and Dr. XXX suggested less table food and more exercise. The only table scraps I ever gave to Rafa were baked chicken and broccoli or other lean meat and vegetables. Dr. XXX suggested getting a female dog to up his activity level. However, she never suggested testing his thyroid level or doing a full chemistry panel on him. The average age of onset of hypothyroidism is 7 years old. Rafa's unusually high weight gain, his age, his breed, his lack of energy, and his strong reaction to the rabies shot, which is known to sometimes trigger autoimmune disorders such as hypothyroidism, were all clear signs of a potential hypothyroid condition. It's not that this was some unforeseen condition, he was literally wearing the diagnosis around his waistline and Dr. XXX was seemingly oblivious to what should have been an easy diagnosis. I believe this set the stage for him to have inadequate hepatic clearance to handle the isoflurane, a known liver toxin that has to be metabolized or it will result in massive necrosis (tissue death).

On April 6, 2018, I brought Rafa in for his annual visit. His weight had gone from 90 pounds the previous year to 98 pounds. The year before that it had gone from 80 to 90 pounds. I expressed considerable concern and Dr. XXX suggested getting a female dog to increase his level of activity. No suggestion was made to test his thyroid or do a full chemistry panel. She said that his teeth really needed cleaning and a cleaning appointment was scheduled for April 23, 2018. I asked for the blood work to be done before anesthesia.. I had no idea that a shortened chemistry panel would be used that would leave out testing anything that might be important to Rafa's ability to handle the anesthesia. Upon picking Rafa up that afternoon, I noted that Rafa was really out of it so much so that he did not attempt to feed him that night. Two weeks later, he would no longer eat dry dog food. Secretions began coming from his eyes that I had never seen before.

On May 30, 2018, I brought Rafa back to see Dr. XXX explaining that he was not eating well and asked if possibly his gums were sore from the cleaning. He was given clindamycin. I returned with Rafa the following day May 31, 2018 as his condition had worsened. Dr. XXX's vet tech said, upon seeing him, "Oh no, he has had recent anesthesia." Dr. XXX noticeably stiffened up upon hearing this. Rafa had a noticeably swollen abdomen, which is known as ascites and is one of the most common signs of liver failure. I left Rafa with them for the day for a chemistry panel and x-rays. That afternoon, I received a call from Dr. XXX, and she said "Well, I have good news! He has a normal set of x-rays and the only thing that I can find wrong with this blood work is that he has a very low thyroid level, so low that it hardly registers on the scale." I asked if the low thyroid level could cause him to have no appetite. She replied, "yes, it sure could." She then went on to say that "I am going to put him on thyroxine, a synthetic thyroid supplement, and the good news is that he should drop 20 pounds very quickly." She made no mention of x-rays showing extreme hepatomegaly (swollen liver) or any mention of the numerous crashing blood work numbers, that in concert with the x-rays, meant that Rafa's liver was likely failing. I recently learned that weight gain and lethargy are the two most common signs of hypothyroidism and Rafa clearly had both symptoms in a big way.

I believe, Dr. XXX knew that she had missed a thyroid diagnosis that had been staring her in the face for years and that she had now poisoned his liver with a known liver toxin-isoflurane-that had to be metabolized and excreted or it would result in massive necrosis (tissue death). That massive necrosis had already occurred was evidenced clearly by the x-rays. The x-ray shows extreme hepatomegaly with the liver literally pushing his intestines posterior. This x-ray would be any doctor's worst nightmare post surgically having come to the realization that an undiagnosed hypothyroid patient had been put under anesthesia. An anesthesiologist has confirmed that putting a hypothyroid patient under anesthesia should not be done ever for elective surgery and that using full dose isoflurane on a hypothyroid patient is especially bad. Hypothyroid patients are known to be extremely sensitive to anesthesia.

Dr. XXX could have taken the high road and simply told me the truth. Instead, she lied to me about the blood work and x-rays stating they were normal except for the low thyroid level. On Friday, June 1, 2018, I could not get Rafa to eat anything. On June 2, 2018, I returned and expressed my concern to Dr. XXX that "that the anesthesia must have messed him up." She replied, "he doesn't even have elevated liver enzymes, how you gonna hang your hat on that?" In my opinion, Dr. XXX was clearly lying. I believe she knew that, given the totality of his condition, those numbers would be worse and well elevated by then. She still failed to tell me about the x-rays or blood work. She gave me cerenia saying "maybe he is nauseated, and we just don't know it." During the entire time, Rafa never vomited or even acted like he wanted to vomit. In fact, I still have the unopened package of cerenia that Dr. XXX gave him. I believe, Dr. XXX has revised her records to report "some nausea" on June 2, 2018. She was not even around Rafa, except for the 15 or 20 minutes that me and Rafa were in the clinic together. I was with Rafa the entire time he was in the clinic. He was not vomiting and showed no signs of nausea. I believe, Dr. XXX also entered into the records that Rafa be taken to the emergency animal clinic if no improvement. However, she never told me to take Rafa to a specialist or emergency clinic until June 5, 2018. At the June 2 visit, she told me that Rafa could have two problems, the thyroid level and a GI tract stricture. She scheduled him for a barium contrast procedure on June 4, 2018. However, there was no reason to suspect a GI tract stricture.I believe, Dr. XXX had created a ruse, something to blame his loss of appetite on other than his liver being profoundly damaged by the anesthesia.

On June 4, 2018, I returned with Rafa for the barium series. It showed nothing. However, Rafa was given a heavy metal and fluid load that he did not need. A radiologist has confirmed that the fluid load and stress would have been harmful to him. An internal medicine doctor has confirmed that the blood work and x rays made for an unmistakable diagnosis of a failing liver. The stress alone along with the fluid load was horrible for him. Dr. XXX tested everything under the sun looking for something to blame the liver damage on other than the obvious isoflurane. She did a tick panel, checked for leptospirosis and did a urinalysis. Finally, she started him on IV fluids, four days after it I believe should have been commenced. She was content to just go on and let him hemorrhage his guts out, which is what happened over the next two days. She sent Rafa home Monday, still having not informed me of the x-rays or anything about the blood work, other than to say that "well, he does have elevated liver enzymes now." She did not even send him home with IV fluids for me to administer overnight which I easily could have done. I took Rafa home.

On June 5, 2018, I returned with Rafa and he was given more IV fluids. Later that day, I received a call saying that Rafa's liver enzymes were "off the chart" and that Dr. XXX had scheduled an appointment with Dr. YYY at the specialty animal clinic on June 8, 2018. I immediately drove to the specialty animal clinic and tried to move his appointment up as early as possible. They gave him a June 7th appointment. At this point, I had researched acute liver failure and discovered that the success rate for saving a dog in acute liver failure was 1 in 8, even in a university setting. At this point, there was no point in taking Rafa to Auburn or Mississippi State. He would have just gone to die in a strange place surrounded by strangers. Dr. XXX sent Rafa home with IV fluids. I stayed up all night giving Rafa the IV solution that Dr. XXX gave him. The solution was lactated ringer's solution, which, unknown to I, is contraindicated for a patient in acute liver failure as it has to be metabolized. By the morning of June 6, 2018, it was clear that it was all over. I took Rafa back in and left him for more IV fluids. I came back at noon to pick up Rafa, he was not ready. By 3 PM, Dr. XXX had I come to the back. She had shaved one side of his abdomen, and using a vaginal ultrasound wand, she had now determined that Rafa was "full of cancer." A vaginal ultrasound device used in such a manner has no diagnostic capability whatsoever. According to Dr. XXX, he had a normal hematocrit one week earlier and a normal set of x-rays and now one week later she determined that he was full of terminal cancer. She was clearly desperate to find something to blame his liver failure on other than herself. I got the necessary barbiturate from Dr. XXX to put Rafa to sleep and took him home to spend a few hours with him before putting him to sleep at 6 PM that evening.

Dr. XXX failed to diagnose Rafa's thyroid problem, which resulted in the poisoning of his liver and his ultimate death. She then deliberately misled I. Had she told I the truth on May 31, 2018, he could have taken him to Auburn or Mississippi State and put him into a real ICU setting. Dr. XXX lied about his bloodwork and x-rays stating they were normal when they weren't. When she finally recommended seeing a specialist on June 5, it was too late for Rafa. She squandered the window of opportunity to potentially save Rafa. She wasted five days and deprived I of the truth at a time when it was crucial for him to know and steps could have been taken to save Rafa's life. She did unnecessary tests when she knew, or should have known, she had poisoned Rafa's liver herself. She gave him the barium contrast series that were harmful to him at that point. She made no attempts to control his hemorrhaging, despite crashing platelet levels and weight gain of eight pounds from third spacing fluid. She provided no nutrition for him by tube feeding that would have been absolutely necessary for his liver to have any chance to heal. She gave the wrong kind of fluid to him. Even the thyroxine she prescribed to him is at twice the dosage that a sight hound should have. Literally everything this woman did was incompetent but all of that pales in comparison to the moral depravity of lying to me knowing fully well that Rafa's life was on the line. Rafa's only chance to be saved was to have been taken to a true ICU setting at Auburn or Mississippi State on May 31, 2018.

Rafa

CHAPTER TWENTY-ONE

Sugar's Story

Sugar was a beautiful long-haired black and white cat who was approximately 10 years old when she died. We adopted her in December 2014 from a rescue organization in suburban Chicago. She was a sweet, petite cat but also very feisty and independent. Sugar did not like to be held too long but loved to be close to you, snuggling up to you or in her bed. She had the cutest little meow and let you know when she was hungry with her adorable meow. She loved to eat and sleep (especially in the sun in the bay window) and play at times, all the things a normal cat does. Her favorite activities were sitting in the sun in the bay window and playing hide and seek, talking softly in her cute little voice while running quickly around the house, trying to hide from us.

Sugar had a history of chronic upper respiratory issues/rhinitis and chronic GI issues which were managed well with diet, medications, supplements, and nebulizing (she loved to be nebulized which provided relief when she was congested). She had soft stool and sneezed now and then but nothing detrimental. She seemed quite happy and content. In late June 2018, she sneezed (this time a violent sneeze) which caused her eyes to dart back and forth and lose her balance. We brought her to one of our primary veterinarians right away for observation. X-rays of her upper respiratory system as well as blood work were done then. The X-rays of her lungs were clear, and the lab work showed cholesterol levels out of range and high ABS monos levels (indicative of her inflammatory gastrointestinal disease) but was otherwise unremarkable. I mentioned to the primary vet that I take a low dosage of Meclizine (an antihistamine used to treat vertigo caused by vestibular disease that affects the inner ear and helps with motion sickness) for my middle ear issue when I get vertigo every now and then so can we give that to Sugar for her motion sickness? She had not prescribed that before but was open to it and confirmed from her veterinary medical book that this medication was indeed listed. I knew it helped me with my motion sickness and read that it was an excellent drug to use in cats with vestibular disease and suffering from motion sickness. Side effects are few though sedation can occur. (I know it makes me sleepy.) The vet prescribed a low dosage and Sugar improved. I was relieved we could give something to Sugar that was on the safe side and that was helping her, but she was not really eating on her own and had to be syringed fed and given fluids at the vet.

Worried that she was not eating enough and wanting to get another opinion, I brought her to a well-known cat clinic on the northwest side of Chicago on July 12, 2018. The veterinarian there did not perform any tests since they were completed by her primary vet recently. He was just very adamant about Sugar getting enough food, so he strongly urged she get a feeding tube. His vet tech syringed fed her but Sugar was not really liking it. When the vet came back, he said he called a local well-known national ER pet hospital and set up an appointment for the next day, July 13, 2018 at 4pm. I agreed to take her there and get a feeding tube thinking it was the best thing for her since the vet seemed so adamant. I recall holding Sugar and looking through the glass in the exam room we were in at the other people waiting with their pets. She was curious and they all smiled at her, while she peered out at them. It was one of my last, fondest memories of her.

The following day at the ER pet hospital in northeast suburban Chicago, the vet's diagnosis included Sugar's chronic rhinitis, IBD and her recent vestibular event. She suggested a couple of medications for Sugar including, Leukeran, a chemotherapy drug, for her "suspected GI disease" as noted on her medical report. Sugar was not diagnosed with cancer at any time and the other medication, an antibiotic, is horrible on the stomach per Sugar's primary veterinarian so it would not have been good for her, given her very sensitive digestive and gastro system. None of Sugar's vets, primary or specialist, have ever recommended these medications (different antibiotics were administered when Sugar needed it) so these meds were never given to Sugar. The vet did suggest an esophagostomy feeding tube

(E-tube) for Sugar, but she said it will have to be done in the morning since it was getting late and they were not able to perform the procedure then.

The following day, on July 14, after dropping Sugar off at the ER vet hospital for the E-tube placement in the morning and then picking her up in the afternoon, the ER vet's tech showed me how to handle the E-tube feedings. I noticed Sugar seemed rather quiet but figured it was due to the feeding tube. I felt a little rushed and not very comfortable with how things were being explained so when I asked if I could call her or the vet with any questions later, she chuckled slightly saying that they were both heading back to Michigan. She went on to say that they were just there to assist at the suburban Chicago location for a short time and were heading out after Sugar's appointment. But that I can call the vet techs at the suburban Chicago location for help if needed. (Even though the medical reports included a statement from the vet that I could contact her with questions.)

After bringing Sugar home that afternoon, she seemed okay but quiet and kept going into her crate which was unusual for her. I tried feeding her in the early evening when it was time for her feeding but was having trouble getting the food into the tube. I added more water and was following the instructions. I called the ER vet hospital twice that evening saying that I was having issues and that Sugar seemed stressed out about it. The first time I called they said to basically follow the instructions. The second time they said to give it 24 hrs. They also asked if I was following the instructions which I was. The next day, July 15, I tried feeding her, but she would not even come out of her crate. I was able to gently pull her out and tube feed her, but it still was not easy to administer even with adding more water to the food. I looked over the incision to see if it was causing problems, but it was clean and did not look infected. I called the ER pet hospital again that morning but was told to make sure I was syringing water in the tube before and after the food which I was. She was still acting strange and stressed. She would hide in her crate which was not like her at all. I tried feeding her the next feeding around Noon that day, but the food was not going down the tube at all. I called the ER pet hospital again and they said to add Coke to the tube to try to unclog any clogging and wait 30 minutes which I did. It was still clogged.

I brought Sugar back to the ER pet hospital that afternoon on July 15, where the vet tech, after trying to get food down the tube, discovered that there was an issue with it and had to insert a tool (a wire device) to clear the food that was stuck and push it through. She told me that I should not do this at home (using a device to push food down in the tube, which I would not have anyway). I asked her to then try the tube again with food to make sure it worked, but it was *still* clogged. She noted that the tube was extremely narrow and that I should add even more water to the food in order to get it down the tube. I was concerned and told the vet tech that I wanted the vet who took care of Sugar to know what is going on. The vet tech said that she would email her. Later at home, I administered a tube feeding for Sugar. The food went in this time with no issues; however, she was stressed and uncomfortable. She went back into her crate, was not sleeping, was curled up and moaning. I had not seen her like that before. I called the ER pet hospital that night and said I wanted the tube removed but was always firmly told that I needed to give it a little more time and to follow the instructions. There was no compassion or empathy from them in my requests for help.

The next morning, July 16, Sugar was still upset and seemed very uncomfortable so rather than continue with the ER pet hospital, I believed she would receive the attention she needed at a different ER pet hospital, so I brought her to ER pet hospital #2, a separate independently owned pet hospital. After admitting her to the ER there, they discovered that there was air in her stomach, which is why she was so uncomfortable. She was admitted that morning for lethargy, diarrhea, anorexia and issues with the E-tube. The E-tube was removed because they noticed that it was not flowing well, the patient was uncomfortable and had aerophagia. The ER vet recommended the tube be removed that day as it was likely causing discomfort which was unlikely to resolve even with adjustments/tinkering. The curling she was displaying was because she had air in her stomach as a result of too much air getting in the tube and then into her stomach, rather than food. (Important to note that she was not displaying any signs of having air in her stomach prior to the E-tube placement. She was not curling up or moaning then. In fact, she was playing with a straw in the car the night before on July 13, 2018, on the way home from ER pet hospital #1. This was the last time I saw her play.)

While Sugar was being evaluated at ER pet hospital #2 on July 16, I told the ER veterinarian that I did not want her to suffer and that I was open to euthanasia if they deemed her quality of life was poor. The vet agreed. I was concerned that she was not getting enough food/nutrition in her due to a faulty and ineffective E-tube. Because she was anorexic (she was a little under 5 pounds by that point), they recommended a stomach tube (PEG tube) which I agreed to, provided she was strong enough.

Sugar underwent a procedure the next afternoon on July 17 to have a PEG tube placed, an upper GI endoscopy and a nasal flush. After the procedure, they called me with an update saying that she recovered well from anesthesia and that there were no oral or facial abnormalities noted. However, later that night, a vet tech noticed her left eye was bulging and mentioned it to the vet who confirmed that her left eye was indeed enlarged. I was surprised that the vets did not notice this before especially given her rhinitis, thinking they would have seen it either prior to or during her evaluations the day she was admitted or even during the nasal flush. And I was taken aback that they noted there were no facial abnormalities noted just hours before. There was a thought (but the vet ruled it out later) that perhaps the E-tube placed by ER pet hospital #1 caused the infection since the infection was so close to where the tube was placed on her left side. But the fact that it was mentioned as a possibility was somewhat of a concern.

A CT scan of Sugar's head was performed on July 18 which revealed an abscess and swelling behind the left eye, an inflammation in the inner ear and her persistent rhinitis. I called often to check on her. They said she remained stable, that she was feeling well and did not seem to be in any pain, so they withheld her pain medication. She was tolerating her PEG tube feedings well. Aside from the eye change, she remained stable and was neurologically appropriate. I could bring her home in the morning. I reminded them that she loved to crawl under the blankets in her bed. They let me know that she was curled up in a nice bed with a fluffy towel over her and was resting very comfortably.

When I arrived at ER pet hospital #2 early July 19, she was not responsive and completely out of it. The veterinarian said that she was most likely out of it because of a high dosage of pain medication they had given her that morning (Buprenorphine was given at 8AM and then again at 10AM per her medical records) since she was in pain. They had refrained from giving her pain medication overnight because they said she was feeling well as noted previously. I later noticed from her medical records that she was given another dose of Buprenorphine at 1PM that day which I found alarming since the vet said she likely received too much in the morning. I later learned that this drug is 30-50 times stronger than morphine and can be dangerous for pets with respiratory problems. She had chronic respiratory issues which was noted on their summary report.

The vet told me that Sugar was "a sick kitty" but that she was a fighter, and it was decided that it was best to leave her there for further observation. He said that he was not sure if she can pull through this, but we will initiate therapy and see how she responds. I had faith in them when they said she did well overnight. They seemed upbeat. Even the vet tech seemed positive and mentioned that she was just somewhat "drunk" from the pain medication. I continued to put my trust in them thinking they had her best interest in mind. Besides, I had told them on day 1, July 16, as noted in the medical summary, that I did not want her to suffer and was open to euthanasia if her quality of life was poor. I trusted they would tell me when it was time since they were the experts. I have had other vets and specialists tell me when it was time or that they had done all that they could with my other pets. But it seemed by their actions and behavior that Sugar may pull through.

Even though I could not take her home that morning on July 19, the vet tech took the time to show me how to administer the tube feedings and while doing so, one of the office staff members came in to tell me how much was due on my bill. I was thinking at the time that they could have done this at the front desk on my way out or emailed me the balance due, especially since we were administering to Sugar. The staff member apologized for interrupting but said she had to make sure I knew what was due before I left. It was all so surreal, receiving instructions and going through the motions of tube feeding Sugar while she lay there, unresponsiveness and being told how much to pay.

I had called later that day on July 19 to check on Sugar. The vet tech said that she "is perking up but is still pretty drunk" (from the pain medication earlier). When I called the next day, July 20, they said she was stable. I mentioned that I wanted Sugar on IV fluids if she was not. They informed me later that day that her status was unchanged and that she needed heat support. She was still lethargic but handling feedings well. They said they will continue support and reassess her tomorrow. They said she would likely stay in the hospital for a long period of time. I was surprised by this because every time I called, which was often, I was told that Sugar was fine or stable and, in fact, they had prepared her to be released the day before.

I went to visit Sugar late that night on July 20 after work. I had called to let them know I was on my way but still had to wait there for more than 30 minutes which surprised me because not only did I have them a heads up that I was on my way, but the hospital was empty except for two front desk personnel. They brought her out to me in one of the exam rooms and, as I held her, I noticed that she was moving strangely and seemed to be in pain and/or uncomfortable with her eyes darting back and forth as if she was having a vestibular attack or seizure, similar to what she experienced a few weeks ago. I was surprised and concerned that they removed her from the IVs and not attending to her instead. Unsure of what to do, I asked the vet on duty what he recommended. He did not say much and left the room to attend to another patient while I held her. I mentioned to the vet tech present that Meclizine was given to Sugar by one of the primary vets for a similar episode that occurred weeks prior and that it helped Sugar. But the vet tech was instructed by the vet to administer Benadryl, an antihistamine like Meclizine but much more sedating. She injected 5 mg of Benadryl into the back of Sugar's neck. Since I could not stay in the hospital while she was being attended to, I left thinking she would be okay. Besides, the vet did not return so I figured he did not have to speak with me further.

I received a call about an hour later after returning home from the hospital from the same vet. He said that Sugar had gone into respiratory arrest. She had stopped breathing but her heart was still beating. I was shocked and in tears. He gave us the option of continued care or to consider euthanasia and said that if care was continued, she will most likely pass away over the next few minutes. Based on that, the decision was made to euthanize her. Sugar died at 12:20AM on July 21, 2018. (The vet team who treated Sugar July 17-19 were off for 4 days starting July 20 were surprised to learn that she had died when they returned to work the following week.)

We had a private viewing of Sugar's cremation at Hinsdale Pet Cemetery in Illinois. They allowed us to be with her while she was cremated. Since we were not able to be with her when she died, we felt we owed it to her to be with her when she was cremated.

In my search to contact the vet who evaluated Sugar and handled the E-tube placement, I could not find her on their website for either Illinois or Michigan. Further, I discovered from IDFPR's (Illinois Department of Financial and Professional Regulation) website that she was not licensed in Illinois. I could only find that she was licensed in Colorado. Her tech told me that they were going back to Michigan after Sugar's procedure; however, when I searched online, I could not find this vet on any of their hospitals in Michigan either.

Also, there was a lack of communication and follow up for Sugar. Not one person, including the vet who placed the E-tube called to follow up to see how she was doing. I did not hear from anyone from the day the E-tube was placed on July 14 until July 24, when I in fact called them to make sure I received all of her records and to tell them that she had died. I asked for the manager who was unavailable but when she called later, her first question was "how is Sugar?" When I told her that she died, she became quiet, apologized and said she would have her manager call me. I received a call from the lead manager who seemed cold and unconcerned and said that a lead veterinarian would call. I was shocked and disappointed that no one contacted me even after all the calls I made concerned about the tube, her condition and bringing her there on Sunday for help, the day after the E-tube was placed. It was as if she never even existed to them. I have had pets for more than 35 years and I also have a pet-sitting business so when I have had to bring my pets or a customer's pet to an ER pet hospital, a follow up call was and is customary, particularly when a procedure was done and there were issues.

It was not until August 6, 2018, that I heard from the lead veterinarian who was one of the ER pet hospital #1 medical directors. She called to say that she had information for me which, I believe, was all false. She said that based on the information she gathered:

1) the E-tube they put in worked fine.
Based on records I reviewed and my experience, this is NOT TRUE, it was clogged for more than 24 hours as proven by the vet tech having to use a wire device to fix it and was ineffective as supported by ER pet hospital #2 vets who documented that the E-tube was not flowing well and unlikely to resolve with adjustments/tinkering and that it was causing discomfort with the patient being aerophagic as a result).

2) that Sugar did not handle the stomach, or PEG, tube ER pet hospital #2 put in. Based on records I reviewed and my experience, this is NOT TRUE - Sugar handled the PEG feedings well and can be supported by ER pet hospital #2 medical records).

3) that the chemo medication Leukeran was discontinued by the vet at

ER pet hospital #2 Based on records I reviewed and my experience, this is NOT TRUE - this medication was never ordered nor given to her.

I later learned that the medical director had been calling the vets including ER pet hospital #2 to obtain information. One of Sugar's primary vets notified me indicating that she was still getting notes and questions from them after Sugar died, seemingly as if they were trying to cover all bases as to what happened in case, I decided to pursue anything with them. Unbeknownst to me, the medical director had been in contact with one of the primary vets as well as ER pet hospital #2 in order to obtain information when she called me, apparently to make a case. Even though I had not authorized the primary vets nor ER pet hospital #2 to share Sugar's information, ER pet hospital #1 persisted. Both parties agreed to notify me if they continued to receive calls from ER pet hospital #1. One of the primary vets also added that she does not like to refer patients to ER pet hospital #1 but lists them on her website in case a patient has an emergency and needs to get to the closest one. She added that "they are owned by the giant that is…VCA, Banfield, Mars" and that "they have too much money to fight these things."

Lastly, ER pet hospital #1 added a document after Sugar died which were the notes by the vet tech who took care of the clogged tube on July 15. Her notes were dated July 27, 2018, 3 days after I called them to inform them of her death. I did not receive this document until this year when I requested her documents again in preparation for writing her story. In her report, there was no mention of my request to have her notify/email the vet who handled the E-tube procedure.

I later learned that there were lawsuits against this ER pet hospital #1 for. I believe, negligence and malpractice. I learned that the hospitals have spoken out against each other. I also learned that ER pet hospital #2 has had complaints against them within the last 2 years for problems with their products/services and billing/collection issues. I was told that their invoicing was disorganized. I was also told that they have been known to keep pets "going", giving pet parents false hope. I was surprised by all of this because I went to this ER pet hospital based on previous experiences as well as recommendations; however, I did get a sense and was led to believe that Sugar was going to make it at times.

It made me wonder if things were changing at ER pet hospital #2 or if Sugar was indeed too sick but then why keep her going? I looked at Sugar's medical records closer. There was a note that she stopped breathing at 9:30PM on July 20 but then started to take rapid shallow breaths on her own. This occurred about 3 hours before she died and not too long before I saw her. When I read this, I was shocked. I was not informed that she had stopped breathing prior to my visit. The report also indicated that her head bobbed a bit, that she "hard swallowed and her neck stretched" in the morning. Why didn't they tell me any of this? It seemed to me that she might have been declining early on July 20, but I was told that she was stable when I called, that she needed heat support and still very lethargic but handling feedings well and would reassess her the next day. They said that she would likely stay in the hospital a long time. But Sugar passed that night.

One might even question the type of medications that were given to Sugar given her condition. She was given Buprenorphine (a powerful opioid/analgesic that interacts with the nervous system to relieve pain) twice in the morning on July 19, 2018 and then again early afternoon that same day, as previously mentioned. I learned that this opioid should not be given to debilitated pets, those in a weakened state, with nervous system dysfunction or with respiratory issues. I would think that Sugar would have been classified in at least one, if not all, of those categories. They switched her to Gabapentin (an anticonvulsant, affecting the central nervous system, used to treat pain, seizures and reduce anxiety) and administered this at 8PM on July 19, at 8AM on July 20 and another dose at 8PM that night. When I read later about these medications, I was upset to learn that these medications given to Sugar on her last 2 days of her life could have adverse reactions with each other. Keeping in mind that she was given Benadryl shortly before she died, a resource I read stated that pets on medications affecting the central nervous system should not be given Benadryl because of adverse complications. Benadryl was injected into Sugar about two hours after Gabapentin was administered. I did inquire with a couple of veterinarians outside of this pet hospital about these medications, their dosage and interactions with other medications but was basically told that it all depended on the situation but why am I clearly finding that there are issues with the interactions?

There were also confusing and concerning entries on their medical records. Benadryl was administered to Sugar around 10PM on July 20 (while I was there as noted previously) and then listed again as the very last entry on the medical records which would have been the second dosage within an hour. But 1 dose was charged on the invoice so one might assume that only one dosage was administered. There were other medications including one that had 3 dosing entries within an hour while the others had 2 dosing entries within 3 minutes. Hopefully, these were inadvertently added duplicates. It was difficult matching the medical entries to the charges on the invoices.

I filed a complaint with IDFPR once my case with ER pet hospital #1 was closed and ruled in my favor. The IDFPR investigator wanted all records, even the records from ER pet hospital #2 even though my complaint to IDFPR was focused on the wrongdoing by ER pet hospital #1. He told me that he has received and reviewed complaints against both ER pet hospitals in the past, so he wanted to see all records. .

Early this year, the vet board at IDFPR closed Sugar's case without any explanation. (I later learned that this is common – the vet boards do not have to give you a reason). The frustrating thing was I had to email the investigator who told me that they closed the case 10 days previously. No apology, no letter, just a brief email saying "The board/lawyers closed the case on 1/21/20. All over. They never explain why." I was appalled. After many months of back-and-forth communication and follow up with the investigator, only to be told that it is all over without a reason or answer, was just absurd.

The state attorney general also closed my case against ER pet hospital #2. He had been closely following what action IDFPR was taking, often asking me where they were at in the process and to keep him updated. However, during that investigation, the state attorney general advocate had asked me an interesting question: "Had I ever seen Sugar awake or responsive at ER pet hospital #2?" The answer was No.

I sent a FOIA request to IDFPR requesting minutes from Sugar's case. I received an email that the meeting minutes were closed. When I emailed and called to find out why, they said that if the meetings were closed to the public, then the minutes are closed. There was not much more they could do. I was appalled but not surprised. After all, the vet board's response was always brief, vague and non-transparent. It just added to the frustration I was feeling at that point.

It has been more than two years since Sugar's death. What happened to her has been a heartbreaking experience in many ways. I have never experienced anything like this before. I have had dogs and cats most of my life, some healthy and some with chronic illness. But I have never questioned the care my fur babies received up until July 2018 with Sugar's care. There were many emotions during and after her death for a long time - feelings of anger, sadness, hopelessness, confusion, the joy of living had been suppressed. The anger I felt then has subdued somewhat but the pain remains and there is still a void. It was difficult reliving and writing her story, but I had to…for Sugar, for myself, for all pet parents.

I am not one who likes to complain. I am more of a quiet, non-confrontational and non-combative person. I have never posted complaints on social media. But I have never gone through what Sugar and I experienced with her veterinary care and subsequently by the vet board. I have had positive experiences with my pets and their veterinary care. I co-own a dog walking and pet sitting business and have dealt with many pets and their parents and they have shared many positive experiences. But I knew in my heart and gut that what happened at ER pet hospital #1 was wrong and I just had to do something. Reporting them to the vet board was another way to bring light to what happened.

But I need to also question the treatment Sugar received at ER pet hospital #2. I fought ER pet hospital #1 and "won" (in the financial sense but not in the bigger, more important sense since Sugar was gone) but things were more complicated at ER pet hospital #2 where Sugar was for 5 days. I did not question the care there until I heard what attorneys and others had to say and after reading / interpreting her records. I had dealt with ER pet hospital #2 in the past with positive results, but this time was different. Have they fallen from grace? Is money that important to keep pets "going"? Some of the questions and concerns that remain include whether the right medications were given, whether euthanasia should have been suggested earlier and also lack of or poor communication particularly not telling me she stopped breathing prior to my visit on her last day. Her records indicated that her temperature was critical many times from the first day she was there until the last day, 5 days later. In addition, Sugar's attitude was noted as quiet, dull or obtunded the last 2 days even though I was told she was stable. Why wasn't I told these things? She was a fighter, but did they prolong the inevitable?

When you hear and read complaints about the places you put your trust in, it seems you have a moral responsibility to report any wrongdoing whether it be negligence, poor quality and questionable care and in extreme cases, malpractice. One needs to bring the wrongdoing to light and awareness so that changes can be made. Although there are some wonderful vets including Sugar's primary vets, I have been hearing more and more concerns about some ER hospitals who seem to be "in it" for the money, particularly those who have been bought out by a corporation. How could the veterinary industry have changed this much? I am still desperately looking for relief, peace, answers and solutions. Things need to change. I want to make people aware of what happened, despite how painful and difficult it is to talk and write about. I was angry for Sugar. I always respected and admired veterinarians but this experience has left me questioning a lot, left me wondering if things have changed because of greed, power and money. Has the veterinary industry changed since many have become corporatized? And do the independent hospitals feel a need to do what they can to stay in business, competing with these corporations? ER pet hospitals that are corporate owned like ER pet hospital #1 are becoming monopolies. This is not the kind of veterinary care we want. Pressure and action by our government officials is needed to break up these greedy monopolies.

All in all, I have learned from this experience to be a stronger advocate. Make sure you are in constant communication with your veterinarians. Demand to know what medications are being given your 4-legged family member(s). Can the communication be improved? Of course. Perhaps there needs to be stronger documents (including points about euthanasia not only regarding DNR) and online access on pet hospitals website so that pet parents can see their pets' client communication reports, notes report, anesthetic records, hospitalization/medical records, etc. The two ER pet hospitals I brought Sugar to have online access for pet parents but only for ether paying the bill or checking in/getting in line for emergencies due to COVID-19. It would be advantageous and eliminate a lot of confusion and frustration if there was also online access to obtain medical records, like what humans have. I would even go as far as to suggest having pet health care advocates like we have for our human family members who act as liaisons between pet parents and the hospitals. The pet industry has continued to grow every year and with the increase in the number of pets, there is an increase in demand for related products and services. The veterinary has become a big business. I think our pets are unfortunately getting 'lost' in the process of veterinary care when the vet industry becomes that - big business.

I felt I was all alone when I was dealing with Sugar's situation until I heard about Scott Fine and Joey's Legacy this year and realized that there are others who have suffered due to veterinary mistreatment, poor quality of care, negligence or overt malpractice. I believe telling Sugar's story and bringing awareness helps. As the saying goes "Pets are not our whole life, but they make our lives whole." I just want to be whole again

.

I am grateful to Scott Fine of Joey's Legacy and to JL Robb for allowing Sugar's and other pets' stories to be told in this book. I have met other pet parents on Joey's Legacy, and we share many of the same feelings and concerns. We hope things will change for the better after telling our stories. I am hoping Sugar's story will educate and enlighten others. Sugar will not be forgotten. Love you and miss you sweet Sugar.

Sugar

CHAPTER TWENTY-TWO

Brooklyn's Story
Bernadette deCallies

Deception, lies, negligence and the poisoning of our beloved dog, Brooklyn, by a female veterinarian in Brooklyn, N.Y.

Our beautiful dog, Brooklyn, was a female 8-year-old Rhodesian Ridgeback mix dog, which we rescued when she was two months old from North Shore Animal League in Port Washington, N.Y. 11050. We enjoyed a good life together until a so-called veterinarian prescribed a drug that was toxic to Brooklyn. A drug, we believe, which took Brooklyn's life and has forever changed our lives. The loss of an innocent and beautiful soul that left our hearts grieving. An empty space that can never be replaced.

On January 6, 2020, we called a Park Slope veterinarian's office to make an appointment for a wellness checkup. Brooklyn was scheduled for January 7, 2020. To calm Brooklyn's anxiety at the veterinarian's office the receptionist asked for our pharmacy and said the veterinarian would send a prescription that we were to give Brooklyn before she arrived. The drug Trazodone was prescribed. No questions were ever asked in reference to Brooklyn's current health, any medical conditions or other drugs that she may have been taking. She never expressed any concern for prescribing Trazodone. She never informed us of the possible drug interactions or adverse reactions. Brooklyn never took Trazodone in her life before this fatal encounter.

As instructed, we gave Brooklyn the Trazodone in our car 45 minutes before arrival at the veterinarian's. Two blocks away from the veterinarian's office, Brooklyn started shrieking, then collapsed, convulsed, and stopped breathing. We helplessly watched Brooklyn suffer and die in the back seat of our car from a toxic reaction from Trazodone.

Following, was a chaotic scene brought on by the veterinarian. Instead of her showing remorse, compassion, or empathy, we were cruelly treated. We were yelled at and threatened with being reported to the police for asking for Brooklyn's body back. We had to stand and listen to random theories of excuses. Not only is Trazodone not FDA approved for dogs, but one would at least use with caution or have a patient relationship. There is something really wrong in the field of veterinary medicine these days.

Veterinarians are not acting conscientiously while following the standard of care. They are not keeping with the principles of veterinary ethics. The one we encountered with Brooklyn was carless and reckless. Neither is considered using skill for the benefit of animal health or welfare. Our ordeal from beginning to end with this veterinarian demonstrated that she is blatantly wrong for the field of medicine.

Brooklyn

CHAPTER TWENTY-THREE

Maggie's Story
Al Casapulla

Maggie's Story.

Before

Maggie was a little 10-pound, 10-year-old female Shih Tzu that was rescued in Florida. Maggie's life prior to being rescued by us was an extreme case of abuse and neglect. With our love and care, she blossomed into a beautiful little girl full of spunk and love for her daddy. She was the smallest of the pack of four but was the most fearless of the bunch. Maggie had the heart of a lion. But on August 19, 2014, Maggie was given seven vaccinations (Bordetella, Parvo, Lepto, Corona, Distemper, Hepatitis and Parainfluenza). Then 12 months later on August 26, 2015, she was given six more vaccinations (Lepto, Bordetella, Distemper, Hepatitis, Parvo and Parainfluenza).And did you know that a 10lb dog gets the same dose as a 150lb dog? One size fits all. From this day forward, Maggie's life and ours was about to change forever.

By the time we arrived back home from the vet, she started shaking, crying, hiding, not eating and lethargic — a few of her symptoms. Little did we know that this beautiful healthy little girl that we took to the vet for a wellness visit would now, for the next 16 months, be facing the biggest battle of her life — the fight for her life. Even after all of our efforts and trips to so many vets, which included three neurologists, cardiologist, internists, two homeopathic vets, radiologist and many in between, to try to fix what had been broken from all of those vaccinations. Maggie's health continued to decline. It was so hard to watch her shake and cry; stumble and fall in her food and water bowls; and to have her come up in our faces in bed in the middle of the night, crying and shaking, begging us to help her. The journey is far too long to put it all in this letter.

After

On December 30, 2016, Maggie lost the fight. She died peacefully in my arms, surrounded by her family and hearing the last words from my wife and I, telling her we love her. This was the hardest and worst decision I had to make in my life. Here this little girl I frantically tried to save for the last 16 months, and I now had to be the one to end it. And this all could have been prevented if she had not been over vaccinated with 13 vaccinations in 12 months. Far too much for any dog to endure, let alone a little 10-pound house dog. Maggie did not deserve to die this way. It is hard enough to lose a pet from illness and old age, but to lose one from being over vaccinated puts a whole different element on grief and mourning. Maggie may be gone from this earth, but she will live on through me warning others about the many dangers from vaccinations.

If only someone had warned me, she would have never had to endure what she did and would still be by my side where she always was. Also, some vaccines may be good for a lifetime, or for many years after once vaccinated. There is a blood test called a titers test that will check the antibodies in your dog's blood. This has been a life-changing experience that I would not want anyone to have to go through. So please take this warning seriously, and don't let Maggie's death be in vain and let this happen to your pet. Always be their voice, and question everything.

302.381.6377

Al Casapulla's
Subs.
Steaks, & Pizza
Shoppes of Millville | Rt. 26
302.539.5488

CHAPTER TWENTY-FOUR

CHESTER'S STORY
Jill Gorski

My name is Jill Gorski. I am from NH. I am a member of Joey's Legacy. I had a lawsuit against this vet. Her insurance company settled two weeks before the jury trial. I had to sign a non- disclosure after I agreed to the settlement. I filed a complaint with the NH veterinary board. My complaint has been turned over to the Attorney general's prosecution department. They assured me this has not been dismissed. There was a hearing against Deborah Kelloway.

In February 2018, she was found guilty in two cases. In my opinion, the Prosecutory basically gave her a slap on the wrist. She states this in one of the many news articles.

Here is my story. His name was Chester.
He was my little angel RIP.

In May 2016 I brought my 12-year-old miniature schnauzer Chester to AVC 55 Carl Dr Manchester NH. To have the top right tooth examined. After the examination, Dr Deborah Kelloway surgically removed 26 teeth from Chester's mouth. The infected tooth, however was not one of the 26 teeth removed by Dr Deborah Kelloway. When I brought this to the attention of AVC and Dr Deborah Kelloway, I was told to keep an eye on it.

I called AVC and spoke with Hannah the receptionist asked her if I could bring Chester in to see Dr Deborah Kelloway and was told to bring him on October 11, 2016 I was promised Dr Kelloway would handle the procedure and if she was unavailable. I would be given the option to come back another day. This, however, did not occur. But Dr Kelloway was Chester's

Dr her name was also on the bill. During the surgery to remove the previously discussed tooth, Chester died.

At first Dr. Herr declined to tell me how or why Chester died. Dr Herr said to my husband and I it was not the anesthesia. She didn't Know what happened Dr Herr was very jittery. Instead, she brought me my dead dog in a plastic bag stuffed in a box. Dr Herr made a disturbing comment that I should use a board- certified Dr. next time. A week later AVC attempted to explain what had happened. The letter claimed that Chester died by air caused by a power drill used in the procedure. The letter also referenced another individual involved in only identified as Athena.(See attachment). After that I emailed a dog dental specialist in Bedford. Her response made me very suspicious. What I learned from this specialist cast serious doubt on the matter in which Chester died and showed serious negligence.(See attachment. Report)

The specialist informed me that she looked into the high power drill used on Chester and discovered that this device was equipped with a safety device that would make it impossible for an air to be released and kill Chester. This Veterinarian also reached out to certain individuals. Sarah J who witnessed this procedure. Athena K.. previously referenced in the explanation letter from Dr Deborah Kelloway, was at the time an unlicensed unqualified not certified kennel help at AVC and was unlicensed to perform medical procedures. However, Athena had been instructed to participate in the procedure in a capacity well above what she was qualified and certified to do. During the procedure, Athena cut off oxygen to Chester, resulting in him suffocating and dying.

I truly believe, the negligent actions by Dr Kelloway directly resulted in Chester's death. Chester was a healthy active dog . His death was needless , senseless, and completely avoidable. I was forced to bury my family member.

This is what the second vet did. In my opinion, Dr Lee Garrod is a piece of work. She contacted me back when this all happened she offered to review Chester's medical records (she did). Writes a 4-page report on how this is impossible. Then offered to be my expert witness.

Then nothing. It's almost down to the end. Dr Lee Garrod seems to be avoiding us. She goes out of her way to make sure I know what happened to chester. Knowing I hired a lawyer. All because of her. Then she disappears. What kind of person does this?

In my opinion, Lee Garrod saw an opportunity, and took full advantage of getting revenge on her competition at my expense.

<u>Chester</u>

CHAPTER TWENTY-FIVE

KENZIE'S STORY
Mike Minor & Sybille Crom

I am writing this letter to hopefully help bring awareness and future justice to all animals gone too soon due to veterinarian malpractice, negligence and abuse by the hands of bad veterinarians and or assistance.

Not a day passes where I don't see the last look from our dearly loved little dog Kenzie, a little cairn Terrier mix. I rescued Kenzie from our local animal shelter after losing and looking for my lost cat Bindi that I never found, hoping someone took her to the shelter, no such luck, I walked by the dog kennels and there she was tiny sickly and helpless among a few bigger dogs.

I noticed her little whimper and it was love at first sight I asked for her info and was told she was a stray from the middle of an intersection in town and someone dropped her off at the shelter.

I adopted her at the time her name was Betsy, she was already spayed, and I was able to take her home the following day, believing her color was brown I was surprised after bathing her three times in two days that her color was a golden caramel, and I renamed her Kenzie, it seemed like she liked her new name she listens to me call her and she responded right away.

I noticed that Kenzie suffered from very bad breath and she also needed a good grooming for the tri-vexes I followed up with her local county low-cost vaccination clinic. I always took my cats there as they were great and caring with my pets but limited in what they could provide I remembered hearing about a clinic inside PetSmart called Banfield pet Veterinarian clinic, someone I knew took their pets there and they had pet grooming inside PetSmart and Kenzie needing extra TLC and I wanted to make sure I meet her needs.

After her grooming I decided to stop at the Banfield clinic counter and asked if it was possible to see the veterinarian on duty for an exam on Kenzie, she checked and said if I didn't mind waiting, I said OK I didn't mind.

Two hours and 20 minutes later Dr. Sharpe Greeted us and I thought it was cute as three little dogs followed her and peaked around from behind the doorway. She examined Kenzie and told me that she needed a good dental cleaning and more, meds for ear mites and a nail trimming. We made an appointment and left the clinic the following day I noticed that Kenzie had trouble chewing so I was happy for her vet appointment. We arrived and I signed the waiver for the anesthesia after talking it over with the technician, she also told me I could go home, and they would call me as soon as Kenzie was in recovery from the anesthesia. I said I wouldn't mind waiting then she said it would take more than five hours, so I said OK, went home. 2 1/2 hours later I got a call from the veterinarian and she told me Kenzie is doing fine and they had to pull one tooth, but she is doing fine I could pick her up around 2:30 PM pick up was great as both of us felt very insecure being separated and very happy to be reunited. Some of the happiest times followed. My little dog always by my side dreaming next to me during the night enjoying our nightly walks being my therapist when I'm down in the dumps supporting me with her warmth when I had the flu. I Miss you so much Kenzie!!!

Then when I took Kenzie to her follow up appointment I was very surprised that Dr. Sharp was no longer at the clinic but transferred to another Banfield veterinary clinic in Tampa so Kenzie got to meet several new people there and I noticed she didn't like them all, I wish my alarm button had gone off then but it didn't two years later on 4/3/18 Under that clinics wellness plan Kenzie was up for her second dental cleaning and since she had to be under anesthesia for this ordeal I asked if she could also have her dewclaws removed as they were barely attached, at the veterinarian Dr. Harden agreed, this would be fine to do including trimming Kenzie nails the pre-op read that Kenzie was in good health and her blood work came back normal. Drop off was around 8 AM in the morning noticed my Kenzie didn't want to go anywhere that day, she seemed nervous. Why didn't I cancel why didn't I. I wished I could have stayed with her. Stupid rules I was thinking, the technician reassured me and noticing I was also getting nervous like Kenzie she's said she's in good hands and I would get a call in a couple of hours never will I forget the look from my little baby girl her last look at me and me reassuring her kissing her and telling her I would be back picking her up and how much I loved her, her last look I never thought that she would die, why; I received a call just as I was going to call wandering because it took longer to hear from them this time and I heard a lot of background noise and I couldn't hear what the veterinarian was saying at first but I said was Kenzie OK and Dr. Harden said that she passed away and all I could do is scream and repeat myself no no no not my Kenzie, please god no Kenzie why!

4/3/18 at 11:20 AM I was ripped apart and this killed my trust in people forever because of what followed was a huge feeling of hopelessness being repeatedly lied to and really felt more like a bother I started questioning the entire procedure that something had gone wrong, who was to be held accountable, where are the reports, and that the death of Kenzie meant nothing to anyone but my husband Myself and some of my friends who she also loved it has been such a sad journey. I had to wait for my husband that horrible day, he left work early and together we drove to the clinic I noticed that the people are kind of numb to people's emotions we tried to keep our composure but cried a lot trying to get some kind of answers to what really occurred the only thing Dr. Harden talked about is if we would like to say goodbye to Kenzie.

I just couldn't do it, I was shaking and hoping all this was not real I had to get out of the clinic I did and my husband followed we were stopped and asked to look at some pet urns for after the cremation then we were offered a necropsy by Dr. Harden I was not ready to make that decision either at that time we went home two hours later we received a call from a different veterinarian at the clinic she asked when we would pick up our dead dog I told her as soon as I found someone other than Banfield to do the necropsy that's when she told me that it would no longer be accurate because our pet was put in the freezer, that's when I lost it we called lawyers radio stations local news nobody was available to help with info on how and where I could maybe still get a necropsy done I filled a complaint with the local sheriff's department wrote a letter to Pam Bondi the district attorney called the veterinarian licensing board got called back need to get records from Banfield and report followed up with Banfield made sure they reported read laws and regulations about veterinary code of ethics and researched websites on veterinarian malpractices and could not believe how much of it there is and all the deaths by vets at Banfield around the country all the abuse, drug abuse by veterinarians. I am crying every day almost all day for nine weeks and still bawling my eyes out from one moment to the next, anywhere when I see a little dog it's often overwhelming cannot walk by Banfield because I get accused of just wanting money for what, I believe, they did to my companion. I never saw Kenzie as my property she was and always will be like a child to us. Banfield veterinarian clinic never admitted to any wrongful acts.

Dr. Harden was transferred and so was the manager that gave us the neatly type report from 4/3/18 not one handwritten note everything went perfectly according to procedure she had an allergic reaction due to? Her blood work was fine, her throat swelled they said that they did everything they could, CPR, injections not one time did we hear sorry this happened. recently we received the report of the investigation from the department of business and professional regulation and read case dismissed due to insufficient evidence against Laura Harden

We miss you Kenzie with all our arts.
Thank you, Mr. Fine and Joey's Legacy.

<u>Kenzie</u>

CHAPTER TWENTY-SIX

JASPER'S STORY
JoAnn Cochennet

Jasper was our 6-year-old Pomeranian. He was the best fur kid anyone could ask for. He lived with a mild collapsing trachea. If you aren't familiar with this it is where the trachea rings weaken over time and collapses for brief periods of time. Very common in small dogs. He also had allergies. So, we treated him with Zyrtec and Flovent inhaler by Aero Dawg. It was manageable. Certainly not life threatening. His biggest obstacle was not being able to exercise aggressively. So, this was our life. We managed and treated his symptoms. He had a good life; he was such a happy go lucky dog. I miss him so much!!

So, one day I noticed he wasn't eating. Jaspers ALWAYS ate! I knew something was up. So, I called the vet and got him in right away. They diagnosed him with pneumonia. Put him on antibiotics and oxygen therapy. After a few days he stabilized and was able to come home. We continued his antibiotic therapy and he continued to improve. About 2 weeks at home, I noticed his breathing was short again. I called the Vet took him back to oxygen therapy tent. They ran x-rays and sent them off to a Radiologist. They came back and said he needs to see a specialist and we recommend Blue Pearl in Oklahoma City. So, we immediately got him and drove the 4 hours to this hospital.

I called to make sure they knew we were coming. Blue Pearl said when you get here, we will have you drop him off and put him in a cage in the front lobby due to covid-19 restrictions and they would then immediately put him in oxygen. 4 hours later I walked in the front doors of Blue Pearl hospital a decision I will deeply regret forever.

Our vet sent Blue Pearl all of Jaspers prior medical records and x-rays. Dr. Rothenburg from Blue Pearl later called us to find out what was going on.

We had several back-and-forth conversations about how to move forward and what best treatment to help our little guy. We agreed to initial tests like heart worm, blood tests, covid-19 etc. but nothing invasive. We were hoping to try another antibiotic. Thinking maybe his bacteria had grown resistant or something like that. Well Dr Rothenburg told us she HIGHLY recommended he have a $7200 bronchoscopy and cat scan ASAP. She also said she was only available today and tomorrow and after that it would be two weeks.

We spent an entire day going back and forth calling with additional questions. Again, Dr Rothenburg at Blue Pearl assured us the procedure that she was recommending was safe with minimal complications. We asked how minimal? She said less than 10% have complications. She also followed up and indicated the procedure itself is safe. She also said complications if they are going to happen, happen during recovery. She said in her professional opinion this was the best route with the lowest risk to treat Jasper. She said it is the one that would get him back home to us the fastest. With a lot of heartfelt discussion and prayers my husband and I agreed to the procedure.

The next day it was scheduled to be done around 3pm. I had asked if I could see him before the procedure, they told me no. I asked if they would call me before they started. She said yes to that. I told them to tell Jasper I loved him and was praying for a good outcome. An hour and a half later I got a call from Dr Rothenburg saying she doesn't have very good news about Jasper. They aren't sure exactly what happened. She didn't know if they punctured a lung or it just ruptured. His oxygen began to drop, and they went to intubate him, and the air filled his chest not his lungs. Which caused both lungs to collapse then his heart stopped. They told me there was nothing they could do.

We rushed to the hospital and this time they let us in and put us in a room. Dr Rothenburg came in and I began to say you told me less than 10% you said he was stable, you told me usually complications come after the procedure not during. I was devastated. Her reply was simply "I told you there was risk" She was totally cold and emotionless.

They brought me Jasper wrapped in a blanket and I ran out the front doors. We drove home 4 hours with him in my lap. I didn't want to say goodbye and let him go. I was there to help him. The worst 4 hours of my life. Not only did they, I believe, take my precious Poms life they took our money too. $8,000 later we drove home to have a funeral. I can't tell you how awful of an experience this was.

We were lied to and manipulated by a high-pressure salesman that didn't care one way or the other what happened to Jasper. We later found out after we researched that there was a risk greater than 50% that Jasper might die during this procedure based on his pre-existing conditions. Some of this research was even found on Blue Pearls own website. In my opinion, they committed fraud and took advantage of us in one of the most vulnerable possible positions.

I am sharing this story to raise awareness. They are a huge corporation, and they need to be exposed. Blue Pearl is owned by the Mars family. They are one of the largest private companies in the world. We have since done a lot of research of the company. We have found hundreds of complaints with very similar experiences to ours. They should not be able to get away with this. I am hoping the more voices we have that come together we can make a difference in Jaspers name for other families.

Please share your Blue Pearl stories with me and share this with your fur friends. It could save a life. Thank you for taking the time to read this.

Jasper

CHAPTER TWENTY-SEVEN

DECKER'S STORY
Holli Stone

On November 5, 2011 I had two dogs that were due for routine shots. A couple of days before their vet appointment one of them started having urine accidents in the house. At the appointment Dr. Spier was asked about the accidents. He asked if one of the dogs had been drinking a lot, and the answer was yes, Decker had been. Dr. Spier pricked Decker for a single blood sample. Decker's blood glucose was 330 and he was diagnosed diabetic. Dr. Spier explained that diabetic dogs were the equivalent of a type I human diabetic because their pancreas stopped producing insulin and they needed injected insulin to survive. Decker was then given his DALPP and three-year rabies vaccinations and sent home. Dr. Spier asked that Decker be brought back on November 7th to be started on "insulin therapy", and he was kept overnight "to be regulated". Having no prior experience or knowledge of diabetes, I was naive enough to believe it was that simple.

Decker had been fed and dropped off on November 7th around 8a. He was 97 pounds of uncontrolled energy and I wished the receptionist good luck as he pulled her towards the back. On November 8th Decker was picked up around 4:30p. He was picked up shaking, saturated in urine, he had blood-shot eyes, a hoarse bark and he could hardly stand/walk. When he did move, he held one rear leg up. Dr. Spier recommended a blood glucose meter be purchased to check Decker's glucose levels at home. Dr. Spier gave written instructions on the veterinary letter-head which said, "normal glucose levels are 60 - 200, give 40u of humulin n insulin every 12 hours (twice daily), insulin requires 6-7 hours to start working, have 3-4 meals available daily, any day you can't be with your dog when insulin starts working, don't give insulin, show me the blood glucose results in one week, give karo syrup (corn syrup) if dog is shaking)."

Decker had a larger-than-life personality yet came home and simply curled up in the corner and slept. A blood glucose meter and insulin were purchased for him that night. Dr. Spier had shaved a patch of fur, so it was clear where to inject Decker's insulin. It took some trial and error (and some tears) to learn to check Decker's levels, and there were times it didn't work out, but his readings for that first week were as follows:

11.9

6a blood glucose 232 (gave 40u of insulin)

6p blood glucose 175 (gave 40u of insulin)

11.10

6a blood glucose 84 (skipped insulin)

6p blood glucose 59 (skipped insulin)

11.11

6a blood glucose 98 (skipped insulin)

6p blood glucose 173 (gave 40u)

11.12

6a were unable to test (skipped insulin)

6p blood glucose 118 (skipped insulin)

11.13

6a blood glucose 192 (skipped insulin)

6p blood glucose 216 (gave 40u)

11.14

6a blood glucose 55 (skipped insulin)

6p blood glucose unable to test (skipped insulin)

11.15

6a blood glucose 278 (gave 40u)

6p blood glucose 134 (skipped insulin)

Decker was not doing well at all. He was a dog with strong herding instincts who typically didn't have an off switch, yet when he wasn't drinking buckets of water, he spent most of his time curled up sleeping. The blood glucose readings were called into Dr. Spier. Based on those readings Dr. Spier determined that Decker "may be in honeymoon," meaning he may have still been producing some of his own insulin, and he recommended we continue to test Decker's blood glucose levels, but that we take him from 80u of insulin a day to zero. No follow up instructions were given.

Decker's blood glucose levels continued to rise without insulin. Decker was not doing well, and I started to read to learn more about canine diabetes. I learned that at 97 pounds, most dogs were started somewhere between 11u - 20u of insulin. I learned what a blood glucose curve was. I learned that insulin injections should be determined based on the lowest number of a blood glucose curve (not just a single before meal reading). I learned that food and insulin worked together and that it was best to both feed and inject insulin twice daily (not feed 3-4 times daily). I learned that exercise can lower a dog's blood glucose levels and that it was recommended to have liquid syrup around during periods of exercise. I learned diabetic dogs could be prone to urinary tract infections, and that uncontrolled diabetic dogs could go into ketosis (which could be life threatening). I learned that diabetic dogs often develop cataracts, which lead to blindness. I learned questions to ask to find a new vet who could help us manage Decker's diabetes.

The last time Decker was seen by Dr. Spier was November 8th, 2011, the day he was sent home shaking and saturated in urine. Decker saw his new vet for the first time in December 2011. Decker's new vet called Dr. Spier's practice to have Decker's records faxed to them. I never saw them. The new vet recommended Decker be started on 20u of insulin twice daily. The 20u of insulin turned out to be too much for Decker, and upon the recommendation of his new vet, he was dropped to 11u of insulin twice daily. Decker remained on 11u of insulin for a week and then a full blood glucose curve was run to determine what should happen next. Once his blood glucose stopped bouncing around from being overdosed on insulin, Decker's spunk slowly started to return.

In March 2012 Decker started having some challenges and I had hoped that his original records from Dr. Spier would shed some light on them. Decker's records were faxed to me on March 13, 2012. It was then that I saw for the first time what Dr. Spier had done. I had a second dog and two cats under Dr. Spier's care, and after seeing Decker's records, all of my pets were moved to the new veterinary practice. Decker was fed and dropped off at Dr. Spier's on 11.7.2011. His blood glucose after eating was 263. Dr. Spier started a 97-pound dog on 35u of insulin at 8:45a. A full blood glucose curve was never run. Dr. Spier checked Decker's glucose levels at 12noon (reading was 491), 3p (reading was 241), and 4p (reading was 448). There was no record of Decker being fed or any glucose checks after 4p. There was no record of a second shot of 35u of insulin given. On 11.8.2011, Dr. Spier checked Decker's glucose at 8:50a (reading was 470) and raised Decker's insulin dose to 40u. Dr. Spier checked him at 12noon (reading was 220), 2:30p (reading was 145), 3:30p (reading was LO, meaning under 20, a life-threatening hypoglycemic range). There is no record of any treatment for the life-threatening hypoglycemia. There is no record of a second dose of 40u of insulin being given to Decker. The records show that Dr. Spier wrote "Keep on 40u humulin n BID" BID means twice daily. Dr. Spier put in writing for Decker to be given 40u of insulin twice daily and sent him home. The last thing Dr. Spier wrote in

Decker's records is, "after showing the blood glucose results, I suggested stop the insulin and just test. Dog may be in honeymoon." The blood glucose readings he based that decision on were not in the records. There was no follow up information in the records. The final note is that the records were faxed to the new veterinary practice on 12.20.11.

In March 2012 Decker's health began to take a nosedive. Dr. Spier had never recommended or run any blood work or other diagnostics on Decker. Which meant that he had no baseline information for his new veterinary team to work with. It took time to sort out what was going on and to work through treatment plans. Decker did end up developing cataracts and by Spring 2012 was completely blind. In January 2013 Decker passed away somewhat unexpectedly at home. I took some time to mourn the loss of my boy and then started to sort through all that he had been through. Dr. Spier was a licensed professional who I paid and trusted to care for Decker. In my opinion, he grossly overdosed Decker on insulin, vaccinated an unwell dog, and failed to maintain accurate treatment records. I had a copy of the handwritten notes on the practice letterhead and a faxed copy of the records.

July 27th, 2013, I submitted a complaint against Dr. Spier to the NYS office of professional discipline. My hope was that no other pet would have to experience what Decker did under Dr. Spier's care. I spoke with the investigator in October 2013 to ask how the investigation was going. I was told that he'd just received all of the information from Dr. Spier. On November 21, 2013 I received a letter from the Office of Professional Discipline which read, "This office has completed the investigation of your complaint against the above named individual (Dr. Spier). Our investigation did not disclose any violation of either the New York Education Law or the Rules or Regulations of the Board of Regents and the Commissioner of Education. We are closing our file on this matter." Just like that my complaint had been dismissed.

On February 11, 2014 I called the investigator and asked if Dr. Spier had submitted the same handwritten records as I had. I was told yes, but in addition to those he had submitted typed records. May 2014 I again requested Decker's records. Decker had last been seen by Dr. Spier on 11.8.2011. I received the original handwritten records in March 2012. My complaint was filed 7.27.2013. The records I received in May 2014 were the same handwritten records as March 2012, however, they had alterations on them, showing IV treatment for hypoglycemia (the LO blood glucose reading). Decker had no longer been under Dr. Spier's care and there is no reason the records should have been altered.

November 2014, I learned that Dr. Spier had sold his practice. I went in and asked the new owner for a copy of Decker's records. The only records that existed in his file were the same handwritten records with the alterations on them. If typed records do exist, they only exist in a manner that I do not have access to.

I had been warned by others that veterinary boards are known for protecting their own. As a pet owner, I did what I thought was right. I took my dog to a licensed professional. I kept and followed Dr. Spier's written instructions. When things seemed off, I asked for a copy of the treatment records. Decker was under the care of Dr. Spier for seven years and the hand-written treatment records were less than a page and a half. I believed the review of Decker's complaint would bring disciplinary action. My hope was that Dr. Spier would be required to take additional education courses to update his management of diabetic pets so that no other pet would have to suffer as Decker did. That didn't happen. My complaint was dismissed. Dr. Spier got to continue practicing as he wished.

I cried when I saw that the handwritten records showed a licensed professional had started a 97-pound dog on 35u of insulin, failed to run a full glucose curve, and raised his dose to 40u the next day. AAHA guidelines recommend starting a 97-pound dog on 11u of insulin, yet Dr. Spier started Decker on more than three times that amount. Dr. Spier again failed to run a full glucose curve. He dropped my dog's blood glucose to LO (under 20, life threatening hypoglycemia), failed to document any treatment for the hypoglycemia, and sent him home an hour later with written instructions to give 40u twice daily (though one dose had put Decker into a life-threatening hypoglycemic state). I cried again when I realized that Dr. Spier was not even minimally cited for record keeping - the page and a half of hand-written treatment records which did not have the blood glucose readings in them were considered to be satisfactory. I cried when I realized that upon diagnosing Decker diabetic, Dr. Spier could have chosen to hold off on vaccinating Decker as he was unwell at the time, or he could have spaced out the vaccinations. Instead, he gave an unwell dog a series of six vaccinations all at once (in the same general area the insulin injections were given). I cried again when I realized the written instructions for giving Decker 40u of insulin BID was not considered to be a single act of gross negligence. I cried again when I saw the alterations on the May 2014 records. I saw firsthand the impact Dr. Spier's treatment choices had on Decker. I saw my dog suffer because of those choices. By law Decker may be considered a piece of property, but to his family his life mattered. He deserved better!

Decker

CHAPTER TWENTY-EIGHT

SMOKEY'S STORY
Kathy Webb

2 years ago, I lost a 13-year-old sweet female cat. I now truly believe after many months of research, that it was a rabies shot that was the demise of her. At first, I thought maybe it could have been cancer that the internal vets did not pick up on, but I believe, I am sure it was the rabies shot that killed

her. After I lost her, I wrote a thank-you letter to the internal vet that tried to save her, but, at the same time shamed them for not following up on things I brought to their attention, and for not including treatments in her plan. I also shamed the vet that pushed that rabies shot on her. I made sure all vets involved in her care, received the email that I sent to all, so they could see each other's mistakes. To this date, I still blame myself for not walking out of that vet's office and saying no to that rabies shot. My sweet cat was at the end of a major FHV flare up. That shot should never have been pushed on her. I still go over her ultrasound pictures and have found nothing. The day I brought her to the er, I just needed anti biotics. The regular vet could not see her right away, so I had to go the er. The er vet said she was the healthiest cat he had ever seen, besides the FHV flare up. I was told to bring her to my regular vet in a month for a follow up after the antibiotics.

When I brought her for the follow up, she had gained back 1 lb. of weight, and the nasal drip was clear. That was the day the vet pushed the rabies shot on her. 1 month later, my sweet girl was going downhill fast. The regular vet said they could see her in 2 months, that they were booked. I made an appointment with an internal vet. I was in panic mode, due to how fast she was going downhill. By the time the internal vet ran blood tests, the tests were out of whack, with highs and lows. Every test for illness, came back negative. They could only guess what was wrong. I did not believe their guesses. I have found vets will tell you the titer cost hundreds and the rabies only cost 40.00. I learned about titers from my research, after I lost my sweet girl. Thank-you in advance for reading my story.

Smokey

CHAPTER TWENTY-NINE

LILLY'S STORY
Josephine Garlick

It was 4 years ago I took Lily to the vets early morning as she was having breathing problems, they kept her all day saying they were doing tests, I was phoned at 5pm to say they were sending her to be treated by Vets Now corporation overnight. The vet who admitted her did not want to treat her and suggested she be put to sleep as she was leaking blood, but my vet said she would be drained and stabilized and was going on to another vet for surgery, so I said no I wanted her to be treated. she was put in an oxygen tent and left till 2am in the morning it was 9 hours from admission before giving her plasma. I was phoned a couple of times through the night first to put her to sleep second to give her a blood transfusion not realizing they were filling her up further with more blood as she was still leaking. When I picked her up next morning she could not walk and had to be carried and looked like a beached whale, I could not see her till I paid the bill of £2000 to go on to another vet for surgery to be told they could not do anything for her as she was too far gone and full of blood. I went through all the complaints I was advised to do to RCVS, after a year said they had done nothing wrong and closed the case, Vets Now refused arbitration

Lilly

CHAPTER THIRTY

LOGAN'S STORY
Darlene Shea

We got Logan in April 2007 when he was 17 weeks old. He was a rescue from Louisiana that I found on PetFinder. When deciding on what type of dog we wanted, we agreed we loved the husky we used to dog sit for, so looked for that breed. Logan was a husky "mix". Out of the thousands of dogs on PetFinder, his was the face I fell in love with.

I just knew he was the one we were meant to have. Having both grown up with dogs, we had wanted to get one for our family but with young children, activities, and long work hours we waited to adopt until we could spend more time with a dog. The right time came when our children were older, and my husband and I started working opposite shifts. That meant that one of us would most always be home with Logan.

Please know that I speak to all pet parents who will understand when I say that Logan was my heart and soul dog. I've had other dogs and currently have 2 dogs. Logan slept on our bed. No matter where I was in the house or yard, Logan was with me. He was there when I was sick or sad or tired. He was our daughter's confidant and my grandchildren loved him.

Shortly after being prescribed a certain medication, we lost our beloved dog Logan. We lost him in January of 2017. He had just turned 9 one month prior. After his sudden and unexpected death, I learned the following: Pet owners must insist on receiving information about EVERY medication that is prescribed for their pet.

Your veterinarian has all the important information on a Consumer Data Sheet. Many veterinarians fail to issue these important data sheets, thinking they will just be thrown away despite containing very important health and safety data for your pet.

These data sheets or Consumer Medicine Information are published on behalf of Pharmaceutical Companies that list indications for medication, how to take medication, what adverse reactions/side effects to look for, how the medication is eliminated from the body (what organ) and more. Just like when a person picks up a prescription and get all those papers attached.

Medications are eliminated through various organs. Liver, kidney, etc. It is important to not only know side effects, but also to request that baseline testing and monitoring testing are completed BEFORE, DURING AND AFTER being prescribed medications.

I also cannot express enough how important it is to have pet insurance. We didn't then but we do now.

Logan

CHAPTER THIRTY-ONE

BUDDY'S STORY
Melissa Ganim

I have had a lot of dogs in my life, but Buddy was my soul dog. I rescued him and I can honestly say Buddy rescued me as well. We were a team. Buddy was the most special gift I have ever received. He was my whole world. He was my teddy bear. He was my pride and joy. He was my best friend.

Buddy was not your typical Yorkie. He had quite the personality with just the right amount of sass. He had no fear; he knew he ran the show. He knew that he could get away with anything. If he could talk, he would say, "I am all that and a bag of chips!" Buddy was quite the beggar, too. He would sit up and stick his tongue out, and it worked, he got his way! Who could say no to that cuteness?

The longer I had him the more I realized how much I needed him. He helped me with my mental health. He was my therapy. He would snuggle right on my lap and I felt at peace. I was always a worry wart fur mom; I think we all are to some extent. He would sleep in my bed with me and in the middle of the night I would rub his belly and feel his chest to make sure he was breathing. He was my baby boy, and I would do anything for him. Buddy brought out the best in me. I never took one day for granted as I valued the gift of his presence every day. I was his mom, and I was there for everything. Every vet visit, when he was sick, in sickness and in health, I was always by his side. It was my job to keep him safe and protected. I never needed anything else in life because I had Buddy. And then tragedy struck. I am left now heartbroken and suffering unbearable pain. My world is empty and lost without him. I still do not know how to get up each day and face the world without him by my side. Life has become very lonely to say the least.

I never thought something like this could or would happen to me. I never knew evil existed until that one night. It was then I found out what real evil was, in human form from someone I thought I could trust. I lost something I never thought I would lose so soon.

Buddy was only about 5-years old. I never thought this would or could ever happen to me. Everyone goes through hardships in life, but this one has ripped me to the core. Buddy has been gone for 2.5 years, but I am still consumed with immense grief that overcomes me. The way I lost Buddy was very detrimental to me and affected me in every way possible. I had no idea that there was an ongoing problem with negligent veterinarians. I was blown away and in complete shock that, in my opinion, my veterinarian had been doing immoral and unethical practices for quite some time. I learned more and more what a true monster he was as I did my research when I was working on filing my complaint against the vet I had blindly trusted. I kept asking myself, if someone else who had lost their pet secondary to this incompetent had filed a complaint, would Buddy still be here? Could this vet have been stopped earlier?

One of the things that keeps me going these days is my newfound purpose and life mission. Which is to spread the word as far as possible to pet parents so that this will never happen to another pet again. Buddy was and still is my hero and he did not die in vain.

I educated myself in every aspect possible as it relates to veterinary medicine. I feel I have learned everything I need to learn. For example, I Interviewed vets in my community and in doing so, I educated myself on veterinary ethical guidelines, protocols, equipment standards, educational requirements, and standard of care. Armed with a wealth of new knowledge, I have transformed into a passionate educator to pet parents. Buddy is not here in the present, but he has a voice. I am his voice. I intend to continue my advocacy. I will raise awareness for the rest of my time on this Earth.

The Tragedy Unfolds:

I had been taking my dog, Buddy, to Allen Veterinary Hospital since August 2014. I had never had any problems and I trusted the staff implicitly. I believe the majority of pet parents automatically trust their vet, but I have learned in the most painful way that they should not. A vet needs to earn your respect, it should not be immediately given.

On August 5, 2015, Dr. Holland, a veterinarian who is no longer part of the practice, wrote in Buddy's chart that he had 3rd degree dental disease during a routine exam. This was never discussed with me and dental x-rays were never taken to arrive at this diagnosis. Naturally a veterinarian would discuss his findings, yet this one did not. In August 2017 Dr. Hall told me that Buddy had some teeth that needed to be extracted due to decay. At the time I did not do it because I thought it would be expensive, but in January I was told that they do not charge for extractions. This is an example of one of the many inconsistencies in communication and collaboration. I was left in the dark. Buddy was an established patient, and this is something that should have been brought to my attention. These two veterinarians clearly were not a collaborative team.

On Wednesday January 10, 2018 around 9:00am, I brought Buddy in for a dental tooth cleaning and polishing. I was under the impression that Dr. Coffman would extract three teeth since this was a surgical procedure. Buddy underwent the procedure and was discharged home to me that afternoon.

On the morning of January 11th, Buddy was whimpering mildly. He was not struggling to breathe. I believed Buddy must be feeling pain, so I gave him pain medication as prescribed by Dr. Coffman. I became concerned as I watched Buddy become what can only be described as disoriented. While watching him at 4:00pm, I looked on in horror as Buddy started rolling around in his crate, unable to breathe on his own. He began gasping for air. His tongue was purple, and he had what I had thought was a seizure. He was not able to control his bodily functions. He would sit up only to collapse. He defecated in his bed while I was grabbing my keys and preparing to take him to the vet. I immediately called the vet. I put the phone on speakerphone so the receptionist could hear how serious this was and that he was gasping for air loudly. The receptionist said to bring him in. I left immediately and raced to the vet. I carried Buddy into the back office on his bed with his blanket covering him. The technician, Zac Thomas, said I could be in the back with Buddy while he was in the incubator. Dr. Shiplov said, "But be careful, I don't want him to see you and get worked up or exerted." They took him to the treatment area in the back of the clinic and I went with him. I saw everything that happened. It was Dr. Coffman's day off, so he was not present although he had performed the dental extraction. The people who were involved in his care on January 11, 2018 were 2 veterinarians, Dr. Anthony Hall and Dr. Brian Shiplov, and a veterinary technician, Zac Thomas. I honestly do not know if Dr. Coffman personally did the dental cleaning and extraction or if a vet tech did the procedure.

They did not take his blood pressure or his oxygen saturation, they only took his temperature. They noticed his tongue was purple and I saw that it looked like they were trying to put a tube down his throat, but it didn't stay in his throat. They immediately put him in the incubator. Then they tried to take him out three times to see if he would breathe on his own, but he was unable to do so. At 4:35pm I was in the back room with Buddy in his incubator when Zac told me to turn on the TV and sit back and relax. They said to talk to Buddy so that he can hear me, and I can pull up a chair. They handed me the remote control. I did not watch television, but I did take pictures and videos of my dog and talked to him. The television was extremely loud but no one adjusted the volume. They removed Buddy from the incubator 5 times to see how he breathed outside of the incubator. Other than observing his breathing, there was no monitoring of his respiratory rate or effort. Early on, they shut the lights off in the rest of the facility. About

1 hour before the time they told me they were closing, the lights had already been shut off at 5:07pm. After removing him from the incubator for the 4th time, they did an x-ray. Dr. Shiplov ordered x-rays so they took x-rays and Dr. Shiplov asked me if he had a history of heart failure or heart disease. I told him not to my knowledge, no. I was surprised they were asking me since Buddy has not seen any other veterinarian except them since 2014. He said, "it looks like an enlarged heart, if it is an enlarged heart it means chronic heart failure." During all of his past exams and bloodwork at the clinic I had never been told he had heart disease. They asked me if he was diabetic and I said no. Dr. Shiplov told me that if Buddy wasn't better by 6:00pm when they close then I will have to take Buddy to the emergency vet hospital.

I did not see Dr. Shiplov after 5:15pm. No one came to monitor Buddy from 5:20pm until 6pm. Buddy continued to have a pink tongue while in the incubator and from what I observed, he was breathing at a normal rate. Then, vet tech came out and told me it was 6pm and since Buddy still wasn't better or improving that I had to go to the ER because they were closing.

They removed him from the incubator, placed him in my arms and asked me to pay. I was standing there holding Buddy in his bed with his blanket when I noticed his tongue was purple and he looked like he was struggling to breathe. I ran to look for someone and saw the vet tech and Dr. Hall. They looked at Buddy and I asked them if I could keep Buddy in the incubator while I finished paying and checked out. The vet tech very casually allowed this, and I noted she was rather and was nonchalant about it. This actually made me feel a little less stressed as I assumed his condition was not life threatening based on the demeanor of the staff as a whole. All of the lights were off and the rooms' doors were closed. There were no other patients in the clinic. It was very evident that they did not seem to care that this was an emergency situation. Looking back, I now know that they should have done everything in their power to treat his life-threatening condition instead of asking me to pay the bill and transport him across town by myself. I paid and went through the discharge process while Dr. Hall talked to me. I felt very confused, unsure if this was an emergency, and asked Dr. Hall if I needed to speed to the ER and have my hazard lights on. "Sure," Dr. Hall told me, "have your hazard lights on, but be safe and drive carefully. And if the cops pull you over then they will just escort you to the ER." I asked if they would call the ER and tell them that we are coming and he said, "Sure." My concern was that Buddy would be uncomfortable while he was breathing like this. I didn't feel panicked or worried because I didn't think this was an emergency, I just thought that I had to go to the ER because Allen Veterinary Hospital was closing. I felt confident that Buddy would be okay so that I could get him to another doctor. I did not receive written discharge papers.

At 6:15 pm on Thursday January 11t, 2018, the temperature outside was 13 degrees Fahrenheit. I raced to the Emergency Animal Hospital. I was wanting to make sure that Buddy would be comfortable as soon as possible. I talked to him the entire time and held his paw. I kept the radio off so that I could hear him breathing and any sounds he made. I grabbed Buddy out of the car and rushed into the Emergency room. Before this, I didn't have a chance to look at Buddy as it was dark outside, and I was focusing on driving on the road. The Emergency Room staff was immediately panicked and ran back to work on him. I was confused because I didn't realize this was a life or death situation. I was not told that Buddy was unable to survive without an incubator or oxygen mask. I was still in the lobby when a female technician asked for my phone number and told me to come back to the room. The second my feet hit the doorway Dr. Rainey came up to me and said, "Ms. Ganim, I'm sorry, Buddy passed." The world stood still. I was in complete shock and an emotional wreck. The ER staff was confused and didn't know why I was shocked. Dr. Rainey explained to me, "Well, this was a life or death, a life-threatening situation. This was very serious and critical." I was very emotional but asked if I could borrow a phone charger because my phone battery was low. I called my vet's office around 6:50pm. Someone picked up immediately which surprised me because I thought they were closed. I told the woman on the phone that I was just up there with Buddy, I was at the ER and Buddy is dead." I asked if Dr. Hall was there and she said he was and put me on hold. Dr. Hall got on the phone and I told him Buddy was dead. I asked him if he knew Buddy could die from this and clarified if he knew that this was a life or death situation. He said, "yes." I became very upset and began to yell, asking him why he didn't tell me this. I told him I never would have left and would have insisted they help him if I had known he could have died. Dr. Hall said that he could have died because of pneumonia and that this could be one of many possible causes.

The ER staff realized why I was as shocked by Buddy's death as they overheard my loud, emotional conversation. I spoke with Dr. Hall for 15 to 20 minutes. The entire time he was very calm and quiet, soft-spoken like we were just having a friendly conversation. I was in disbelief. I asked the ER Vet if he thought pneumonia could have caused Buddy's death. He said no. I was shocked that Dr. Hall would have such a calm demeanor hearing that my dog had died under his care. I asked the ER Vet to call Dr. Hall and what he thought about Dr. Hall's mannerisms. He did and the ER Vet reported to me that Dr. Hall sounded very "mellow". Despite their conversation, Dr. Hall did not send any chart records or x-rays to the ER Vet at the emergency room. I asked the technician about the details of their conversation and she told me that it was a confidential conversation and could not be revealed to me. I asked the tech if Allen Veterinary Hospital had called to speak to the ER Vet and his staff before we arrived at the hospital and the technician said that Dr. Hall had only spoken to the receptionist that night and told the receptionist that Buddy needed an incubator without other details regarding his condition.

I was so emotionally distraught by Buddy's death that I stayed in the Emergency Room until midnight. Finally, one of the staff members came to talk to me and mentioned that my car lights were left on since I was in a hurry when I arrived with Buddy. I mustered the courage to leave the room and I got in my car and left with severe emotional distress. I found myself replaying the conversation I had with Dr. Hall on the phone when he told me that he knew that Buddy could have died when I left the Allen

Veterinary Hospital. I've learned since all of this happened that information that should be included in the notes is not there.

I decided to no longer take my two other living dogs to the Allen Veterinary Hospital, and I started interviewing other vets to learn how they practice. In all of the conversations with them they all said that it is important to not perform dental surgery on a dog with the problems Buddy had.

Now that I have been looking over Buddy's records under Dr. Shiplov's care I truly believe that Dr. Shiplov provided substandard care. After Buddy died, I did extensive research to learn more about Buddy's condition. Looking back, Dr. Shiplov seemed to recognize that there was a problem on the x-ray and should have informed me and documented that Buddy was suffering from cardiogenic pulmonary edema. Dr. Shiplov has been practicing veterinary medicine since 2007 and has more experience than Dr. Hall. I presume that Dr. Shiplov left around 5 pm since I did not see him after this and I was in the back room and did not see him when I was told to leave the hospital at 6 pm. Dr. Shiplov should have properly instructed Dr. Hall, a veterinarian who had only been licensed for 11 months at the time of the incident, what medications were necessary to administer. From my research and reflection of the encounter and the questions Dr. Shiplov asked me, I have realized that Buddy likely had pulmonary edema and congestive heart failure. I was never told that Buddy had congestive heart failure during any of the many times that I had visited Allen Veterinary Hospital, the sole provider of Buddy's care. I have discovered the standard of care for emergent congestive heart failure and believed that Dr. Shiplov should have been able to use his medical expertise to suggest industry standard recommendations to care for Buddy's emergency situation on January 11, 2018. Instead, in my opinion, Dr. Shiplov provided substandard care.

The following interventions are what Dr. Shiplov should have told Dr. Hall to do, but what he failed to do. Dr. Shiplov had the opportunity to intervene and involve himself in the case by interpreting the x-ray.

As final word of advice, I implore you to ask questions, be assertive, do not feel shy to seek a second opinion, and stand your ground!

I love you, Buddy. Love never dies.

Moving Forward

I advocate excellent veterinary care. I know it is scary to trust a veterinarian when you have been betrayed, but as a pet owner, I believe it is important to have a veterinarian. The difference between before Buddy's death and after Buddy's death is that now, I know what to look for when choosing a veterinarian.

Why do you use your veterinarian? And what is the first thing that pops into your head if you were to refer a friend to your vet? Common answers to the questions are:
1. Location is convenient
2. Prices are cheap
3. Vet is a family friend or relative
4. Vet shares my religious views and is considered a "Great person of faith."
5. A vet saved your dog's life one time, so you continue to go to them
6. You have heard they are trusted and well-respected   in the community.
7. You have used the same vet for 20+ years

Which number did I use when choosing my vet? If you guessed number 7, you are right. I used a vet from my hometown. I felt safe with someone I had known since we had pets during my childhood. I grew up in Allen, Texas. It's about 10 minutes North of Dallas. Back in the early 90s there were only a couple of practices open in my town. Growing up my family would take my dog, Shadow, to the local vet in the area. Once I was an adult with 3 fur-babies of my own, I continued to take my dogs to the same place. I didn't know any better or any different. I had only used one Veterinarian and had no other experience to compare this practice to. It never occurred to me or entered my mind that overtime technology changes and becomes more advanced. I stayed with what I knew and didn't question it. To me, outdated equipment and treatment approaches were familiar, not archaic. Familiarity and comfort would come to haunt me. It would be the greatest devastation and loss I would ever suffer from. I didn't know evil existed until I lost Buddy due to the incompetence of a trusted veterinarian. I would be getting hit with a fatal tragedy that would forever change my life in a matter of seconds.

Things you need to know about your rights when choosing a veterinarian:

1. Schedule a meet and greet appointment
2. Interview the veterinarian
3. Tour the facility
4. Note any red flags such as limited access to certain rooms in the facility and dirty equipment
5. Share your story and watch for reassurance
6. Ask about their policies and procedures
7. Notice if the waiting room is overcrowded
8. Are they knowledgeable and friendly?
9. If they don't know an answer, do they offer to find out?
10. What does your gut say?

To the Ethical Veterinarians

I know excellent, ethical and competent veterinarians exist. I now have one. Knowing that my dogs are given the best standard of care is reassuring and healing. It took a long time to trust and a lot of therapy to move forward, but I am taking it one step at a time and making progress. My new veterinarian is a part of my journey.

<u>Buddy</u>

CHAPTER THIRTY-TWO

VANILLABEAN'S STORY
Sharon Athanasiou

VANILLABEAN ATHANASIOU (maltese)
FRIDAY, MARCH 22nd, 2013
at E.H. ANIMAL HOSPITAL
Hollywood, FL 33021

*Brought in Vanillabean for dental cleaning at 10:30am
*Was taken in at approx 10:50am by dental tech. (Gas anesthesia was used)
*I was waited there until the dental was completed, so as to be there during Vanillabean's recovery.
*Dental tech brought him out to me to recover at approx 11:40am. Said he did fine but was "JUMPY" as he came out of the anesthesia.
*He was making a VERY bizarre sound. A hollow-sounding rasping, and his body showed that his breathing was very intense. I asked what that sound was, and was told it was completely normal after coming out of the dental.
*Approx 10 mins later the noise did not stop. I asked for vet. He came in, and I was told by him, as well, that it was "completely normal". He said that Vanillabean was "protesting coming out of the anesthesia." I still showed concern so he has me place Vanillabean on the table, at which time, while he was standing, the noise diminished. Vet said there was nothing to worry about but that I could still stay in recovery room as long as I wished.
*Noise began again as soon as I placed Vanillabean on my lap or held him after vet left the room. I went out to the front desk to ask the girls if this was normal, and they said to ask vet (which I had already done). So I returned to room to recover. He spits up a little clear fluid.
*I held him for another 20 approx minutes, noise still did not cease, I called in the dental tech. She once again said the sound was "normal" and

not to worry but that I can stay in recovery room as long as I wanted.

*Approximately 45 minutes to one hour later I am still there, and call in vet again. He once again reassured me it was nothing to worry about, and left the room.

*About a half hour after that — a total of me waiting in recovery with Vanillabean for approximately one-and-a-half hours (I normally am able to take Vanillabean home 20-30 minutes after he is brought out to me after all of his dentals), vet comes into room again, and pulls out the stethoscope, but then just tells me to take Vanillabean home. His words were "Take him home so he can relax." He DID NOT actually ever USE the stethoscope or put it up to his heart, but instead sent me home.

*On drive home, he is still making the same sounds, although they are a little less frequent.

*When we arrive home, he is able to walk in the door fine, pee and poop on his wee wee pad. He cannot walk up the ramp to our bed. So I carry him up so he can relax in his favorite spot.

*He is still making noises and he is still breathing heavy. I call vet from home, he says, "I figured it out, it's tracheal irritation. It can last about 5 days, and he'll probably have it through the weekend. But call me at home if you need me."

*Vanillabean is spitting up very diluted blood, mostly clear fluid with light blood. I figure it is from the "tracheal irritation."

*I call Vanillabean in for a treat, he does not come. VERY alarming, as he never ever refuses a treat. I call vet immediately again, at approx 2pm, he is not available. The receptionist says they will have him call me in an hour.

*I try to give him a treat in bed, and he does not take it there either.

*I offer some peanut butter on a spoon, he licks it very slightly and turns his head away from it.

*Hollow-raspy sound is diminishing a bit, and there are even periods with no strange sound coming from him at all.

*Vet calls me back 2 hours later and says all that Vanillabean is doing is normal.

*My husband comes home and I tell him what is going on. He holds Vanillabean and Vanillabean completely stops making those sounds.
*I go to take a shower as my husband holds Vanillabean, and when I come out, I check his gums. His gums are completely grey. I call vet office and tell them I am coming over.
*Upon arrival, I am placed into a room. Vet looks at gums and tongue....both of which are grey.
*Does an X-ray. It.shows that one lung has collapsed due to fluid. Vet says he WILL be okay.
*He also says that he "regrets that he did not call me back sooner."
*I call my holistic vet in Tampa to consult with this vet, regarding drugs to be used for this, as at this point I do not trust this vet to do the right thing, since he clearly misdiagnosed Vanillabean earlier by telling me he was "protesting coming out of anesthesia" and had "tracheal irritation", while all along, it was a collapsed lung.
*Vet comes in and says he will be okay, then, 5 minutes later, comes in and says he almost didn't make it and that he (the vet) "got scared', but now he got his gums more pink. He walks out of room again.
*I have him talk to my holistic vet again, and this time he asks me to give him my holistic vet's phone number, and calls him from another room.
*We ask vet is he is going to make it, and now he says "50/50"
*He tells me to call my holistic vet, and then walks out of the room.
*My holistic vet tells me to get into the room with Vanillabean immediately, as he IS NOT going to make it.
AGAIN, TO CLARIFY, my holistic vet in TAMPA was the one who had to tell me BY PHONE that my Vanillabean was dying...NOT THE VET IN THE CLINIC WITH ME WHO DID THE DENTAL, who chose to, instead, walk out of the room with no updated news.
*I go in and Vanillabean is almost in a coma. Oxygen is still being administered. I hold him and sing to him as he is dying in my arms, Tommy is in front of him looking into his face. My friend Lisa is behind me, holding me as I hold Vanillabean. As I am singing to Vanillabean, vet says (for reasons I will never comprehend), "He can't hear you."
Vanillabean passes away shortly thereafter (at 6pm).

*We hold his little body and go into a room, and vet has no answers except to say this "never happened to him" before, and that he has not had a death as a result of a dental in 8 years. He says, "Well my record is now broken." He said he has no answers.

*I called and left a message for vet on BOTH his home line AND his office line the very next day (Saturday), as my husband and I had questions for him that remained unanswered.

*Neither the vet, nor his office, call us all weekend.

*He did not call until Monday, saying he "was going to call us Saturday" but decided to give us "some time"....despite the fact that I left TWO messages for him Saturday (the day after Vanillabean passed), requesting a phone call back.

*His message also just said "I'm sorry for you guys," and that he was going to "try to find out what happened."

*He surprisingly called back in just a very, very short time after his first call. Although he said he was going to "try to find out what happened," all he said in his message was that Vanillabean had 15 dentals at his office. That was all. Then he finished with the same thing as before, "I"m sorry for you guys."

Vanillabean

CHAPTER THIRTY-THREE

ELLIE MAE'S STORY
Matt Frederick

On Monday July 16th, my wife and I took Ellie (our 11-year-old Border Collie Lab Mix) to Animalia Health and Wellness in Franklin, Tennessee for an abdominal ultrasound when her previous bloodwork revealed her ALP, ALT, and cholesterol levels were elevated Dr. Lisa Martin performed the abdominal ultrasound and reported finding a small mass on Ellie's liver. Dr. Martin stated that the next step to reach a definitive diagnosis was to perform a 'Tru-Cut' liver biopsy. I asked about a fine needle aspirate in lieu of the 'Tru-Cut' but was told that the fine needle aspirate produced samples of inferior histopathological quality. When I inquired about the risks associated with the procedure, I was told that the only risk was hemorrhage, and was assured that Ellie would be monitored very closely before, during, and after the procedure. We scheduled the procedure and took her to Animalia at 7:55 am on Friday, July 20th, for Dr. Martin to perform the biopsy. They stated that they would keep Ellie until 4 pm to monitor her for potential hemorrhaging. I called Animalia at 11:53 to check on Ellie and was told that everything was fine.

Dr. Martin's report states that she had Dr. Sarah Mosher call me at 3:35 to inform me of the situation, which is not true. I called Animalia to see if Ellie was ready to be picked up. Dr. Martin did not come to the phone, instead Dr. Moser informed me that Dr. Martin had found fluid in Ellie's abdomen which they suspected to be bile and stated that they would take a sample and run a test to confirm. Dr. Moser stated that Ellie would be ok, and if they needed me to take her to the emergency vet they would call. Dr. Martin's Addendum shows that she waited for 1 hour and 11 minutes before she even attempted to consult with another vet about Ellie's case. (3:35 to 4:46.) I asked Dr. Moser why I shouldn't pick Ellie up right then and take her to Blue Pearl immediately, and again Dr. Moser stated that Ellie would be okay and there was no cause for concern. According to the attached phone records, I did not hear back from Dr. Mosher until 5:09 (their timeline says Dr. Mosher called at 4:55, which again, is not accurate) to confirm that the fluid in Ellie's abdomen was bile and said that I should take Ellie to the Emergency Vet.

They continually reassured me that everything would be fine. They told me that they had just spoken with Blue Pearl and that when I took her, they would evaluate Ellie and then decide if she would undergo surgery that night or the next morning to remove her gall bladder. They said this was a significant surgery, but nothing to be worried about, and that she would be in the hospital to recover for a couple of days. She also stated that they would remove the liver mass at the same time if possible. She gave no indication as to the severity or time sensitive nature of Ellie's injury at the hands of Dr. Martin. In addition, Dr. Moser stated that Dr. Martin claimed that the bile in her abdomen was most likely from the liver mass pressing on the gallbladder, and not what I believe was a 3mm injury from Dr. Martin puncturing Ellie's gallbladder.

Dr. Martin's statement seemed highly suspect for an extremely healthy dog with no prior history of any gallbladder issues. Dr. Moser did not act alarmed or concerned at all. I stated that I wanted to pick Ellie up immediately, and Dr. Moser again stated that I did not have to worry, and they would again call when she was ready to be released.
I could not deal with the uncertainty any longer. I drove to Animalia and demanded that Ellie be released.

Dr. Martin's timeline states that Ellie was picked up at 5:47. When I saw Ellie she was completely unresponsive. I was extremely upset and asked where Dr. Martin was. I was informed by the receptionist that she was "tied up". Dr. Martin did not even have the decency to show her face.

While Ellie was carried by a vet tech to my car, Dr. Mosher followed me out to the car and said that "there is nothing to worry about, we caught this early."

Ellie's mouth was open, and I noticed she was gasping softly, and that her gums were discolored. She did not respond when I cupped her face and called her name. Her eyes were open, and she was not blinking. I asked why she was unresponsive, and Dr. Mosher stated it was because of the hydromorphone that Dr. Martin had given her for pain. I rushed Ellie from Animalia to the emergency facility and arrived at the Emergency vet at 5:54.
When Ellie was triaged the Emergency vet's Report listed her as "comatose, cyanotic and in agonal respiration."

They rushed her into critical care, intubated her and got her breathing on her own again. Because she arrived in such critical condition she was never fully stable, and several more critical hours were lost before surgery could be performed at 8:30. It then became a race against time to get the bile that had leaked into her abdomen neutralized so it did not cause major organ damage and further shock to her system.

The surgeon on Ellie's case reported that when they were closing her incision she went into cardiac arrest. They restarted her heart and then stated that she had lost neurological function. She was placed in ICU, not fully breathing on her own and her prognosis was grim. After numerous subsequent cardiac arrests, Ellie died at 10:36 on Saturday night July.

The unexpected loss of Ellie has been and continues to be devastating for our entire family. I immediately requested Ellie's records, as well as a clinical timeline from Dr. Martin regarding an explanation of the events that day. We found it very concerning that there were over 49 images on record from Dr. Martin's original ultrasound of Ellie from July 16th, yet there was not a single stored image from Dr. Martin's actual Tru-Cut Biopsy performed on Ellie on July 20th.

Upon review of the records, I uncovered some very disturbing facts. Sue Hutton told us that after the procedure, Dr. Martin left the clinic for a few hours. Ellie was left in the care of a vet tech. It also came to light through my wife's conversation with Ms. Hutton, that there was not even a single veterinarian in the clinic for several hours due to an off-site Doctor's Meeting.

Had we known this was the case, we would have taken Ellie to a specialist. Had we done that; she might very well be here with us today. Ms. Hutton made a very telling comment during her conversation with my wife: "The only right thing that we did really at the end of the day was send her to the Emergency vet, because that was the care that she needed."

That comment begs the questions: What else has been overlooked, undocumented, and concealed by Dr. Martin? How many other beloved companions have suffered a similar outcome? I requested a sit-down meeting with Dr. Martin, but was refused, as Animalia leadership felt that it would be "counterproductive."

The Subjective/History section of Emergency vet's Report states that "During the procedure (which we assume is the post ultrasound), the gallbladder reportedly got smaller in size and free fluid began to accumulate in the abdomen."

Dr. Martin's Medical Note/Addendum states "Approximately 6 hours post biopsy, a brief ultrasound was performed to evaluate for hemorrhage. A moderate amount of fluid was noted in all four quadrants of the abdomen and a small amount was aspirated for analysis. The gall bladder at this time was empty compared to its pre-biopsy size."

If these major changes were noticed by Dr. Martin during the post-op procedure, and she knew that most likely it was bile, with her training and expertise, knowing full well that Animalia was not equipped to handle such an emergency, she should have sent Ellie to Emergency vet at 3:35 instead of 2 hours later when she was in agonal respiration. It has also been stated to us by Animalia, that Dr. Martin was aware that Ellie's condition was very serious during the ultrasound check at 3:35, despite what her actions, or rather, her lack of appropriate clinical response showed, as well as what she communicated through Dr. Moser on the phone.

We believe it is also telling that Dr. Martin did not speak to us once since she realized that she had made a potentially life-threatening mistake but had someone else speak to us for all further communication.

In reviewing Dr. Martin's Medical Note/Addendum, it became clear that Dr. Martin's facility did not have the ability to reliably test the bilirubin level of the fluid sample from Ellie's abdomen. As Dr. Martin herself wrote: "unknown on the reliability of this measurement because our bloodwork machines are only calibrated for blood."

Our primary doctor at Animalia, the Medical Director at the Emergency vet, and several other veterinarians we have consulted have told us that these 2 hours were most likely the difference between life and death for Ellie. Along with the 2 hours that Dr. Martin should have sent Ellie to the emergency clinic, Ellie should have been rechecked via ultrasound for any problems well before 5 hours post biopsy. Even Animalia has realized that this should have been done and has since changed the protocol for all Tru-Cut biopsies to be rechecked by ultrasound immediately after the procedure, and at 2- and 5-hours post-op. This is of little consolation to us.

Ellie was an incredibly important member of our family. She was adored. She deserved Dr. Martin's best care and attention and died, we believe, because Dr. Lisa Martin failed on several critical fronts. In my opinion, Dr. Martin failed to appropriately monitor Ellie after the procedure, leaving the clinic for several hours. Dr. Martin then failed to respond quickly and decisively to a life-threatening mistake, instead waiting for 2 more critical hours to pass.

Ellie arrived at the Emergency vet in such poor condition that several more hours passed before the surgeon could even attempt to save her life, and when he tried, she suffered the first of a series of cardiac arrests from which she would never recover. In my opinion, Dr. Martin's negligence, poor decision making, and failure to act are the reasons that Ellie died. It is beyond unacceptable.

Ellie Mae

CHAPTER THIRTY-FOUR

PAULIE'S STORY
Jessica Pearson

Paulie was a healthy, incredibly silly 3yo French Bulldog. He was a gift from my husband when we got engaged. Paulie was with us for every major life event. Our engagement, marriage, birth of our son, and deaths of our loved ones. He was truly our "child". On June 6, 2020 we took Paulie to Oak Hill Animal Hospital because he was licking his paws. Nothing major, we assumed it was allergies. This was to be his first visit there, and when I scheduled I was told due to COVID-19 we would not be allowed in the building. I was not comfortable with this but trusted that he would be in good hands. It was a veterinarian, and they love our animals, right? I even wrote a handwritten letter stating that Paulie gets easily worked up, and under NO CIRCUMSTANCE to put him in a cage.

My husband took Paulie to his 5:00 appointment. At 6pm he called me to say they still had not come to get him. I had a bad feeling. Eventually they came out and my husband handed Paulie over along with my note. My husband watched as Paulie trotted along with the tech, happy as can be. About an hour passed, and no one gave us an update. My husband went to the door to see what was taking so long. The receptionist would not let him in and said Paulie was getting his collar on and would be right out. Seconds later, the doctor came outside and simply said "well, Paulie's dead". He explained he got "worked up" and his heart exploded. There was nothing he could do.

Devastated, I refused to accept that answer. An independent vet reviewed his medical report and stated absolutely nothing was done to save Paulie. Further, a tech working that day reached out to me and stated she witnessed Dr Walsh punch Paulie in the head because he would not sit still, then forcefully throw him in a cage (after we specifically told them not to). The tech came to check on Paulie and found him in his cage, dead from a heart attack due to anxiety.

I pursued a lawsuit against Dr Walsh, which resulted in closing his clinic and he is no longer practicing veterinary medicine. Thank you for taking the time to read about Paulie.

<u>Paulie</u>

CHAPTER THIRTY-FIVE

MAX'S STORY
Mary and Richard Belyski

The time was September 2014. We had just got married on a cruise ship in Miami, and we were driving home to Myrtle Beach, SC. We had our Boston Terrier, Chopper in a kennel, while we went away for our wedding and honeymoon. Chopper, the Boston terrier, would be alone for the first time in the kennel without his brother. We had lost our boxer named Buster one year ago to cancer.

My husband had researched the Florida area prior to us leaving for our wedding. He found a reputable seller of puppies. After we left the cruise ship, he wanted to stop, just to see what type of puppies they had. We stopped on the way home and saw two pug puppies. One was black, and very hyper, and the other was fawn, and calmer. The owner gladly took them to an area, that we could play with them, to see if we wanted to buy one of them. We played with them for 3 hours. They were so adorable. I then came to my senses, and said no, we can't get another dog. We just got married, let's just go home. We got in our car and left. I wanted to get a coffee before we got back on the road. Coffee in hand, we were headed toward the entrance of I-95. Just before my husband got onto the entrance, I said, "Wait, let's go back and get the fawn-colored puppy". We made a U turn, and back to the puppy store we went.

We pick up that adorable, loving fawn colored pug, and he licked us both. This was the best wedding present we could give each other, and our other dog Chopper. We felt blessed to have chosen him.

We got all the food, puppy gear, harness, and lease. The owner gave us a box to put in the back seat, and we had a blanket that we put in the box. We place the little pug into the box, and he began to cry, "yip yip, yap, yap". I picked that little fur baby up, got the blanket, and put him in my lap. We began the 8-hour trip back home, and I carried the precious fur baby the whole way! On the long ride home, we discussed puppy names. When I first met my husband, he had another boxer, named Max, or Maxie as I called her, as she was a girl. We decided to call our new fur baby the name of Max.

When we picked up Chopper the next day, he didn't know what to think of this new little fur ball. We slowly introduced them to each other, and they became best friends. Our family was complete was complete.
Max started to develop problems on December 9, 2017. He woke up and was in severe pain. He was having either low back or right back leg pain. The vet could not pinpoint what was wrong with the dog. We were given Carprofen, Buprenorphine, and Benadryl. We were told to restrict his activity and keep him on crate rest. December 29, 2017, he vomited food. Vet thought it was pancreatitis. He was started on a specialty dog. Last dose of Carprofen was on January 4, 2018. They advised to bring him to a specialty vet two hours away for further evaluation. It was Christmas time, and he could not be seen until January 9, 2018. Max was starting to improve when we brought him to the specialty vet. We decided to treat him conservatively.

October 2019, he started to have pain again. We brough him back to the specialty vet. The dog was now given prednisone and gabapentin by our local vet prior to going to the specialty vet. Again, we were told because he is improving, to treat him conservatively.

Aug 23, 2020 Max was in pain again. He started to whimper loudly and was very uncomfortable. We started him on crate rest, to let his body heal. We set up his crate, with extra blankets, so he would be comfortable. He could not get comfortable. I called the specialty vets emergency number. I could not remember what we were told the last time we went there. We never got discharge paperwork, just prescriptions of Carprofen and Gabapentin. The bottles were given had no instructions or warning on them. I called the emergency number this specialty vet had, and the girl that answered read from the medical records. She said the doctor prescribed the two medications to be given if a flare ups occurred. She said, I would have to go to my local vet, and get another referral to come back to the specialty vet.

The next day, I brought him to our local vet. I brought all of his past medications with me and put them on the examination table for the vet to see. They were: Carprofen, Gabapentin, Tramadol, and Buprenorphine HCL. The vet could not conclude what was wrong with the dog. She told me to give him all of the medications that I brought in. She prescribed more Buprenorphine HCL and Tramadol. She did not tell me any warnings, just said to give all the medications. She did say make sure you give Carprofen 12 hours apart. She advised crate rest, and off I went. Max has never seen this vet before. I said we wanted to bring him to the specialty vet, and to do a referral. She said she was an intern there, and advised that if we went, they will most likely want to do all these tests. She has seen it before, that they will order MRI's, then tell us they can't do surgery, discharge us, then we would have to go back to them. We would then be told they have to do another MRI and tests. It was nice she was telling us this, but as I told her, this has been happening for 3 years, and we need to have him get all the tests needed to help him. We just needed a referral. I went home, made a chart to give our dog Max all of these medications, so me and my husband could keep track of what we were giving him.

Max was getting worst, not better. We had finally got the Tramadol filled at the pharmacy. My husband gave him one dose, and I gave him another that night. That night I put him in his crate and laid awake all night with him. He was panting and looked in distress. He could not get comfortable at all. He would get up, yelp loudly, then lay down. I was at a loss. My poor baby, all this medication, and you are still in pain.

Early the next morning, we brought him to the local emergency vet. Due to COVID-19 19, we could not go in. I had previously typed out a list of all the medications we were giving him and gave this to the girl that came to our car to get our information. She then took our Max, and carried him in. The vet inside the facility called us. She carried Max into the office. The vet called us on the phone, while we waited in our car. She said she would add yet another medication for our dog. She gave him a muscle relaxer. She did say not to give Tramadol with the other medications. She never warned us of any of the medications that we were giving.

We got him home and gave him the new medication. He was resting or was forced to from all the medication he was on.

This rest did not last long. He began to yelp louder and louder. We agreed to get him to the specialty vet 2 hours away. We knew we had to get an MRI and surgery to help our little guy. He could not be in this type of pain. None of the medications were helping him.

We got him in the car that morning. He did not look good and was very quiet. I thought this was from the new medication that was prescribed for him. 9/2/2020 - We made our way to the specialty vet. We had to wait in our car for them to come out to take Max due to COVID-19 19. We were having him met again with the Neurologist, in hope to have him get his MRI that day, and whatever else it took to get our dog out of pain. If surgery was recommended, we were ready to have him have surgery, and be out of pain. We waited patiently in the car for the vet to call us after she examined him. What followed we never expected. The Neurologist called us, to tell us he is lethargic and anemic. Everything went downhill from there. We were told he needed to go to the ER there, as he was very unstable. They said he was anemia and had to do a blood transfusion. An ultrasound showed a perforated bowel. We were told he would have to have emergency surgery to stop the bleeding. We were told to go home, and the vet surgeon would call us that evening with an update. We got the call that evening. She said he has a huge ulcer "she had never seen an ulcer that big before", that went into his lower intestine. She closed the ulcer, and he will have to be watched. She said it would be a 50% chance he would survive. We were devastated. We began to pray for a miracle. Vet told us before the surgery was done on the phone, the dog would be in a guarded condition. The medical records show otherwise that the dog is in poor/guarded prognosis. We were not informed prior to the surgery the prognosis was poor, just guarded. Each day the vet would call us in the morning and night with an update. Things were looking up, but he was not out of the woods. On September 4, 2020, the vet surgeon called that morning. She said he was not responding to the antibiotics, but maybe changing to a different one would help him. A hyperbaric chamber was discussed to help him heal. We agreed. She called us back in one hour to say his blood pressure was dropping. They would treat that right away. She consulted another vet, who recommended bringing him back to surgery. The other vet did not recommend a different antibiotic. The vet surgeon could not see having him opened up again to be operated on, to assure she closed up the ulcer. She called us back in another hour, stating his blood pressure went back up, but now it is going down again. She was not hopeful this time. He was in the process of dying and was suffering. We agreed euthanize him, after discussing this with the vet surgeon.

We were two hours away, so we could not be with him. I asked to have a phone call, so we could speak to our baby Max. The technician called us, so we could tell him how much we loved him, how sorry we were that this happened. I said a prayer for my baby pug Max. He was listening, he lifted his head from the blanket he was one, then put it back down. He was very sick, and his little body couldn't fight anymore. We said our goodbyes to our beautiful pug Max. I said, "Daddy and Mommy know you in a lot of pain. We are so sorry baby; we will see you again in heaven one day. We both love you very much" He was then euthanized on September 4, 2020.

The next week we were in shock and dismay. We couldn't even function or come to a realization our dog was gone. I asked for the medical records for his visit to be sent to us. The medical records read GI Bleed due to

Carprofen! There it was in black and white, and we were never warned this could have happened. How could this of happened!

We had Max cremated and picked out a beautiful urn. We all got into the car, including his brother, Chopper, the Boston terrier to go get Max two hours away. We picked Max up in a bag, with his ashes inside the urn. We went to a park overlooking the ocean. It was a peaceful day. We talked about all the good memories of Max, all the things he did to bring us joy, and our unconditional love for him. It is only the three of us now. Our anniversary on September 13, 2020 has passed. Even though our baby is gone, and a piece of our heart if broken, we will always remember our fur baby, Max.

Max

CHAPTER THIRTY-SIX

LUKE'S STORY
Alicia Brindisi

Luke was a beautiful mastiff rescued from a high kill shelter after his owner passed and he was left by family members at the shelter. He came to me in 2015, barely 2 years old, and just 3 days before he was scheduled to be euthanized, we had both suffered a loss and to find each other in such a time of need, it was fate. He became a bright light of hope for me and so I named him Luke, meaning 'to bring light'.

I've had several mastiffs previously and was comfortable with the breed. They are highly intelligent and strong willed, yet it was clear from the early days that while Luke was true to his breed, he was also very afraid of the world around him. For the next several years I dedicated many resources to teaching him, protecting him, and giving him his best life possible. His joy was my joy. I believed in him and I knew he just needed the right skills and the confidence to live his best life. I planned activities and trips for us so that he could travel and explore nature without fear. We were together all the time – traveling and experiencing new things. Our bond was strong. We supported each other day to day. It was clear he was a special dog and I considered myself blessed to have found him and honored that I was able to give him the life he so deserved.

Luke was happy and playful and extremely smart. He excelled in obedience classes. He loved scent work. He was a friend and playmate to other dogs and animals. And though he was confident in the animal world, he was more fearful and distrusting of people. His circle of trust was small and for that reason I worked very hard with him under the guidance of a behavioral veterinarian to make certain that Luke was safe and so were the people around him. He continued to blossom and become more at ease with new people and new experiences.

Unfortunately, the one place that Luke could not feel safe was during veterinarian visits. He was happy to walk into the office and greet the staff with paws and kisses. However, when it came time for the exam, he became frightened and aggressive. Routine exams and vaccinations required muzzles and restraint and eventually sedation. It was highly stressful for him, and for me, and it pained me to see him in such distress.

I chose to share this backstory because I think it's important to understand that while Luke was a large dog who could be fearful and aggressive in stressful situations, he was also a good dog who was gentle and smart. He loved to play with his toys, roll around on his back in the grass on summer days, and snuggle on my lap during car rides. Like most mastiffs, he was loyal to his person, yet in the company of strangers he preferred his space. He looked to me for guidance and served as my protector. We were a team. We helped each other navigate the more challenging days, celebrating the successes along the way. I could easily read his signs and help him through a difficult situation. I did all I could to mitigate his stress and stress to others who had to care for him. I dedicated our time together to teaching him but also to keeping him safe.

About the age of 6 years old, Luke developed a very treatable infection. Yet over a period of 2 weeks, we were dismissed by multiple vets who did not want to see him in the office or provide treatment, I believe, because they knew he was a more challenging patient. These were trusted doctors, many whom we had known for decades. We were simply told to "keep an eye on things" and "call back in a few days" … But as we watched and waited, the infection grew worse. When he was finally prescribed medication over the phone, Luke was only able to take one dose as the infection had now become too painful for him to swallow or eat.

Within 24 hours of being prescribed medication over the phone, it was clear that Luke was in distress. I took him into the emergency vet that evening – a well-known, and seemingly reputable hospital that I had used many times before. When we finally were seen, close to midnight, we were denied treatment and left with instructions to call our regular doctor in the morning. We had already gone this route and had not been successful.

After returning home and Luke suffering through the night, I made the mistake of returning to the same ER the next day. Luke's infection required immediate surgery. I spoke at length with the ER vet about Luke's fear in the hospital and my concerns about over sedation. I was assured he would be monitored closely. When I left him that day I patted and kissed his head and told him what I always did when I left him "Momma will see you soon" — I never imagined it would be the last time I actually saw him.

Luke had surgery and all went well. He would need to stay one or two days in the hospital. I opted not to visit him after surgery because I knew he would become excited and protective of me and I wanted him to rest so he could come home. I received updates that he was doing well. The morning after his surgery I was told he was resting comfortably but the hospital wanted to keep him another day.

Just a few hours later in the afternoon on the day after his surgery, I received another phone call. It was the surgeon in charge of Luke's case. He told me Luke was found unresponsive in his kennel. He said they were administering CPR but were unsuccessful and he was gone. In disbelief I sped to the hospital. Surely someone had made a mistake. There was no way my healthy dog who had been recovering from a simple surgery a few hours ago was now dead!

I waited almost 30 minutes alone in a room for some information and to see him. No one came, no one explained anything. Finally, after an agonizing wait, his dead body was brought into the room. My worst fears were confirmed. He was gone. My world stopped spinning at that moment. The air came out of my lungs. My beautiful baby was gone. The bright light that he was had been extinguished. I knew immediately something had gone very wrong. I was left with a bill for thousands of dollars, no dog, and no explanation of what truly transpired.

After a careful review of his medical records by independent veterinarians not affiliated with this hospital or having any knowledge of Luke's care or condition prior to this incident, it was presumed that during a procedure to tend to his wound, Luke was given a series of sedatives/anesthetics. When the initial dose of sedatives did not take effect quickly enough to control him, he was given more. The combination of sedatives/anesthetics (dexmedetomidine, propofol, ketamine, and alfaxalone) administered intramuscularly proved to be fatal. With no reversal agent administered, no monitoring or airway support in place, his unconscious body was left in a kennel where he presumably suffocated and he was later found dead. He was gone too long for CPR to be successful. It would have been difficult to revive him under the amount of sedatives he received and that he had been dead for a period of time before the hospital staff had noticed.

There is nothing that can prepare you for an event like this. I did all that I could for Luke during his short life with me - even saving him from death once before, and yet I could not save him from this fate.

I feel a huge sense of betrayal. I was robbed of my last goodbye with my precious Luke. Robbed of more years of life. He was young and healthy otherwise. He was happy and joyful. He was not a monster. He was loved and gave so much more love in return.

I will continue to seek the truth for Luke, and honor his memory by advocating for better healthcare standards and veterinarian oversight. Pet caregivers and the pets they love need more advocates to protect them from tragedies like this.

"My sunshine doesn't come from the skies, it comes from the light in my dog's eyes. You will forever be my light, my love, my Luke"

Thank you for reading Luke's story.

CHAPTER THIRTY-SEVEN

JENNA'S STORY
Kyndall and Shannon Bowen

Jenna was a hound mix that was almost thirteen years old. She was a family pet that was deeply loved and was always happy. As someone said, "To know Jenna, was to love Jenna." She had an unbreakable spirit that never failed to love you beyond belief. We are deeply saddened by the loss of her and it has torn our family up in more ways than one. I felt it was necessary to tell Jenna's story as a tribute to her, in hopes that the vet that hurt her won't be able to hurt anyone else's beloved family pet. Jenna had a fatty lipoma on her stomach that I felt needed to be looked at to see if it was able to be removed. It had gotten a little bit bigger and I didn't want it to affect her in the future. I noticed that it would hang down some and I was worried that it was making it harder on her. I took her to Benessere Animal Hospital in Greensboro, North Carolina on April 9th, 2020 for a consultation to see if the fatty lipoma could be removed. We were seen by the vet who goes by Dr. Janine Oliver. Little did we know this was just the start of something that would end so badly, and cause Jenna senseless suffering and pain. This was just the start of something that now consumes our lives and started a campaign to get justice for Jenna.

On the day of April 9th, Jenna was taken in for a consultation at Benessere Animal Hospital. Due to COVID we weren't allowed inside, so a tech came out and did the initial check-in questions. The tech then took Jenna inside the hospital where Dr. Janine Oliver was going to look at her and pull some cells out to confirm that this was a fatty lipoma. A little while later Jenna was returned to us by the tech, and we waited to talk to Dr. Oliver. When she finally came outside she was adamant that she could remove the main lipoma, but she ensured that she could also remove the other two smaller ones on her side. She boasted "I can take all 3 of these lipomas off at one time. I once did a Schnauzer who was more tumor than dog," and "I removed one from an older dog one time that interfered with movement and this dog's quality of life improved." See I did not take Jenna in for a removal surgery of all three, and even said "Only do that if it is safe." Dr. Oliver made a point to tell me she would only do it if it was safe and ensured me, she would run an ultrasound over her abdomen to make sure everything looked alright before proceeding, as well as pull blood work before the surgery. She told us the cells showed as just a fatty lipoma and that was the extent of the conversation. While outside she barely felt Jenna's abdomen except for a quick squeeze and proceeded to tell us to bring her back on April the 13th for the surgery. At this point we had no reason to doubt that Dr. Janine Oliver was incompetent in her profession.

Jenna was dropped off for her surgery on April 13th, 2020 and she had the surgery performed on the 14th. She had the surgery, which they said went well and that she did good. She was picked up from Benessere Animal Hospital on the 15th. Dr. Oliver was not there on the day of release so an employee returned Jenna to us with a bag of medications and a soft, blue e-collar. At this point we still believe Dr. Janine Oliver is a competent doctor who helped Jenna and furthered her quality of life, but we sure were wrong. Jenna went home for a few days and had an uneventful time. She drank well while she was at home and used the bathroom as usual. Jenna wore her e-collar the whole time she was home and rested. Otherwise, she would make a slow circle outside to use the bathroom and then would return to get on her soft, orthopedic bed. We started noticing on the first day she was home that Jenna's surgical incisions were really dark black and didn't seem to be done well. They almost looked like a child could have done a better job stitching them back up.

On April 18th, 2020, which was a Saturday, I noticed that Jenna's surgical incision was beginning to open back up around the edges of the skin that was already turning black. This was just three days after the initial surgery. I grabbed my phone and looked up the hours for Benessere and they were already closed. Not knowing if another vet would want to look at this on a weekend and with COVID happening, I opted to keep the area clean until Monday when Benessere opened back up. I personally worked at a vet for fifteen years, so I am no novice at keeping surgical areas clean. The spot at this point was about the size of a fifty-cent piece that had opened up on a few stitches. I did send Dr. Oliver a message on Facebook, which will come back in to play in Jenna's story later on. On April 20th, I called the animal hospital and talked to the receptionist about bringing Jenna back in to have her place re-sewn. Jenna was dropped off on this Monday at 8:31 AM, and we would never have imagined the condition she would be in ten days later.

I called on April 20th at 3:41 PM to check on the status of Jenna and was informed that she had not yet had the surgery but would be having it shortly. At 5:09 PM an employee called me to tell me that Jenna had gotten her surgery, but that there was a fifty-cent hole still left that wasn't able to be closed, so they were going to hold onto Jenna for a few more days to make sure she healed properly. Please note this was the only time I ever received any communication (other than a Facebook message from Dr. Oliver on the 23rd) from Benessere Animal Hospital during the ten days she was there, which occurred on the first day by an employee. While Jenna was under the care of Dr. Oliver I called to check on her eleven different times and was always told the same scripted answer which was "Jenna is eating, drinking, and doing well. She should be ready to go home soon." Mind you I was never told this by Dr. Oliver, but by her staff members. Every time you would call they would say "Hold on let me go ask Dr.O/ Dr.Oliver." Twice I was told I could bring Jenna some food or treats that she liked by the staff members. I now know that it was an attempt to get me to come and see the horrible condition that she was in. I was reluctant to go and do this though, as she was an older girl and I didn't want to upset her. I knew she would think she was going home and would be upset when she wasn't able to yet. After all, at this point I still think Jenna is healing and should be ready to go home shortly, as I keep getting repeatedly told every time I call.

On April 30th, 2020 I took the advice of the receptionist and decided to take Jenna some snacks. I pulled up with all her favorite treats and called to let them know that I was there to see her and brought her some treats. At this point it is around 12 PM, so I felt this was a perfect time to visit her, as she should be cared for already for the morning. I was told to pull around back and that they would bring her out. When she was brought out she was walking slowly, but I chalked it up to her being sore from being up there for a period of time in a cage. She was also wrapped in a pink bandage and saran wrap that wrapped around her stomach area and down her back leg. I just assumed it was around the back leg to keep it from sliding off her stomach. After visiting her for a few minutes I started to notice a strong smell coming from her bandage, that I can only describe as smelling like death. I took a closer look and noticed that her bandages were covered in pus and filthy. After a few minutes an employee that I had never spoken to before came out. She started leaning against the outside railing and stated "There are cameras everywhere out here, so I have to be careful what I say." I of course immediately asked if my dog is okay. A worried look went across her face and she said "I know you can't see what is under those bandages, but if you leave your dog here, I'm scared she is going to die. Dr. Oliver has let your dog's incision open up everywhere. Every surgical site that she has done has reopened. She is open everywhere under there and she needs a wound vac" She then stated she would go get Dr. Oliver from surgery to talk with me about the condition of my pet, and to please not believe anything Dr. Oliver was fixing to tell me. Dr. Oliver came outside a little while later dressed in a cap and gown. I questioned Dr. Oliver on why Jenna smelled so bad and why her bandage wasn't changed. She claimed that she would change it later in the day when she got done with surgery. I did not feel comfortable with the fact that the hospitalized animals weren't being cared for first thing and expressed that I was going to take Jenna for a second opinion at a different vet. Dr. Oliver was adamant that I do not remove Jenna from her care and stated "No one else is doing wound care. I know all my colleagues and everyone else would tell you to euthanize this dog. I have got your dog halfway healed. Why would I tell you otherwise? What would I have to gain? I'm not even charging you. I wish I would have taken pictures of your dog when she came in. She looks so much better." This of course raised red flags, because I know vets all over the world do wound care. I also started questioning myself, because why would she be doing this to an animal. I thought you were supposed to trust your vet, right? I then expressed that no one ever communicated with me that Jenna's whole stomach and leg was split open under the bandage. This was the only time Dr. Oliver actually looked surprised in this conversation, because she didn't know how I knew this nor did she know that her employee told me this information. Dr. Oliver then started listing a number of excuses as to why I was never told the condition of my dog and continued to be dismissive of every concern that I was having and the fact that this poor dog smelled like she was slowly rotting away. She instead blamed the smell on Jenna and that she was peeing and laying in it. I of course just got more worried, because who lets a dog with now open wounds sit and lay in their own urine?

At this point I was equally confused as I was stressed about the condition that Jenna was in. Dr. Oliver went back inside and thought I had agreed on leaving Jenna with her and expressed she would have someone come out and get her. She thought she had talked me into leaving Jenna in her care. A little while later the practice manager came out and expressed to me to get her out of there. So, now two people are telling me to get Jenna out before something bad happens. They helped me load her into my vehicle and I immediately called an Emergency vet who said they would be waiting on her. Her leg had doubled in size under the care of Dr. Oliver so when I arrived, they had to take her in on a stretcher, as she was having trouble walking. After about five hours of Jenna being inside, they came back with a report of purulent discharge in and around the wound and necrotic tissue at wound edges and deep inside. The abdomen was one open wound and there was severe necrosis to the superficial tissues. Their final assessment was dehiscence and infection of surgical wounds including catastrophic areas of skin. She received two doses of morphine while there and was said to be in a lot of pain. She was given a grave prognosis and the treatment they said they could try (two wound vacs and wet to dry bandages) would cost anywhere from 8-12 thousand dollars. They recommended, in her current state, that I should put her down. Keep in mind they also took pictures for me, without me asking. I will include the most shocking image taken, and let you decide if Jenna was really cared for at Benessere Animal

Hospital by Dr. Janine Oliver. Due to COVID I wasn't allowed to go into the building, so I still hadn't seen the grave state Jenna was in and did not understand why they were telling me to put her down. I had dropped her off with a small surgical area that had reopened, but now ten days later they are describing it as a catastrophic area. I guess the only factual thing Dr. Oliver ever said was that her colleagues would recommend euthanasia, and I would later find out why. I opted to let them clean her and give her medications, and I made an appointment for 8 AM the next morning at my local vet to try wet to dry bandages. I took her home and she had one final night of resting in her own bed.

At 8 AM on May 1st, she was seen at a local vet and had her bandages removed. I then realized why the emergency vet gave the grave prognosis. Jenna's whole stomach area and leg area was gaped open. Jenna could not walk that morning and was non-ambulatory. Due to the fact that Dr. Oliver chose to lie for ten days Jenna was now beyond any help that would be useful. Dr. Oliver claims we knew all along that she had informed us that Jenna was declining so badly. She claims we knew Jenna was in bad condition. That is a blatant lie because if I knew my dog was like this, then we would have removed her from the start. I walked into my local vet convinced I would be bringing Jenna back home with me. No one had any clue that Jenna looked the way she did. We decided to end Jenna's pain and suffering as we cried and told her how sorry we were. Sorry, I ever saw this vet. Sorry, I trusted this vet. Sorry, I didn't know sooner. (How could I?) Sorry, I had to tell her goodbye. Sorry, we put her in the hands of a person we believe to be a monster. I truly hope that Janine Oliver is proud of herself for putting a stain on the vet profession. While most vets strive for perfection, I believe she strives for much less. In my opinion, she doesn't even get close to being an adequate veterinarian.

I have never been lied to so much by someone that took an oath to do no harm and be honest. Dr. Oliver lied about the condition of my dog, lied and tried to say I knew her condition, etc. I believe she even fabricated Jenna's records. One obvious example that I found was that she put Jenna under anesthesia one day and then the surgery was done on the next day, so apparently she can't even remember when she did the procedure. She also claimed in her notes that if Jenna came back hypothyroid that she would not do the surgery as the thyroid was essential to the health and healing of the skin. She did come back hypothyroid, but the surgery was still performed and in fact she never mentioned this information to me and proceeded with the surgery. I never saw her bloodwork to know this. I also have a text, in which Dr. Oliver refuses to let a relief vet treat Jenna and even states " I don't need Dr. (name left out for confidentiality) involved. I will deal with her tomorrow." The staff told me Jenna would be put in a drain tub and have pieces of skin cut from her wounds while fully awake, without any anesthesia. Perhaps, though the most blatant lie was that I knew the condition Jenna was in. As I previously mentioned I had only ever gotten a Facebook message from Dr. Oliver in which she stated Jenna was doing good and healing. I will include the image of said message. The message was sent on the 23rd and claimed Jenna was healing, I later learned from an anonymous source that the day before on the 22nd Jenna had started to break down and open on her incisions. I have time stamped pictures that prove this was false and in fact she was deteriorating rapidly. Dr. Oliver had every chance in all the times when I called to come clean and confess, she didn't know what she was doing and couldn't heal Jenna. I feel as though she signed her death certificate by hiding her condition from me for so long. Now more horrifying cases and stories have come out; however I can't speak on them. I am simply here to tell the story of how, in my opinion, Dr. Oliver failed Jenna and caused her to suffer senselessly. I hope Jenna always remembers how much we loved her and that we will see her again. You can lie, you can falsify, you can do whatever you want, but if I have anything to do with it you won't hurt anymore pets. Jenna deserved so much more than a vet that is a butcher and a liar. I hope Jenna's name stays stamped in your memory and that you never forget the pain and suffering that you caused her.

I removed her on April 30th after ten days under the care of a vet. This image was taken by the Emergency vet. You can see the saran wrap, pus coming from the wounds, and the filth on the bandage Dr. Oliver claimed she cleaned every day. Does this look like it was cleaned every day?

Does this look like something a vet would consider acceptable? To me it looks like Jenna layed, rotted, and wasted away for ten days.

Jenna

CHAPTER THIRTY-EIGHT

SCOUT'S STORY
Dolly Centella

My Scout

On March 7, 2006, I came across a dog named Misty, of interest to me, who was at the local shelter.

After talking to her and petting her, she still did not shut up. I flagged down the attendant to make him aware of my interest in this 2-year-old female dog.

New home, new name, Misty was now Scout. I always wanted to name a pet after the little girl in the movie To Kill a Mockingbird. For a week in her new home all she did was cry after those people who had dumped her. I did toy with the idea of naming her Mrs. Ima Whiner....but Scout won.

Care for Scout over the years was kibble with no chemicals, dyes, or artificial preservatives, with a bit of table food or high quality can food for a topper. During her time with me Scout was fed Innova, until the company was sold, then Acana, Wellness, or Honest Kitchen. Scout's nails were not clipped, I would use a grinder on her nails. As soon as she saw the grinder come out, she would jump on the sofa and tuck her front feet under her body, wanting no part of the grinder. I used a children's electric toothbrush to clean her teeth.

Scout received added supplements, over the years. Always pro-biotics, fish oil, Cranberry extract when struvites had showed up. The Cranberry extract along with distilled water added to her food temporarily, flushed the struvites right out. Dasuquin or Cosequin as she got older, Denamarin at times for liver support. I had routine blood work done every year and twice a year as she got older. Heartworm medication was given seasonal, and Scout would be re-tested each spring.

Also, Scout received her yearly DHLP booster at the shelter before adoption, and again she received a booster at her Vet the following year, 2007. That was the last time she had a yearly booster. I had titers done every year only to find the vaccine was still in her system. Except for Leptospirosis, which ran out in 2 years. Since Scout was not high risk, I chose not to get that vaccine as it can be fatal in some breeds. During the remainder of her life, Scout never had another booster.

I did not know for sure her true breed until near the end. Scout was a mix, exactly the type dog I love. DNA showed she was what I always suspected, and what Vets had seen in her over the years. Scout was a mix of Aussie, Lab, Collie, German Shepherd, and Rottie. A true mix that can never be replaced. That also accounts for why she was so smart and cute. She was small in stature even with this large breed mix. She always checked in somewhere between 37 lbs. to 45 lbs. She was 35 lbs. when she left me.

By law, rabies vaccine was given every 3 years until she came down with a medical problem when she was 15 years old. Vaccines are to be given to healthy animals, and she was due that year. I refused and the local Vet was nice enough to research having a titer done. We did that, it was expensive, a result over 0.1 was good. Scout's result was 2.2, also the local township accepted the report for her yearly license.

The first medical problem of concern happened in April 2019, one month after Scout turned 15 years old. A tumor on the spleen was found. I was told this happens with certain breeds. With Scouts age I did not want a biopsy done under anesthesia. It was 50/50, cancer or not cancer. We took a gamble. Over the next several months we did about 5 ultrasounds at the Animal Hospital to monitor for any changes. Scout was seen 2x by Surgical Oncology there, and they determined no cancer. There were no changes to this tumor, it remained the same. We were good, with just the monitoring for any possible bleeding of the tumor.

Heading towards 16 years old, Scout still romped around a huge yard chasing squirrels.

In December 2019, I noticed Scout, who was never a really big water drinker, started drinking more water than usual. We had a scheduled appointment just before Christmas for her routine ultrasound. When there, I mentioned my concerns to the Vet and with just relying on routine blood work the Vet told me there was nothing wrong with her kidneys. That conclusion might have been different if she had done a SDMA a better indicator of kidney disease. Till today I still have her email to me telling me Scout was fine and that she could be drinking DOUBLE the amount of water I related to her and Scout would still be fine.

The Vet did diagnose Scout at that time with a possible underlying gastrointestinal disease, possibly contributing to her gradual weight loss. She put Scout on Hydrolyzed protein food, however I now believe Scout was gradually losing weight due to the onset of Chronic Kidney disease.

As the month of January wore on, I noticed a continued gradual increase in water drinking. On February 6, 2020 Scout had an appointment at the local Vet for a B12 shot. I mentioned the water drinking and he did a SDMA. The result showed a slight elevation indicating a kidney problem he determined was due to her age. He put her on a Renal Diet.

As with the Hydrolyzed Protein food, Scout was not too crazy about this Renal food either. I introduced a little at a time, at one point she was getting half and half or a little less of her regular food.

Scout's appetite had been decreasing daily. On February 26, 2020, that afternoon she was crying and appeared uncomfortable. I bypassed her regular local Vet as they would be closing soon and drove her to the closest Emergency Vet. After giving a history, they did blood work, an SDMA, and found it to be a bit more elevated than when it was done 20 days earlier at our local Vet. There they did nothing for her but give Scout a shot for pain and told me to feed her carbohydrates.

At home Scout did not eat and cried all night. February 27, 2020, I drove Scout 90 miles to the Animal Hospital Emergency Room. There she was admitted, dehydrated, elevated kidney levels, put on IV Fluids, and they did many tests. Scout was diagnosed with Chronic Kidney Disease. Days later she was discharged, sent home with an appetite stimulant and 3 medications for GI upset and a pain medication. The best part was the IV fluids returned her kidney values back to normal. "We were in a good place."

The Animal Hospital Vet ordered blood work done in two weeks. We were back home. On March 12, 2020 I took Scout to the local Vet for the blood work and another B12 shot. The results were to be forwarded to the ordering Vet at the Animal Hospital.

On March 22, 2020 I emailed the Animal Hospital Vet that Scout again was not eating nor feeling well. She emailed me back on March 23rd. March 24, 2020, I again drove 90 miles back to the Animal Hospital Emergency. When I had opened my email, I found an email dated March 18, 2020 from the Animal Hospital Vet telling me she received Scouts results from the local Vet, excerpts: "I received Scout's blood work results from your primary care veterinarian. Unsurprisingly, her kidney values are elevated being off IV fluids at discharge; however, they are much higher from her previous baseline. Her SDMA, a more sensitive marker of kidney disease, is progressively elevated." ..... "I am concerned about progressive kidney disease given her values since we ruled out most other causes of acute kidney injury (infections, obstructions, etc.)." .... So, the Vet was not surprised of Scout's elevation in Kidney values since being off of IV fluids. Indication the need to keep her hydrated.

Scout was again admitted to this hospital and put on IV fluids. Discharged a few days later. Again with appetite stimulant, a pain medication, and even more GI medications instructed to be given 5 doses a day. This time her kidney values had not returned to normal but were slightly elevated past normal.

Again, she ate well after being discharged, then the appetite declined each day. She slept a lot, drinking even less water. All those GI medications seemed to make her sleepy, keeping her away from the water bowl.
Six days after this 2nd discharge on April 3, 2020 I took Scout to a local Vet in that area. Vet did blood work, then told me Scout's kidney values were high. As this facility was not a 24-hour operation, she instructed me to take Scout back to the Animal Hospital, have them put her again on IV Fluids, then discharged on SubQ fluids. This was the first I had heard of the SubQ fluid issue.

In the aftermath I googled home therapy protocol for the treatment of Chronic Kidney Disease in dogs. What I found was information entitled for example "Fluids, Fluids, Fluids" for home therapy and that most Vets send pets home with a way to keep the pet hydrated. Unless there a medical condition that would contraindicate this. Scout had no issue to contraindicate her receiving SubQ fluids at home, and I have now found out, that was the best option for Scout at that time with her disease.

We left the local Vet and drove straight to the Animal Hospital Emergency, Scout again admitted, and put on IV Fluids. The next day April 4th, I get a call from the Vet that Scout's values are not coming down, and that I should consider putting her down.

I didn't want Scout to suffer. She had been doing intermittent crying at home like she was in pain. I went to the hospital on April 5th to do that. They wheeled Scout in on a table, I was shocked to see her so alert, she ate the treats I had brought for her, and she was very interested in what was going on at the curb outside the window.

I could not put her down. I asked them to keep her on the fluids a bit longer to see if the values would come down. They were not happy about my decision. They called in the social worker and had a contract drawn up. They would keep Scout on the Fluids, no intensive care for Scout if it were necessary, they made Scout a DNR, and I had 48 hours to either put her down or take her home.

During that period of time, I contacted another 24-hour Animal Hospital some miles away. I had the Animal Hospital send all Scout's current records to them. I then paid for a telephone consultation with the Kidney doctor. He said at this point the only option for Scout was dialysis or kidney transplant.

Dialysis entailed 5 hours a day 3 times a week for X number of weeks, then afterwards maybe it could drop to 2 times a week...What kind of life was that for Scout. Flying her to Texas for a kidney transplant was also out of the question.

This Vet having reviewed all the records said other than the above options the choices I had was home hospice or put her down. He mentioned at this point Scout's kidney values would not be coming down. He expressed how sorry he was about Scout's situation.

This was all going on during COVID-19, so I could not freely walk in to visit Scout. April 8th, I arrived at the Animal Hospital before the end of the contract deadline they drew up. I had decided I would take Scout home for Hospice. They brought Scout in the room; she was laying on her side in a huge pillow.

Her breathing was labored. I asked about that and was told she just started that this morning. Scout cried (it did sound like a cry of pain) & she was pawing at me. She ate treats I brought with me. They told me she had not been eating for them, and I do believe it because I was unable to get her to eat at home.

I told them I was considering taking her home, I was told "then you should have done that on Friday instead of bringing her back here". They said, they could have a Vet come to the house the next day to put her down. Led me to believe there definitely was no other option. The Vet told me that Scout was on the strongest pain medication possible. To make a long story short, they offered me nothing stronger for pain than what I had at home for her, offered nothing more than previous medications which did not work. It was then I questioned why she was never given SubQ fluids for home as the local Vet had recommended the Friday before I had brought her back here. The response was, "let's not deal with that now, let's deal with this". I am a disabled senior, I had been able to lift Scout into the car, but right then I could not lift her. She seemed like dead weight. I inquired about her lab results taken that morning. The kidney values only reduced a small fraction but were still above anywhere that Scout would feel well again. They offered me no therapeutic support for me taking her home, other than what they already tried which did not work.

Her kidneys were close to gone, I had to let her go. She left me that morning.

Afterwards, I sent an email to the Director of the hospital, and to the Head of the Department charged with Scout's care. Detailing four failures I felt occurred with Scout's care. The first email went unanswered. Four weeks later I sent it again, labeling Second Request.

This time my emails were re-directed to their Social Worker. She later replied with a detailed email full of BS. The inquiry of SubQ fluids was not addressed and ignored. I emailed her back telling her the reply was unacceptable and I would be in touch.

Then I found Joey's Legacy through the Regret-A-Vet Facebook site. Where I would boast about where I take my dog for specialties, and the wonderful care we always received. Words I would live to regret. I had used this facility for specialty care for 41 years, never was dissatisfied, never had a problem...until this time.

Upon investigating into this further, I was told by an independent Vet after reviewing the records, that Scout had been treated for Acute Kidney Crisis and not Chronic Kidney Disease. The Animal Hospital diagnosed her, why did they not provide the best treatment for her disease?

In the absence of SubQ fluids, which like I mentioned was protocol for treating her disease, as she was becoming dehydrated, her kidney values would rise, her appetite would decline. I was giving her GI upset medications as they instructed. If they had provided me with a way in keeping her hydrated, the kidney values may have remained low, she would have eaten, and GI upset medications would not have to be given on a daily basis as instructed. I believe my dog died from a Lack of Fluids.

They had the treatment backwards. This was my first experience with a dog with Kidney disease. Now I know when something is going wrong. I followed their instructions and my dog died prematurely. At her age, now with this disease, I did not expect many more years, however I did hope for a few more months to get her through the summer which she loved. I certainly did not expect only the 4 weeks that we got out of this.

An important point in this story is that prior to Scout's last admission when she left me, the local Vet did say " have her discharged on SubQ fluids". In the aftermath of all this, another Two Vets told me SubQ Fluids would have benefited Scout and should have been provided for her with the disease she was suffering from. She did suffer, she was not comfortable at all during the month of March 2020. I truly believe, this was pure neglect on the part of the Animal Hospital.

I took extraordinary care of Scout to provide her with longevity. If Scout spit up, I took her to the Vet. I always wanted to be on top of any issue going on with her. All that was destroyed in 4 weeks, in my opinion, due to the negligence of the Vets at this facility.

When you think of Scout, at her age of 16, please do not think of an old graying dog just shuffling along. Scout was not yet gray. While she did not take off at rapid speed as when she was young, she still ran around the yard, and in a different direction when I would try to herd her into the house. Her favorite spot was lying in a hole she had dug out years earlier, under a bush. That is where I would usually find Scout when looking for her in the yard.

When we were at the local Vet on March 12th, 2020, in assessing her over all condition, when I asked, the Vet responded that Scout was nowhere near the time to be put down. Three weeks later after the Animal Hospital, in my opinion, completely destroyed her remaining Kidney function, Scout was put down.

Thank you for reading our story......

Scout

CHAPTER THIRTY-NINE

KIKO ROMEO'S STORY
Linda Nischan

In February of 2014, we adopted a 7-month-old mixed-breed puppy named Keno from a kill shelter in North Carolina. He was delivered to us at 3:00 am on February 22.

Kiko was born on July 4, 2013. A new name was needed to commemorate his new life, and "Kiko" was chosen. Translated from Japanese, the meaning is "be glad rejoicing child." No other name could have been more appropriate.

Sometime after he came into our lives, I heard the story of A Wolf Called Romeo, a wolf that lived in Alaska that would come into town and play with other dogs at the park. He visited for about six years. He never threatened anyone and became somewhat of a local celebrity. One day a young man shot and killed Romeo for no reason. I gave Kiko the middle name of Romeo in honor of that beloved wolf, so his memory would live forever.

Kiko quickly adapted to his new forever home and life. He had plenty of tasty nutritional food, beds, toys, treats, and love. It was obvious that he knew it, too. I swear he went around with a smile on his face!
Kiko was the most patient dog I have ever seen. As shown in the attached photos, he would wear a hat or sunglasses, at least long enough to have his picture taken. He also doubled as a pillow. There was not another dog or person whom he did not befriend.

He was extremely intelligent and lived to please his Mommy and Daddy. He learned the basics of sit, stay, roll over, etc. within just a few days. He listened so well that within weeks he could walk off lead. He would stop chasing a squirrel or rabbit dead in his tracks on the "stop" command. Kiko would roll over on voice command, as well as a silent hand gesture, making a circular motion with your hand! He was simply amazing.

Kiko absolutely loved to go for walks with his Daddy. He would hear his leash being rattled and would come running with a smile on his face, because he knew it meant time with his Daddy and doggy friends.

Because he had a thick black fur coat, winter was his favorite season. He would run through the snow with his mouth open, scooping up as much as he could.

Kiko did not like hoses. If someone had a hose out washing a car or watering a lawn, he would get as far away from it as possible. We suspect that the shelter that held him would clean the cages with a hose, without taking the dogs out first.

As a result, he was not fond of water other than rain. It took us over a year to get him to get in the shower without offering a treat, but he never went in willingly. We live near the water and always walked him along the shore. When waves broke at his paws, he would jump back like he saw a snake. He eventually got over his aversion and would go into the water. He usually would not go in further than belly deep, though. The picture of him standing in the water at dusk with his reflection is one of our favorites.

He loved attention, but he was also aloof at times. Most nights after dinner, we would relax in front of the TV for a little while before bedtime, but Kiko would not stay in the living room with us. He would disappear into another room and lie down. Usually, he would go into a bedroom and lie on the floor with only his head under the bed. He looked like he had been guillotined.

Sadly, we only had the pleasure of sharing our lives with Kiko for about five years. He allegedly developed lymphoma, although the diagnosing DVM could not definitively say it was lymphoma, because she could never aspirate any tumor. Kiko had skin allergies and received Cytopoint injections periodically throughout his life to deal with his itching. We had no idea the damage it would do to his body. There is some dispute as to whether or not the cancer was caused by over-vaccinations but is beyond debate that a DVM gave him an unnecessary Leptospirosis/Lyme Disease combination vaccination when he was obviously not well. The effect of the vaccine exacerbated a bad situation. It caused a rapid deterioration in his health, and effectively pushed his condition past the point where he could have been successfully treated.

That is not to say we gave up. We took him to a local veterinary hospital that specializes in cancer treatment. He was placed in a hyperbaric chamber, which helped for short periods of time. We took him to a holistic vet who used Chinese herbs, ozone insufflation therapy, and acupuncture to treat him. It soon became painfully obvious that all we could do was keep him comfortable for the little time we had left.

We took him to the holistic vet for the last time on August 7, 2019. His lymph nodes were so inflamed they could be seen with the naked eye. On our way there, were said we were bringing him home that night, no matter what. However, the vet took one look and him and told us he was suffering, and nothing else could be done. The thought of him suffering any more was more than we could bear, so we made the heartbreaking decision at that time to have him put to rest. It was the hardest decision we ever had to make. I am crying again as I write this. We miss that little boy so much.

<u>Kiko Romeo</u>

CHAPTER FORTY

KOLBE'S STORY
Julie Anne Garlit

Kolbe was 10 years and 10 months old when he died unexpectedly on July 19, 2013. He was extremely healthy with a wellness checkup and bloodwork to prove it. He walked 4 miles a day, rain or shine. At his wellness exam in April of 2013, the vet told me that fleas and ticks were going to be exceptionally bad in our area that season and that there was a new drug on the market, Trifexis. I politely declined because it cost twice as much for half the amount of medicine. We had been going to the same vet for years and we trusted and liked him. He always seemed to have the best interest of our Goldens at heart. He was persistent so we compromised, and I agreed to try Trifexis during the summer months and Heartgard the rest of the year. I had two other Goldens, Cassie and Cole, to take for their wellness exams so I was going to start the medication at the same time for all three. I gave dose 1, a chewable, to all three in June. Kolbe spit it out twice and I tried to cleverly disguise it until it was finally ingested. There were no noticeable differences in any of the three dogs in month one. I gave dose 2 in July and the nightmare began. I will let the memorial I wrote for Kolbe tell the rest of his story.

In Memory of Kolbe

"Trifexis Kills" were the words that leapt out at me after searching the Internet about the cause for the recent death of our 10-year 10-month-old Golden Retriever, Kolbe. On Friday, we went to the vet with a slight cough. We were given an antibiotic and a cough expectorant, and the vet said he would be as good as new in 10 days. It was a respiratory infection that was confirmed by an x-ray. On the weekend he was lethargic and not his usual self but the cough seemed to subside. He did not want to go for his walk. We were allowing him to rest and giving the medicine some time to take effect. On Monday, the vet added Lasix to the prescribed medicine

because Kolbe seemed to have trouble breathing. By Monday night he could not lie down and was panting heavily. We rushed to the vet on Tuesday morning. It was now diagnosed as pneumonia and anemia. He was hospitalized and given IV medication. The vet was still hopeful he could be home by Friday. On Wednesday morning he bled out and passed away. The vet said it was not what he anticipated. After being given a clean bill of health in April with a wellness panel to prove it, we were devastated. For three weeks I googled everything I could possibly think of and that is when I came across story after story like mine about dogs who were perfectly healthy before starting on the heartworm prevention/flea protection medicine, Trifexis. I contacted the vet who had since pulled the medication from their shelves, the manufacturing company, Elanco, the FDA, and a consumer protection agency. There was no autopsy so the vet representing Elanco said Trifexis was not responsible for Kolbe's death. The FDA released the drug to the general population after a safety study that only involved 352 dogs that were given 3 doses and 1/2 of those dogs were the control group. There are hundreds of anecdotal stories like my own on the Internet. Please do your own research first and make an informed decision. I feel sad and guilty that I did not look on the Internet before giving my wonderful dog this drug. Kolbe was the one who made us laugh each and every day. He was a silly, kind, gentle soul that loved walking with me and his best canine friend, Murphy. He was the one that knew exactly how to behave around my fragile 87-year-old mom even though he could still do wild puppy like laps around the backyard when he pleased. He was the only Golden that we have ever had that took very good care of his toys. No squeakectomies for his stuffed toys. He had lived with other families for the first five years of his life and then he marched into our family and our hearts and stayed for 5 years and a few months. He was a great pet and we loved him dearly. He was an important part of our family. Are you going to risk your pet's health or life with this drug?

After Kolbe's death, it took me 2-3 weeks of internet searching using hemolytic anemia and pneumonia as keywords to find the Facebook page,

"Does Trifexis Kill Dogs?" and then I made the connection. Trifexis was the only new factor in our pets' lives.

Peach's story was our story. I printed everything I could find and went to the vet's office as soon as they opened on a Monday.

All of the advertisements on the wall and signs at the reception counter for Trifexis were gone. I was visibly shaken when I told them the medicine, they gave us killed my dog. They quickly escorted me out of the waiting area so as not to alarm the other clients. The office manager's dog had suffered a seizure after taking the Trifexis and they removed it from their shelves.

I asked if they were going to warn others and they said it involved hundreds of dogs and would be a substantial loss to the clinic not to mention time consuming. They would discuss the issue. After a couple of days, they informed me they were calling other clients to warn them of possible side effects and offering a refund for any unused Trifexis as a credit towards future services. The vet who prescribed the medication called to speak to me to offer his condolences. I was heartbroken but also very concerned about my other 2 Goldens. I had given Cassie and Cole dose 3 prior to making the connection.

Cassie had uncontrollable vomiting and diarrhea for three months after dose 3. She went to the vet numerous times. Her stool and bloodwork were sent to a lab in California because none of the routine medications were working. One night she was very weak because she was vomiting and having diarrhea at the same time. I called the office manager for the vet hospital only to be told the vet wanted me to go to an emergency clinic. I lost it. She called me back to say she and the vet would meet us at the clinic. She also warned me not to make eye contact with or speak to the vet's wife because she was very upset that he was going to the clinic at 10 pm at night. We happened to be one of the first clients for this vet when he began his practice, so he made a decision to meet us since he knew the history instead of repeating everything at the emergency vet at great expense.

I was informed that night that the credit from the unused Trifexis for 3 dogs was used up in that one visit. After Cassie was put on a probiotic to build up her immune system and an antibiotic recommended by the California clinic, she recovered in mid-September.

After Cassie's recovery, we got two puppies. I could not bring myself to return to my long-term vet. I actually interviewed vets before selecting a new clinic.

Cassie lived to be 13.

Cole dragged his rear left leg slightly on walks after the three doses of Trifexis. He passed away suddenly and unexpectedly at age 10 one year and 3 months after Kolbe. One morning he just refused to eat. His demeanor was good and he was urinating and defecating as usual so our vet appointment was for the next day at 11. He started breathing heavily and passed away in my arms that night before we could get him to an emergency vet.

I filed a report with the local FDA office, and they went to the vet's office to retrieve Kolbe's medical records. The office manager offered the FDA agent the records of over 100 other dogs who like Cassie had uncontrollable diarrhea.

Three dogs who were prescribed Trifexis died. Our Kolbe and two others. Since I was the only person to call the local FDA office to file a complaint, the agent refused the other records and only took Kolbe's documentation. The agent called to inform me that they had the health records and I never heard from them again with a follow-up.

I had three case numbers from Elanco for Kolbe, Cassie and Cole. Since there was no necropsy, the vet representing Elanco said it could not be the Trifexis that was the cause of Kolbe's death. They stated he must have had an unknown pre-existing condition and that he had lived beyond the life expectancy for a Golden Retriever.

After Kolbe's death and in the middle of Cassie's health issues, I told the Elanco vet that if another one of my dogs died from that poison, I would be suicidal for dispensing the poison to my canine family. They called to check on me once or twice and offered me a small amount of money towards Cassie's ongoing medical bills if I would sign a waiver agreeing not to discuss Kolbe's death. I refused. Cases closed.

I contacted attorney after attorney to see if there was a case against Elanco, the manufacturer of the drug. Elanco is the pet division of Eli Lilly and Company. Finally, an attorney named Barbara Quinn Smith, offered to help. She said she would need a representative from each state willing to make a deposition. I signed documents agreeing to do that and she said she would be in touch with a court date and I never heard from the attorney again.

I wrote to publishers from magazines that had Trifexis ads and they replied that the FDA had approved the drug.

I contacted the media. The Indy Star was the only newspaper that was interested and published an article titled, "Pets at Risk", in 2015. Kolbe is mentioned in that article.

I promised Kolbe that his death would not be in vain and that I would share his story until the day I die. I know for a fact that sharing Kolbe's story has saved lives and I have formed some wonderful long-distance friendships with people who have had similar experiences or who can offer natural means to offer protection to our pets.

I blindly trusted my vet believing he had the best interest of my pets at heart and that he was an educated professional in a field that I knew little about. I learned the hard way that this was not the case. I am quite sure I am my current vet's worst nightmare because I question everything and do not give medication until I have researched the side effects for myself.

The biggest lesson I have learned is that there is no healthy amount of poison. The life expectancies of our pets have decreased for a reason in spite of all of our medical advancements. Food, medications, vaccinations, environmental pesticides are all factors in the longevity of our pets. Our goal needs to be to get the word out through our stories and that is why this book is crucial.

Kolbe

CHAPTER FORTY-ONE

MOLLY'S STORY
Susan Malone

In late October of 2017, I saw flyers posted for a "Super Dog Adoption Day" nearby. I had moved alone to a new area in 2015, had not made friends, and was lonely. It is apparently difficult to make friends as an adult in your 30's. I grew up with dogs, loved them, and longed for the companionship of a dog. However, I have battled chronic suicidal thoughts and ideation since I was 12 years old. I knew in my heart that I would never leave a dog, as I knew how deep that love would be. Adopting a dog meant committing to life. I was pre-approved for the adoption day and decided I would go, while knowing I was not obligated to adopt at the event.

Over 350 dogs were spayed and neutered, received healthcare from shelters in the South, and were transported to Rhode Island to be adopted. The event was held at a local farm. Then there was Molly, or "Maude" as she was referred to by the rescue at the time. She came from Athens, Tennessee. Molly was sweet, shy, and so tired. She was 1.5 years-old, had just had a litter, was malnourished, sick, and terrified of everything. I walked around the space for a while, knowing Molly was for me, but I was nervous to commit. I decided to go for it. I had no idea you took the dog home the same day! I was completely unprepared in terms of supplies, but I very well knew how to take care of a dog. A kind volunteer helped Molly and I to my car. I cleared out the back seat, as I did not know I would be taking her home with me. The volunteer left. I got into the driver's seat, and Molly immediately climbed over the console and curled up right next to me. From that moment on, Molly and I were inseparable. The date was November 4th, 2017.

I was raised in a family that did not understand mental illness. At the time, over twenty years ago, it was not well understood by society either. In addition to the suicidal thoughts, I developed anorexia at the age of 12. At my annual physical, the pediatrician noted that I was far below the normal

BMI range for my size. No one spoke to me about anorexia or asked about my mental health. The pediatrician instructed me to increase my daily caloric intake, and to come to their offie for weekly weigh-ins. My mother responded by consistently filling the freezer with ice cream, as she knew I would assuredly eat that and gain weight. I ate ice cream, was weighed weekly at the pediatrician's office, and eventually my BMI was in the normal range. No more weekly weigh-ins. I did not receive the treatment I needed.

I do not blame my mom or anyone in my family for this. I have an amazing mom and family that I love very much. I believe we all do the best we can for our loved ones with the information we have. At the age of 18 I developed bulimia and had severe symptoms through the age of 26. In my early twenties I usually worked 10-12 hours, six days per week. On my day off, I would spend the entire day eating and vomiting. Bulimia is a vicious cycle. I ran 5-15 miles every day. I fainted at work one day while speaking to the CEO. In my late twenties, I educated myself and committed to treatment while in graduate school. For those who are not familiar with eating disorders, there are similarities to addiction. It is an addictive behavior that becomes a very harmful and negative coping mechanism. Similar to addiction, individuals with eating disorders may relapse. Life hands us challenges, and we resort to maladaptive, habitual behaviors, as that is what our brain knows at that time. Having experienced all types of eating disorders, I personally feel bulimia is by far the worst. A relapse requires an immediate stop, otherwise the behaviors will cycle.

I was mostly stable in my late twenties to early thirties, with a few relapses; one shortly before adopting Molly. After adopting Molly, I vividly remember going to the bathroom and making myself vomit into the toilet. While doing so, I heard the pitter patter of Molly's feet coming towards the bathroom. The door was open. She looked at me with her ears perked up and her head tilted; an expression that communicated concern. The first time this happened, I immediately stopped and fell on the floor crying with her by my side. It happened two more times. I heard the pitter patter of her little feet, and she showed up each time. Molly always showed up. Molly did not want me to make myself sick or to hurt myself. Molly loved me, and I loved her. I needed her, and she needed me.

I have not experienced any symptoms of bulimia since that time. Molly was a significant part of my healing. I am of course extremely grateful for everything she brought into my life. At the same time, with this realization, the emptiness and heaviness in my heart somehow feels even greater. This exemplifies the intrinsic value of companion animals.

When I adopted Molly, she was traumatized. Molly developed severe separation anxiety. I asked her veterinarian at the time- not the one who took responsibility for her death- for guidance. The practice recommended natural supplements. I tried everything I could find, to no avail. Molly broke out of metal crates when I left for work. Every morning I cleared everything out of her reach, and restricted her to one area before leaving for work. One morning in late January of 2018, I made a terrible mistake. I left ibuprofen on the counter before leaving for work. I took Molly to the 24/7 animal hospital by myself on a Friday night, hysterically crying. Molly was hospitalized and treated for an acute kidney injury. I was told she likely would not make it, and to take her to Tuft's Medical in Boston where they could put her on dialysis. I could not afford it. I had already opened a new credit card to pay for the hospitalization. To everyone's surprise, Molly somehow pulled through. She was discharged after three days in the hospital. As directed, I administered subcutaneous fluids to Molly twice daily in my apartment, by myself. I tied her leash tightly to the door, hung the bags of fluid from the hinge, and desperately tried to hold the needle in her. I took her to her former veterinarian to have her kidney levels checked very frequently for a few months. I changed her diet as recommended, and after a few months of healthy levels, her former veterinarian decreased the appointments with the commitment to monitor her levels regularly, and for me to bring Molly in immediately if I noticed any symptoms of kidney disease. It was hell, but I would have done it all over again in a heartbeat.

With a lot of love, care, and time, Molly's beautiful soul that was always on the inside, shined so brightly on the outside. Molly finally learned to trust. She learned to accept and give love, and she eventually experienced true happiness and joy. Molly was the sweetest, kindest, most intuitive soul I have ever met. She went everywhere with me, and we did everything together. Molly was one of a kind. Molly was pure love.

In 2019 I moved in with my partner and his two dogs. Molly and his younger dog quickly became the best of friends. In November of 2019, I decided to switch Molly to the same veterinary clinic my partner brought his dogs to. The clinic was closer, recommended, and they were able to run all blood work in- house (this was very appealing as I could get her kidney value results immediately). The clinic is owned by one veterinarian, the one who took responsibility for Molly's death, with several veterinarians working for her at the clinic. I scheduled an appointment on November 13th, 2019 to establish a relationship with the practice, to discuss Molly's health history, and to have her kidney function and bloodwork checked. Molly was seen on November 13th, 2019 by a new, young veterinarian at the clinic. Molly's records were faxed to their office prior to the appointment. After taking Molly's blood, the veterinarian said we could wait in the office area for the results. I of course chose to do so, as I was hyper-vigilant (or so I thought). Shortly thereafter, the young veterinarian came out and reported that Molly's bloodwork was completely normal. She said Molly's kidney values were normal, and there were no concerns. She said that Molly's liver enzyme values were slightly elevated, but that their testing machine had been frequently making this mistake, and that it was not a cause for concern. Molly's lab reports were not shared with me. I trusted the young veterinarian's words. Molly and I went home.

On May 26th, 2020, I called the clinic because Molly had been eating less and was lethargic for a few days. This was unusual, as Molly loved to run, was always very playful, and loved to eat. The soonest appointment offered was May 28th at 10:15AM. I of course took the appointment time, and immediately informed my supervisor and co-workers that I would be taking PTO in order to bring Molly to the appointment.

The veterinarian and owner of the practice saw Molly on the morning of May 28th, 2020. I explained Molly's symptoms, expressed concern for unusual, white thick discharge from Molly's eyes and nose, and of course brought up Molly's history and past acute kidney injury. I did not assume that the veterinarian read Molly's records prior to seeing her. The veterinarian asked if I knew Molly's age. I said yes, as her adoption paperwork came with a DOB of 5/6/2016. Molly had just turned four. The veterinarian did not respond to my answer, nor acknowledge Molly's health history and past injury. She looked at Molly and said: "Are you just much older than we think you are", in a child-like tone of voice. The veterinarian physically examined Molly. She then started giving Molly an injection. She did not tell me what it was, or why she was giving it to Molly. I asked what it was while she was administering the injection. The veterinarian said: "Good ole penicillin. In case there are any infections". She took blood and urine samples for laboratory testing.The veterinarian did not make eye contact with me at any time during the appointment. She instructed me to feed Molly chicken and sweet potatoes, and told me she would call me when she had the test results.

The veterinarian/clinic owner called me the following morning, Friday May 29th, 2020 at 10:15AM. She diagnosed Molly with Addison's Disease. She said: "Side note, President Kennedy had this disease", undermining the severity of the disease. She did not share the lab reports with me. She did not inform me about how quickly a dog with Addison's Disease can decline and die. She did not seem concerned at all. She asked for my permission to run (and pay for) an additional cortisol test, which I of course agreed to. The veterinarian said she would call me immediately when she had the results of the additional test. She prescribed Molly 5mg of prednisone 2x daily. I immediately filled the prescription and administered it to Molly as prescribed. I continued to feed Molly chicken and sweet potatoes, as directed.

On Sunday May 31st, the day before Molly died, I held her sweet face looking at the discharge from her nose and eyes. I was so worried and upset, but reminded myself that the veterinarian was not concerned and would be calling very soon. I will never forget holding her face that day, the experience of our eye contact, and how sick she looked.

The veterinarian/clinic owner did not call me back on Friday May 29th, and she did not call me over the weekend. She did not call me back on Monday, June 1st, 2020, although she was at the clinic working that day. I called the clinic and asked to speak to her at 3:50PM on Monday, June 1st. The staff member I spoke to confirmed that they had the additional cortisol test result. The staff member told me that the veterinarian/clinic owner was with a client when I called. The staff member told me the veterinarian/clinic owner was working until 6:00PM, and that she would return my call before leaving work. The staff member assured me that if the veterinarian/clinic owner did not call me back before 6:00PM, she would definitely call me during her commute home. She never called. Four hours after I called the clinic that afternoon, Molly died very suddenly at home.

At 7:30PM on June 1st, 2020, Molly went outside. She walked down the deck stairs on her own, urinated, and slowly came back up the stairs. Molly hesitated to take the step up into the house. I gently guided her inside and she immediately laid down. Molly was not herself. I asked my partner to carry her to her dog bed that she loved. About one minute after he placed her in the bed, I noticed she had not moved, and walked over to check on her. Molly was dead. Her tongue was purple and hanging out. I could not wake her. I could not feel a heartbeat. I was in shock. My partner immediately called the 24/7 animal hospital. We rushed her there. I held Molly in the back seat of the car in her dog bed, while my partner drove. I started googling how to tell if a dog is dead. I read something about pulling a dog's eyelids to see if their eyes move. Molly's eyes did not move when I pulled gently on her eyelids. Molly's eyes were black, glassy, and open.

When we arrived at the hospital, a staff member came out to the car immediately upon arrival, and carried Molly in right away. CPR was initiated and maintained and several rounds of epinephrine, atropine and dextrose were given in an attempt to resuscitate Molly. It was too late. Less than 30 minutes later, my partner and I were told to enter a small room to say goodbye. Molly's 48lb body was rolled in on a small gurney. Her neck and legs were shaven and bloody from the injections. Her tongue was still purple and still hanging out. Molly had two carnations under her shoulder, and a blanket covered the rest of her body. I fell on the floor of the hospital. I screamed, I hyperventilated, and I sobbed.

The doctor who saw Molly at the hospital and wrote her report, stated: "The Na:K ratio was 15.3 The hyperkalemia was suspected to be the cause of her cardiac arrest at home". Molly ate dinner and treats two hours prior to her death. I had no idea she was in crisis, nor how suddenly fatal Addison's Disease could be. However, the veterinarian/clinic owner that saw Molly four and a half days prior to her death, had the test results and had this knowledge. She knew that dogs with Addison's disease can decline rapidly and die. She knew that the disease requires immediate attention. She admitted this to me when she finally called me two days after Molly died. She told me that she should have sent Molly to the hospital when she saw her lab reports, and that if she had done so, Molly would still be alive.

I emailed the veterinarian from the hospital after seeing Molly's dead body, and informed her that Molly died. I did not receive a response. On the following day, June 2nd, I called the clinic and requested copies of all lab reports and records. I asked to speak to the veterinarian/clinic owner. The staff member I spoke to immediately sent the records to me via email and assured me that the veterinarian/clinic owner would call me back that same day. She did not call me back on June 2nd.

When I received the records, I saw that there were abnormalities in Molly's test results from November 13th, 2019 that indicated kidney disease. The young veterinarian who saw Molly on November 13th even wrote a note for the visit that says: "kidney profile?" and the lab report itself says: "Evaluate a complete urinalysis and confirm there is no other evidence of kidney disease". This was never communicated to me. The lab reports were not shared with me. Instead, I was told that Molly was healthy, and there were no concerns.

Molly's lab reports from May 28th, 2020 contain many values extremely out of the reference ranges, indicating kidney disease, Addison's disease, and electrolyte imbalances. On Wednesday morning, June 3rd, two days after Molly died, the veterinarian/clinic owner finally called me. She said: "I did not call you yesterday because I was crying and did not know what to say to you". I asked about the significantly out of range values on the lab reports. She said: "I know. It is inexcusable. I hope one day you will be able to forgive me". She told me that she should have immediately sent Molly to the hospital after seeing the lab results. She told me that Molly's death was completely preventable.

The clinic's practice manager contacted me by email and informed me that the veterinarian/clinic owner was going to send a reimbursement check to me. The veterinarian/clinic owner reimbursed me for both of Molly's appointments at her clinic, including the costs of all laboratory tests. In addition, she reimbursed me for the resuscitative efforts at the hospital on 6/1/20 and for Molly's cremation. The practice manager told me the veterinarian/clinic owner agreed to this "in honor of Molly's death". This amount totaled $1,007. 67. The reimbursement means nothing to me. It is however, a clear admission of guilt.

A symptom of Addison's Disease is a change in a dog's coat. Molly's coat completely changed in early 2020. She shed all of her coarse wiry hair, mostly black and a patch of white hair on her chest. Her new coat was soft, thin, and fluffy. I assumed this was due to moving and living in a new environment. The veterinarian/clinic owner did not ask if Molly's coat had changed. I have only vacuumed part of the house once since Molly died, and have not vacuumed the bedroom a single time. I spend hours picking up beautiful pieces of her hair one at a time, treasuring each one, and store them in glass containers. I am desperately trying to hold onto any piece of her that I can, while knowing that more and more of her slips away each day. Molly is no longer a part of my life and is now becoming a memory. It hurts so much to write that.

On June 3rd I filed a complaint with the state licensing board. I have not heard anything back from them. It has been over six months since Molly died. I called the state bar association on June 10th, and spoke to an attorney for legal advice. The attorney told me: "Although I do not agree with this, I am sorry to say that legally dogs are considered pieces of property. Molly was a piece of property valued at $0". I was advised not to proceed, as I was told the outcome would not be helpful and the legal fees would be costly. A piece of property valued at $0. This disgusts me. The public should be aware of this law and the lack of legal protections for companion animals, as this law stands in the vast majority of states in this country.

I loved Molly more than anything or anyone in the world. I told my partner every day how much I loved her. I told him a few times that the day she dies, I would be destroyed. He always assured me that she would live at least another ten years as she was so young, and so we thought, healthy. I was so afraid to lose her. At times I even said that I wished I never adopted her, as I knew losing her would be too painful. The loss of Molly was far worse than I ever could have imagined.

On August 14th of 2020, I was diagnosed with PTSD. I continue to struggle with flashbacks, disturbing images, insomnia, and emotional outbursts when I experience triggers. I am being treated for clinical depression specific to Molly's death. Every day is a struggle. I was right when I said the day Molly died I would be destroyed. I however, had no idea that it would be at this level, due to the circumstances of her death. It has impacted my my ability to function, my mental health, my physical health, my relationships, and my career.

I would have done anything in the world to save Molly. I was not given that opportunity. Molly deserved so many more happy days, so many more happy years. I am aware that I am grieving far more than the loss of a dog, and far more than the loss of a piece of property valued at $0. I am grieving the loss of my best friend, the loss of my soulmate, and the loss of Molly's daily unconditional love and affection.

Thank you for taking the time to read Molly's story. I will forever be broken. The only thing I can do is to have her story heard, in an effort to make much needed change. Please immediately ask for copies of your loved one's lab reports at every visit. If I had seen those numbers, I would have taken Molly to the hospital immediately.

Molly

CHAPTER FORTY-TWO

SILVER PUFF'S STORY
Nikki Wharton-Eby

Writing my sorrowful story meant revisiting the harrowing nightmare that took the precious life of my healthy 14-year-old cat companion, also my emotional support --- especially after my beloved husband, Carl, was unexpectedly diagnosed with stage 4 lung cancer less than two weeks after our 25th wedding anniversary. My sweetheart passed away only four months later, October 18, 2012. Carl was a health enthusiast, hard worker and in great physical condition. My heart was broken, my world shattered, and my mind wanted to escape the profound grief, but my hurting heart kept reminding me of it. My cats were very special to me --- not pets, but loving family members. Our Persian, Nosa, was fifteen years old when "Dad" passed away...and Siberian, Nikarl Silver Puff, was seven years old.

Weeks and months passed, turning into years...and, with my mind turned off to the world around me, I suffered the shocking betrayal of a trusted family member who cheated me out of a tremendous amount of money. My heart was further shattered. I spent my days reaching for a light on the other side of the darkness, pursuing my goal of returning to my art (painting and drawing portraits of people and animals). My cats were always by my side, comforting me. During a couple of visits to my home early in 2018, my daughter, Ronda, told me that Nosa was weak and dying...that I should think about making an appointment with her veterinarian to help her journey to the other side of this life. Ronda was right. On June 4, 2018, I took my precious Nosa to her veterinarian, Dr Tom Mowery, and a neighbor friend, Marta, drove us. My grief was extraordinary! Nosa had been with me for 21 years!

When Ronda came to visit me a few days later, she saw my sadness and brought Silver Puff over to me. It was then I knew I had Silver Puff to comfort me and be with me for a long time. My heart felt the pain of grief with Nosa's death, but she had lived a long life and I was with her at the end of her journey.

Silver Puff was always deeply special to my heart --- another emotional support family member. When her mother, a purebred Siberian I had adopted from a breeder in Russia, was in labor to deliver her first litter, I was by her side, encouraging her to stay in the cozy birthing bed I created for her in my guest bathroom. Keeping a pregnant cat ready to give birth in an isolated area of the home creates a more relaxing environment for her...and eliminates opportunities for Mama Cat to choose an unsafe place to deliver her kittens.

It was 2005, August. Mama Cat delivered her first baby, a female, at around two o'clock in the morning. She refused to nurture the infant kitten after cleaning her, and she wouldn't let her nurse. When I tried to encourage Mama to nurse her baby, she made it clear she wanted nothing to do with the newborn. After the mother cat bit the baby kitten, I took the tiny one away to take care of her. She was my baby now. I cleaned her more and gave her nutrition. Then, I made a warm cozy nesting place for her in a small cat bed and settled her in my office. I placed a Ty stuffed kitty toy with her as a surrogate litter mate. I waited a while longer to see if Mama Cat was going to deliver any more babies. A couple of hours later I went to bed. When I awoke later in the morning, I immediately checked on Mama Cat --- and discovered she had given birth to another baby. The newborn kitten was in the birthing box alone, still damp and very cold! I scooped her up in my hands and rubbed her tiny body, warming her. I cleaned her and wrapped her in a little baby blanket.

I gave her fluids and food prior to placing her with her sister. This second kitten was Silver Puff. My husband and I cared for them throughout the days and weeks ahead, even sometimes taking them with us when we visited family. One evening, while relaxing together on the couch in our living room, Carl suggested we name the babies "Hi-Yo Silver" and "Tonto." Since I had nicknamed the second kitten born, who was the fluffiest, "Puff," she became "Silver Puff." "Tonto" remained Tonto until a family adopted her.

The months turned to years. Silver Puff became a Mama Cat to 3 kittens but had lost 3 as a result of a difficult delivery. She had been pregnant with six male babies. I decided to have her spayed. Silver Puff was a caring mother to her kittens...and became "Aunt Puff" to the other kittens born to another Siberian. Everyone loved Puff! She was loving, playful and fun! I took her to a couple of cat shows to show her in the Premier Division...and my Champion Nikarl Silver Puff was a Regional Winner for Second Best Siberian Alter!

Silver Puff enjoyed being the Queen of our home, especially after Nosa had completed her journey here. Puff was now the only Queen. When I rescued a male kitten in 2014 and two females later on from my back yard, Silver Puff was cordial to them, but she let them all know she was boss! I loved coming home and being welcomed by her. She usually followed me around and enjoyed cuddling while I read or watched television. I loved snuggling with her for cat naps... and at night for bedtime. She was warm and cuddly, either sleeping on top of me or next to me, sometimes holding my hand with her paw...or laying her head on my arm. Her vibrant purr lulled me to sleep.

In December of 2019 I experienced a horrific loss of my beloved Silver Puff. The details of Puff's horrific experience are devastating... and veterinarians from two clinics are at fault. I am still so immersed in shock, sorrow and despair!

I took Silver Puff to my veterinarian for a general check-up. The vet recommended a dental and assured me it would be safe. I was not sure I wanted to subject her to this, especially just before the Christmas holiday. On December 17, I took Silver Puff early in the morning to the veterinary hospital for her dental. When I picked her up later, the doctor told me in a hushed voice that he was looking forward to travel with his wife and would not be in the office until the next April. (Was he telling me he was not planning to be available for my cat's after care if I had questions?)

The next day Puff was playing and acting normal, except she wasn't eating much. I understood that as normal, since the veterinarian had pulled a couple of her teeth. The following day I noticed she was making raspy sounds in her throat and I worried that something was wrong. Perhaps her larynx was injured during the dental, or she had an infection. On Friday I took her to see another veterinarian at the hospital. He had no answers to my questions. He recommended Science Diet ad canned food to entice her to eat more. I took Puff home, but still had unanswered questions. Later that day, I called the veterinary hospital and spoke with a veterinary tech about my concerns. She made an appointment for me to come in the following morning. (It was Saturday, so they were open only until noon.)

When I arrived at the veterinary hospital, I was ushered into an exam room with Silver Puff. No veterinarian came in to examine her. No one took her temperature. I trusted the veterinary technician when she came in and gave Silver Puff an injection of an antibiotic. I did wonder why, since I was not told she was diagnosed with an infection. I regret not asking more questions!

I took my sweet cat home and fed her some soft food. She was eating better now…but she still made the deep raspy sound in her throat, which I still had no answers for. Silver Puff was a little active before snuggling down for a nap in my bedroom. Later that night I heard her yowling and I ran to see what was wrong! My sweet precious kitty was running crazily around the house, totally flipping out! I was in agony needing desperately to help her! I called the Emergency Clinic, about 20 minutes' drive from my house. Then I called my neighbor and friend, Marta Pionke, who came and picked us up. I had Puff wrapped in a small blanket, but she could not be still! She kept throwing her head back, trying to breathe!

When Marta and I arrived at the clinic with Silver Puff, we rang the bell outside. It was nearly midnight. Before the veterinarian would look at my gasping kitty, I had to give them my credit card so they could charge me

$500. (The final charge was over $1000.) We were then led into a room and the vet tech took Puff to the back, something that has always bothered me. In a little while the veterinarian came into the exam room to tell me that my cat is feeling better, that she was given sedation and is resting. I was also informed that she had bitten the tech when she stuck her finger down her throat! The tech was sent to the ER. The veterinarian said she wanted to keep Silver Puff on oxygen for the night. I wanted to see my darling kitty before leaving for home with my friend. Puff seemed to be resting but was obviously sedated. Marta was upset at how I was treated. I was so afraid!

Early in the morning on Sunday I was given a grim update on Silver Puff's condition. I was told other tests were being done. Later in the morning I received another call from the veterinarian, this time throwing me into shock by telling me that Silver Puff was not going to make it, that she had fluid on her lungs...and that, since she needed oxygen constantly, she would not survive if I picked her up to bring her home (or take her to my own veterinarian). I could not imagine that my Silver Puff would die --- days after having a dental! Nothing made any sense! Later in the day I received a phone call from a different veterinarian at the clinic, who spoke in a softer tone and appeared more empathetic. She manipulated me to believe my cherished Silver Puff could die without me and that it would be best for her if I came in and permitted them to euthanize her. Oh, my God, what have these veterinarians and techs done in destroying my beloved Silver Puff's life --- and making me a part of it!?!

Early Monday morning I picked up my precious cat's body and took her to another veterinarian who I had known for many years, especially during my cat rescue, rehabilitation and rehome years. Dr. Bob Esplin would do Puff's necropsy. To add to my horrific nightmare and trauma, I was told by Dr. Bob that he was required to send her head away to determine if she had rabies! I was torn into shreds inside! Silver Puff was current on her rabies vaccine --- and never went outside! I was told it was the law because she had bitten the vet technician at the emergency clinic. If that is the law, why are we required to keep our furry family members vaccinated?

Dr. Bob assured me he would have her all together and wrapped up when I picked up her body for burial. I was like a zombie moving through the days and weeks, my sorrowful soul seeking answers in a maze of malevolent arrows aimed at my battered broken heart! When I had spoken to Dr. Tom who had recommended the dental, I asked him," If I had not brought Puff in for the dental, would she be alive today?" He replied, "Yes."

After placing a Memorial to Silver Puff on one of my Facebook sites, an insightful, caring woman named Carol Morris contacted me. She asked me if the injection administered to Silver Puff by the veterinary technician was Convenia. After checking, I told her that it was and asked her why she asked. She referred me to a site with detailed information on Convenia, including the horrid possible side effects. I thank Carol for contacting me… and for the touching poem she composed for Silver Puff and me.

Carol also referred me to Joey's Legacy and Scott Fine, the wonderful, empathetic man who created it in honor and memory of Joey, a precious dachshund he and his wife sadly lost to egregious veterinary malpractice. With all my heart, I thank Scott for his help, his empathy and compassion for my sweet cat's heartbreaking experience that cost her and me her life. Every day I pray for everyone who is heartbroken from injury, even death of a beloved animal family member as a shocking result of maltreatment or neglect by veterinarians or anyone in the animal care industry. With all the tremendous love in my heart for Silver Puff and with all the profound pain surrounding me from witnessing her horrific nightmare and death, I pray for the day when everyone in animal care will understand the significance of "pets" to pet parents and families…that they are family! I pray for more diligence, more genuine love and dedication when caring for a client's cherished family member…and more respect, honesty and compassion for the families.

I also pray for Convenia to be banned from use; or, at the very least, to have a law that clients be informed of all the possible side effects, including anaphylaxis, and that a signature be required before it can be administered. It should only be given by a licensed veterinarian, and never to older patients.

Scott referred me to a grief counselor, Sarah Byrd, who was personable and compassionate. We talked a while and she showed empathy, bringing me some comfort. Sarah suggested an activity that can be healing for me…painting Silver Puff's portrait that displays her essence, expressing her dignity and sweetness. I also plan to paint Joey's portrait and will do that before Puff's. I planned to get busy at my art after shoulder replacement for bone-on-bone arthritis in my left shoulder…however, our world became paralyzed by a coronavirus pandemic.

I see my beloved cherished Silver Puff in my thoughts, my prayers, in the depth of my soul…and I see her images as I shall paint her in my mind and engraved on the walls of my heart. Silver Puff, it was not time for you to go, but I know someday we will be together again to enjoy the warm resplendent rays of the sun. Until then, run and play with Nosa and the other angels.

Silver Puff

CHAPTER FORTY-THREE

OTIS' STORY
Kristie Lynn Sharon
Otis "Oatmeal"
He existed- He has a soul- He is loved- He is our family.
1/24/10- 2/1/2020

Otis was a once in a lifetime dog. He was not just any ordinary pug, he was a super pug! Otis was so in love with life, he was the best little man ever. He loved his mommy, daddy, two younger brothers –Rajer and Max- his nana and her dog, Sabrina. But at the end of the day he was a mommy's boy, we were two peas in a pod. We did everything together. I brought him to work with me. He went on all vacations with us. Otis was the best man at our wedding! He took his role very seriously! Otis traveled to more places than many people have! He was our "king of the castle" and he had just the right amount of mischievousness in him that was absolutely loveable and gave him quite the personality. You could never be mad at him! He was like a little old man! Otis brought smiles to everyone he encountered. We used to take him to Pug parties in Chicago, and let's just say, Otis was the one who got the party started! He was so full of life and made everything better. He loved his long walks, loved to cool down in the lake or river. He loved adventures, loved to smell, and smell some more. We would walk and always have to back track 10 feet so he could sniff a particular tree and mark it. I remember one-time Otis and I went for a long walk in a large forest preserve. We got completely lost and water was in short supply. I looked at Otis and said "find the way out" and he would sniff at cross points and give me the look of "follow me" and sure enough he got us out! At bedtime he always was under the covers snuggled into me and I would fall asleep to his extremely loud and passionate snoring. I am so lucky to be his mommy. He is the best thing that ever happened to me. He is the love of our lives.

For Otis, more than one vet failed him, so I refer to it as the "system" failed him. In February 2019, I brought Otis to our 'former' primary vet of 4 years, (IPAH), for an ear infection. During the exam we decided Otis needed to have his teeth cleaned. Since he was 9 he had to have routine blood work. I got a call from IPAH vet, Dr. C, stating that Otis's liver enzymes were elevated. Something told me to have an ultrasound performed. After the ultrasound we got a call from Dr. C stating that Otis had a form of cancer called Hemangiosarcoma and expressed his condolences. He made that diagnosis based on the ultrasound results. He stated Otis had a mass on his spleen and nodules on his liver. The next day we brought Otis in for a chest x-ray to see if the cancer had spread to his heart and lungs. It did not. Dr. C did not offer us any options, such as going to a specialist. He authoritatively stated that Otis needed his spleen removed, and that it was the clear course of action. That Monday Otis went in for an emergency splenectomy. A biopsy was taken of the mass and the nodules on his liver and after what felt like a year, we finally got the call from Dr. C. Everything came back benign! My husband and I cried tears of joy. I believe, Dr. C, however, failed to find out what caused the mass on his spleen and nodules on his liver. Dr. C also did not discuss with us any potential/future consequences, etc. No follow up or guidance post-operative. Sadly, we blindly trusted him to act in Otis's best interest.

In September 2019, Otis was diagnosed with anemia and diabetes after I brought him in to IPAH for bloodwork. The night prior he strangely collapsed and had a hard time for a few minutes gaining his composure. We saw a Dr. B at IPAH (our first time with this vet as Dr. C was off that day), and he put Otis on 20 mg dosage of Prednisone and Vetsulin. Otis did not do well on the Prednisone. Almost immediately we were alarmed by Otis's behavior and voiced our concerns about prednisone. I called several times to Dr. B and Dr. C regarding our observations, but I was dismissed. I was met with no collaboration or any other options. A few weeks after receiving his first dose of prednisone, I rushed Otis back noticing pale gums. Dr. B said we needed to immediately take him down to U of I Champaign. My husband and I raced down there where Otis spent a week undergoing tests and essentially was a guinea pig. U of I came back with an intestinal bleed. Once he was discharged, I made a follow up appointment at IPAH, as U of I instructed us the next step was to have blood work tests in 4 -6 days. Apparently, word got back to IPAH that I told U of I that I was very unhappy with how the Prednisone was being handled. Our follow up appointment in mid-October was with Dr. C. He did not even look at Otis when he entered the exam room. He told me we didn't see "eye to eye" over this medication and that meant "I did not trust him." I asked him if he was terminating us and he said yes, then got up and said, "No further communication" and walked out of the room. I proceeded to have a full-blown panic attack and became hysterical. Dr. C was our vet for 4 years! I could not believe what he had done! I have filed a complaint against IPAH for violation of oaths & principles they swore upon to become veterinarians. Had Otis not been terminated in this regard, we most likely never would have gone to BGVSC. After IPAH did the unthinkable, we had to find Otis a new primary vet quickly as the blood test was needed. IPAH did not give us any referrals and refused to treat Otis until we were set with a new veterinarian. We hustled to find another primary vet by the beginning of the following week. Our new veterinarian initiated testing and monitoring his blood CBC every few days and after that first week, the vet personally contacted me urgently to inform us that "we needed to rush Otis to [BGVSC] for an emergency blood transfusion." I was later told had Otis not been taken, he would have collapsed and died. This ties into how I believe IPHA violated ethics/oaths/principles. You CANNOT terminate a very ill dog. Furthermore, IPAH did not give a referral, nor did they treat him until we could get him into a new vet. The new vets were outraged that IPAH removed Otis's spleen. They told me IPAH should have first done a fine needle aspiration for biopsy. This is how [BGVSC] came into the picture.

FIRST VISIT at BGVSC:

Otis was hospitalized at BGVSC (Northwest suburbs of Chicago) for a blood transfusion on October 22nd, 2019. What caught us completely off guard was a doctor came in for barely 5 minutes to give a clinical impression. Immediately after hearing our boy was going to be hospitalized and the doctor left, two women walked in. The one woman was evaluating our finance plan for the day, ushering us to apply for financial assistance via Care Credit. I was strongly encouraged to "request the highest amount, you never know." The other person was present to give us a written estimate. I realized that they expected us right at that moment to have $2,865.00 for the deposit. We were told if we could not pay, they would bring Otis back out to us (to leave and die). My husband and I knew we were being told we would have to drive an hour home to get our checkbook. They would not even begin treatment until confirmation of payment was received. We frantically drove an hour back home to get finances in order and then called in payment so Otis could begin his blood transfusion. This is One of TEN blood transfusions throughout the experience with BGVSC.

We raised our concern with BGVSC that Otis' prior Splenectomy may have contributed to his current anemia. This became an ongoing curiosity and we questioned repeatedly about this. Was the removal of his spleen the eventual cause of his anemia? Red blood cells are stored by spleen. Internal medicine refused to answer these questions and disregarded it. This was the first question of many that went dismissed and unanswered by BGVSC. My point is we came to BGVSC to get answers since they are a specialty hospital. I do not see why they never questioned or mentioned the splenectomy ONCE. Perhaps if they did further investigation, I may have had some sort of answer. But, in my opinion. BGVSC does not provide answers nor collaborate with patient families. This was our first taste of being left in the dark.

We were referred by our former primary vet because Otis's RBC blood count dropped dangerously low. We were sent to BGVSC for a blood transfusion. We were sent there because they were close in proximity and were known as "the best" and a "level 1 trauma facility". Otis had 10 "partial" blood transfusions at BGVSC during his time with them. We were greeted by Dr. R (internal medicine) during our first or second visit. He informed my husband and I that if Otis needed more than a couple blood transfusions than he would need a FULL blood transfusion (a very risky procedure essentially draining ALL blood out and putting in completely new blood) which is a $12k procedure. We only heard about that ONE time. So why did he have to have TEN "partial" blood transfusions? We never got an answer.

Otis tested positive for the Coombs Test down at U of I Champaign Vet Hospital in early October. His symptoms resembled an auto-immune disorder. Once Dr. R took Otis off his medications for said disorder, Otis's RBC kept dropping at a faster rate. I brought this up at least THREE times to Dr. R. Are we sure this is not IMHA because he tested positive for Coombs, can we retest for Coombs? All questions dismissed immediately. Dr. R had his agenda set on how he was going to treat Otis, and nothing was going to sway him, not even with Otis's life on the line. There is further testing that could have been done to absolutely rule out IMHA but that was never done.

During one of our first visits the only thing I thought was "great" was Dr. R sending our Otis's blood to Cornell University to see where his iron levels were at. Otis had an extremely low iron count at 9. Dr. R gave the full impression to my husband and I that this was the answer. He had an iron deficiency that caused his anemia. Dr. R started to give Otis monthly long-lasting iron injections. However, it did not take too long to find out this was not the cause and it was not helping with his RBC. First occurrence of "false hope."

I believe, due to the high dose of Prednisone and the fact Otis had to be slowly weaned off it, Otis went completely blind in mere hours on December 13th, as the Prednisone had accelerated his diabetes. Blindness came on suddenly and as a complete shock. No veterinarian ever mentioned this possibility, even though it is a common side effect of diabetes/anemia cases. We were instructed to consult an eye specialist to treat Otis. Furthermore, to monitor blood, BGVSC finally applied the

FreeStyle Libre technology to Otis after we had already been there for multiple hospitalizations. They applied it for us to better monitor his glucose without having to prick him for blood. Meaning they were running out of places to extract blood, since they were doing this over an extended period of time. This should have been discussed at the very beginning. However, this is just a classic example on how the doctors improvised as time went on. There was never a clear treatment plan. All we heard was "Otis is a complex case."

 BGVSC suggested "add on" treatments that they swore by. They have this apparent state of the art "oxygen chamber." Otis had about five 1 hour-long treatments in it, when suddenly one day, a nurse tech, not a doctor, told us that they received a "memo" stating the Freestyle Libre could potentially "blow up in the oxygen chamber." So, they had to keep taking it off and reapplying it. We saw no difference in Otis from these "oxygen sessions."

None of the specialists spent any quality time with us. They talked so fast and were in the room and out before you even blinked. Again, the longest a doctor there spoke with us lasted no longer than 5 minutes. All of our questions, or thoughts were immediately dismissed. We were left completely helpless. BGVSC at no time offered any guidance, support, or counsel. I had to consult with a third- party vet (out of state) to help me interpret test results and explain it so I could understand. I cannot understand a veterinarian at BGVSC who talks like they are on "speed" and then exits the room before you even realize the one-sided conversation has ended. The third-party vet we worked with to consult and get guidance felt it was a definite case of IMHA and the findings of scope were mere "coincidental." Hence why I kept asking about the IMHA and Coombs testing. I felt I was talking to the wall. It was beyond frustrating and I cannot explain how helpless my husband and I felt. I had reached out to some alternative specialty hospitals'; however, we are very limited geographically, especially when Otis RBC dropped to fatal levels. In addition, if we went somewhere else, they would have had to repeat all the testing. I could not put Otis through it again and we could not afford to pay for repeat testing.

In January 2020 Otis had the upper GI scope with BGVSC. The results of the upper scope stated Otis had an "ulcerated mass" in his upper intestines. Dr. R said it was a "risky" surgery as the mass was located right by his pancreas. Dr. R never got into detail about the risks involved or how any complications could be fatal. We were under impression it was "risky" due to the fact Otis was age 9 and already had multiple procedures. Enter Dr. M. Dr. M (co-owner of BGVSC) removed the mass that was found during the scope. It was Dr. R's impression this was causing the internal bleeding, even though the report of the GI indicated no fluids around the mass. Mind you, my husband and I never actually met Dr. M at any time in person. He telephoned us only at surgery time. I asked why this mass did not show up on ultrasounds, x-rays, CT scans, etc. I never got an answer. Dr. M merely called me to say, "We got it all out." It was a two-minute one-way conversation. I was never able to get the full clinical summary or any details on this "duodenal resection" surgery. What I do know is Otis developed a severe case of pancreatitis. Honestly, at this point, we are completely skeptical as to what has unfolded. Congruently, I diligently worked with my third party outside vet (not our primary vet) to try to put together exactly what happened to Otis. We were seeking alternative professional opinions.

We had one last procedure performed. Again, Dr. R failed to be upfront that this procedure carried a lot of controversy (a common theme) as I later learned from my own research. He placed tubes in Otis's stomach region to bypass the pancreas, essentially shutting it down to recover. Prior to the procedure, Dr. R stated a "resident" suggested "draining Otis's gallbladder to help offer relief." I would expect that to come from Dr. R and not a resident. Another "resident" recommended to Dr. R to get a kangaroo pump feeding tube. This way Otis could receive his food nutrients as fluids for a 12-hour continuous block while he slept. Otherwise, I would have been trying to administer his nutrition all day as he wouldn't eat on his own. All Dr. R said to us about the gallbladder was that "a lot of fluid came out." Also, I need to emphasize that after the procedure was complete, Dr. R told us he would have "a fresh start," regarding Otis's condition. Here we are again, another example of "false hope." There were so many times my husband and I embraced and cried in joy after hearing "promising news," that led to countless times of "false hope" to only having reality crash down on us.

It was that night when we came to visit Otis a nurse tech that we had never met nor seen before, came out and sat across from us in the lobby area. She stated she was there during the procedure and they got an "enormous amount of black sludge." This was so very concerning to us and caused great panic. Dr. R merely stated "fluids." Finding an "enormous amount of black sludge" is far different than "fluids." Why am I hearing this from a nurse tech and not Dr. R? This nurse tech also said that "Otis has a probable GI bleed." Let us just say that the room started to spin for us. I told her that the WHOLE reason for the removal of mass and Dr. M's surgery was to "STOP the internal bleeding in GI tract" as we were told over and over. How could Otis have a GI bleed now when we were told by Dr. M and Dr. R they got the source of the bleed removed? I felt almost like I was in the Twilight Zone and experienced major Déjà vu. We had done a 360 degree turn and were right back where we started.

When Otis was discharged, they gave us Peptamen, a fluid like Ensure for humans, for his nutrition via tube feeding. After two days I noticed he was leaking the fluid (not digested) through his anus. I called immediately and was told "this is normal, and they actually call it the 'Peptamen poopies.'" They made a joke of something VERY serious. They failed to care that Otis was losing (WHICH I SENT PICTURES OF TO THEM) a great deal of essential nutrition that he desperately needed to keep his strength AND to live. We should have been instructed to give subcutaneous fluids along with the tube feedings. They never gave me an answer about how much water to put in the feeding tube to keep Otis hydrated. I had to wait SIX hours for Dr. A to finally call me back regarding WATER. He stated Otis had been receiving subcutaneous fluids via IV but that he did not think it was necessary to give him more. Further indicating that the Peptamen should keep him hydrated (which it did NOT) and if I wanted to, to administer 10ML of water four times a day. I asked Dr. A in person if we could try an appetite stimulant with him to encourage him to eat. I even stated, "Can we try something like Entyce?" He dismissed that one too merely muttering "we could." But he never did. Here I am and I feel like I am the ONLY ONE fighting for my boy's life. Not one time did they ever make any attempt to collaborate or to even be on the same page with other doctors at the hospital. All of their responses/answers contradicted one another.

I put in at least four phone calls (and e-mails to the internal medicine department) while Dr. R was out of town. He left the day after Otis's tube placement. Dr. A took on the role as Otis's "vet" there. It was clear as day Dr. A and Dr. R had not consulted each other on Otis's case at all. Otis was leaking a clear fluid with a small amount of brown fluid. I was told by Dr. A that "this is normal and unless it smells foul it is not an infection." Two days after this conversation with him, I asked him to look at the pictures of Otis, and commented to him, does this look normal and not infectious to you?

As I stated before, Dr. R was gone for the next week. Apparently prior to leaving, he got the results from the "sludge" culture from Otis's gallbladder. Honestly, it was a fluke the results of culture were even communicated to me, but I happened to be meeting with Dr. A that day. A meeting I insisted on. He brought Dr. J in with him which I found odd. She remained mute and an orderly fixture in the corner, as he did not want to be alone in the room with just myself, clearly. I wonder why not? Dr. A stated Otis still had cancer. I told him Dr. R stated that Otis was "cancer free" that prior Thursday. There was absolutely no explanation or concern on these two strikingly different answers. He proceeded to state that "the fluid in Otis's gallbladder tested high in bacteria," but I was not provided any more information other than about an antibiotic they wanted to put him on. According to a company (that works alongside this vet hospital) this antibiotic "would either kill our dog or help him." We never received this type of warning from Dr. A. In addition, the dosage amount the vet hospital put on clinical summary was way off from what the pharmacy label stated. I called and spoke to a nurse tech who stated to follow the pharmacy label. I feel this was their way of making us go away permanently, prescribing our Otis this very powerful, very dangerous antibiotic. They were aware we were running out of money. As I had since day one, begged and pleaded for a payment plan to be told "they do not offer payment plans." Not until one of our final appointments, when I made a couple of strongly worded comments (not threatening by any means) did they approve a payment plan of sorts. What about the other thousands and thousands of dollars we ran around in a frenzy to collect? When striking up conversations with other clients in the lobby area, we learned about payment plans. We discovered that BGVSC offered payment plans the ENTIRE time, they just offered them selectively.

Otis was dying and three days later I had a vet come to our home to give Otis a shot so he could go to Heaven as I held him in my arms. He was such a fighter through all of this. A rare truth, BGVSC told my husband and I, that Otis was "a very strong little boy." He wanted to LIVE. He was the glue to our family. He knew how loved he was/is and all the plans we had for him and his little Sheltie brother, Maxwell. This veterinarian service that came to our home was referred by BGVSC and it was absolutely awful. The veterinarian rushed us. I wanted to hold my baby boy longer but he was whisked away from me and put in the trunk of her SUV. My husband and I stood on the driveway and watched our beloved boy being driven off. Otis died. And to be quite honest I died with him that day. I was in complete shock by all this and I will never get over the guilt of not being able to hold my boy longer.

We never got an answer as to what took our sweet boys' life. Not one doctor could provide a definitive answer or diagnosis: cancer, infection, auto-immune disease. We were always told "Otis is a complex case." I would think that would motivate the doctor to work harder, sadly no. The doctors were not interested in discovering more about the complexity of his condition. Otis was just another number to them. We did not receive ANY condolences. BGVSC knew we were going to be putting Otis to sleep, yet they had some employee call us to "confirm Otis's appointment with Dr. R that Monday." I was shaking, talk about horrible. My husband got on the phone and demanded to know if they "actually read any of the files at all," but the tongue-tied woman on the other line, per usual, could not answer the question!

To this day, I continue to research my sweet Otis's case trying to determine exactly what happened to my boy. He was ill but stable when we first brought him to BGVSC, but as time progressed, his condition seemingly went downhill under the care of BGVSC.

Pets admitted to hospitals are going to have serious ailments that can be easily diagnosed. Some pets arrive with complex cases that are more subjective. If humans can have multiple health ailments and be treated with transparency, why are pets any different? They are not immune from multiple issues happening at once. These "veterinarians" do not want to be bothered with additional work and accountability. Then when you lose your beloved pet they can rely on their "we told you it was a complex case." It is 2020, how are vets not trained appropriately in complex cases? And what exactly defines a complex case? It appears to us Otis's case was complex because they did not know how to handle it and did not want to be bothered. Therefore, we should have been referred to someone who could handle it. Veterinarians need to do what is in the pets' best interest. Dr. R, 100% could have referred Otis to another specialist. He made it clear he had his agenda set on how to treat Otis. We never had a chance. Looking back, we wish we would have taken him to my husband's alma mater UW-Madison. We are tormented on what we could/should have done. But the simple fact is we trusted, that as veterinarians, they would be able to help our boy and that they care about the animals they worked with. We falsely believed they became veterinarians because they truly "cared." Sadly, the veterinary world (as odd as it sounds) has become increasingly corrupt and veterinarian hospitals are financially motivated and morally lackluster.

Corporatization is hitting the veterinary industry. My husband and I saw upfront in full display the toxic lack of emotional intelligence. In my opinion, BGVSC is guilty of being only interested in hospitalizing your pet for profit. Specialty centers have high level specialists and superior tech tools granting them the ability to stabilize your pet. There are large financial windfalls in hospice…hospitalization, as pharmaceuticals can be administered adlib while under practitioner care. Please be vigilant about questioning all procedures and tests the doctors recommend. Yet keep in mind, they do not like these types of pet owners. To them, it is a waste of their time. As their mind and agenda has been set in a manner that does not always correlate with that of pet owners. Not their problem.

Our beautiful little family is now brutally broken. I cannot handle nice days. They are Otis days and I am SO angry that he is not here to enjoy, he SHOULD be. Otis was robbed of his right to enjoy and live out his senior years. His little brother, Maxwell, is very depressed too. He spends most of his time snuggling into Otis's special pillows. When I can get Maxwell to play, he chooses Otis's favorite toys. The house has become so quiet and lonely. I will never see my boy again; he is gone forever.

However, I am determined to get justice for my boy. I started a Facebook advocacy group. I was blown away by how many families came forward to share their story of how they believe BGVSC harmed their pet. It was quite shocking. I soon realized that this seems to be a national epidemic, revealing, I believe, unethical and immoral veterinary practices. Misleading, price gouging, incompetence, and flat-out blatant lies have corrupted the veterinary industry. It is my mission and goal to expose the dark side of the veterinary industry. I am not saying all vets are bad. What I am saying is there are too many "bad actors" and their fellow colleagues should be holding them accountable. The Veterinary Board, state licensing board, etc. needs to hold these vets accountable. What I want pet parents to take away from this is to never blindly trust your vet.

are not entitled to respect, they need to earn it. Stand your ground, ask questions, and be assertive. Allow yourself to have the option of a second opinion. Do not let the broken system do to you what it did to us. They manipulated us in our hours of darkness, at our most vulnerable.

I know Otis is watching down and proud of me for raising awareness. I know he is still with me everywhere I go. Love never dies. And I know we will be reunited again, one sweet day. We love you Otis.

Otis

CHAPTER FORTY-FOUR

MUTLEY'S STORY
Patricia Deeds Smith

My sweet dog Mutley died from what I believe was an overdose from a veterinarian that did not know anything about a very antiquated and dangerous drug called, Xylazine. It was used off label to sedate my 18 lb., Cockapoo, Mutley for a neuter surgery that never occurred. This drug is used for sedation of cattle, horses and deer.

He passed away within 15 minutes after I left him at the Waldorf Well pet clinic, run by a rescue group, called Last Chance Pet Rescue. I was not aware of this at the time. They called me and said they had lost my dog, I didn't understand, then, Dr Owoeye said he couldn't save him. I was in total shock, numb and screaming.

I left to go to the clinic to see if they had made a mistake.

His lifeless body lay on a table, I ran in unescorted to discover it was indeed true. My world changed that moment FOREVER. I was sick, and in a dream like state. I have suffered every day since. The mental and physical trauma has diminished my quality of life. I lost my wellbeing, my happiness, my trust in veterinary medicine from that moment on April 18th, 2008. Mutley did not get to live his life, he was only 2 years old. They immediately told me they did nothing wrong and the veterinarian had to get back to work. Their actions supported my belief that they overdosed my Mutley immediately. I didn't know what or how to do anything. I had a necropsy to show he was a healthy young dog. It showed he was a healthy dog.

I wrote the Maryland veterinary board who just dismissed the case. I sued the veterinarian and the owner of the clinic. I provided an expert witness in veterinary anesthesia from the University of Virginia veterinary school with over 40 years of experience. It was her opinion that this drug killed my dog, because it was an old and very dangerous drug. I believe the veterinarian used it from a large undiluted bottle.

I had the bottle tested by, Lloyds, the manufacturer of the drug. It showed to not be contaminated. The veterinarian's witness stated they always used this drug in other countries to sedate stray animals mostly cats for spay and neutered surgeries. They stated that they had never had any animal die from Xylazine ever.

The FDA had a list of adverse reactions to this drug, that included the death of horses, pigs, cows, deer, dogs and cats.

In court Dr Owoeye, the veterinarian who administered the fatal dose, stated he used it for pain management. He used this drug because he, likes it, it was cheap, and also for its analgesic properties. My expert witness stated it had no analgesic property whatsoever. I truly believe if my dog hadn't been given this drug, he would still be alive.

I was charged by the clinic for a surgery that never happened.

I felt I was ignored, lied to and treated as if I were a criminal.

No sympathy, just blame that I over fed my dog, and I was the reason he died. I am and will never be the same person I used to be I miss my dog every day. This veterinarian still continues to work on animals.I hope I bring light to an ongoing problem and danger that we as pet owners face every day. Mutley would have been 14 years old now.

CHAPTER FORTY-FIVE

BUDDY'S STORY
Julie Vita

I would like you to read my story about my Buddy.

This is the story of Buddy, an 18-month-old English bulldog who lost his life on July 8, 2020. That is the day that I lost my heart and my mind and the evening I started to blame myself for his death.

Prior to COVID-19, we wanted Buddy neutered. He went to our local vet for blood work and a pre-exam. He checked out perfectly. Then NY state became COVID-19 central and his scheduled surgery was cancelled. I should mention at this point that I currently have 2 other bulldogs and had 4 prior to Buddy. I mention this to illustrate the point that I know this breed.

On June 16, Buddy went to our local vet for his neuter. About 2 hours later she calls to say that she did not do the surgery and that Buddy has an elongated soft palate because after all, "All bulldogs do."

I guess I should tell that to my other bulldogs. I had one with that condition once and it is clearly evident. Buddy didn't suffer that way and the only true way to find out for sure is only when the dog is under sedation. She suggested I take Buddy to a specialist.

I booked a consultation for July 8. Due to COVID-19 I could not go in with my dog but had to wait in the car for the surgeon to call us. Within 10 minutes the surgeon had us on the phone presenting a life and death situation. Dr. Bentley stated that Buddy needed the elongated soft palate surgery, that he had averted saccules and his nares needed to be widened. Oh, and they would neuter him.

I was immediately switched to billing and promptly charged 7600 as a deposit on my credit card. Emotions and nerves were at an all-time high.

J.L. Robb

I would have agreed to any demand. I should mention that I tried to counter Dr. Bentley and tell her that Buddy had no symptoms of this. I had even emailed this prior to the appointment.

Her response was that I wasn't noticing. I trusted what I thought were professionals. Buddy made it through the operation just fine. His surgeon discussed taking him home in about 24 hours, his aftercare, and when he would need a follow-up.

I called the hospital at 9:30 that evening and Buddy was fine. Then, a little after midnight I got the call. They had been doing CPR for 10 minutes and he wasn't responding and what did I want them to do.

What could I have said? The attending vet could only say he probably aspirated. He was under their care, not mine. I waited a full week for anyone from the hospital to call me. No one did. I sent them an email telling them how I felt and that I would be informing my credit card company. Then they wanted to chat.

I have not spoken to them. They killed my dog through negligence, and I killed my dog by trusting them. I not only have the sorrow of losing him, but the pain of never saying goodbye, and the guilt for making the wrong decision.

Buddy

That establishment that took his life is Cornell Vet Specialty Hospital, supposed to be top notch. Only good at running up my credit card. My credit card company is disputing the charge for the whole amount. No amount of money will bring him back or ease my pain. This is Buddy's story.

CHAPTER FORTY-SIX

THE VETERINARY BOARD SWAMP

Veterinary Boards are not your friend. Like Police Unions, they are favorable to their own *kinds*; and hardly ever is the ruling in favor of the victim. The deck is stacked, so to speak and rulings are almost always in favor of the flawed, bad-actor veterinarian.

So what do you do if you believe your veterinarian harmed or killed your beloved pet and lied about it, tried to cover the malpractice up? Plenty, if you have the fortitude and a lot of patience with Veterinary Board rulings.

- File a complaint with your state veterinary licensing board. State licensing boards have the authority to discipline, including revocation of the veterinarian's license, though good luck with that. The boards rarely rule against the veterinarian. Similar to the Good Old Boys Club.
- A lawyer can negotiate a settlement or bring a lawsuit.
- Pursue your case in small claims court.

While pursuing in small claims court is less expensive because you need no lawyer and faster action, the punitive awards are much smaller. Courts consider your furbaby to be *personal property*, not a family member. This is beginning to change.

In the past, punitive awards for veterinary malpractice have been minimal, generally ranging from $100- $500. Since going after the pocketbook of these bad actors is about the only punitive measure one can take, it has proven to hardly be worth the effort. Some folk spend as much as $200,000, and the veterinary board sides with the veterinarian. There was a case in California in which the victims were awarded $39,000, but the legal fees were $250,000. They not only lost their pet to veterinary malpractice, they lost $211,000 in the painful process.

One might ask, "Why do the veterinary boards seem to always side with the veterinarians?"

The answer is simple: The veterinarians pay dues to the veterinary boards. Why would they want to discipline the breadbasket?

From avma.org: Membership Dues for Certified Veterinarians
Dues are determined by the Board of Regents.

- Membership is renewed on a calendar-year basis for all active Diplomates and expires December 31.
- ACVS bills members starting in November each year.
- Annual dues must be paid by, or mailed with a postmark no later than, January 31. After the January 31 postmark deadline, dues will increase by a set amount.
- If dues are not paid in full and postmarked by March 1, the following will occur.
  - Individuals certified prior to 2016 will lose active Diplomate status, but maintain board certification. Reinstatement requires payment of a reinstatement fee and dues for the current year.
  - Individuals certified in 2016 or later will lose active Diplomate status and board certification. Reinstatement requires payment of a reinstatement fee and completion of the applicable reinstatement process as detailed in the *Maintenance of Certification Policies and Procedures.*

From American Veterinary Medical Association web site avma.org
Subject: Complaints Against Veterinarians
Medicine is an art and a science. In medicine, given that we work with biological creatures, from time to time, outcomes are not what any of us

would have hoped. Sometimes undesired outcomes will prompt an owner to question the treatment provided by their veterinarian.

If you are unhappy with an outcome, talk to your veterinarian. After all, if someone had a problem with something you'd done, you'd want them to talk to you about it instead of avoiding you and telling everyone else, right? Many times, what's perceived as an error is actually a failure of communication. The vast majority of situations can be resolved with an open discussion.

If you find that you have remaining concerns, a peer review board may be an option. Some state veterinary medical associations have peer review boards, and their role varies by state. To see if your state has a peer review board and to find out how it functions, contact your state veterinary medical association.

Lastly, if you continue to have significant concerns, you may submit a complaint to the state veterinary licensing board, which enforces state license laws applicable to veterinarians. This is a legal process that may result in disciplinary action against a veterinarian's license or other remedies authorized by the license law.

Key words: May result in disciplinary action.

Following is a case from Kansas:

WE DIDN'T START THE FIRE

We brought our loved ones to you for compassionate care

You provided substandard care that caused permanent injury and death

We expected you to come to us, hat in hand, full of remorse and contrition, offering support in our time of crisis (and what should have been your time of crisis, as well)

You came to us with a cold indifference

We expected you to explain what happened, truthfully and with complete transparency

You came to us with a premeditated, duplicitous account of events

We never expected you to betray our trust

You not only betrayed our trust, but you also made it almost impossible to trust again

We filed complaints with our state boards of veterinary medicine, seeking appropriate redress

Our complaints were summarily dismissed, presumed to be without merit while trampling on our right to due process.

We know that 70-80% of all complaints filed with boards of veterinary medicine are dismissed

We know that about 70% of the cases our vet team reviews reveal veterinary negligence

We expected you to hear our cries, and advocate for us.

You failed to do so.

We expected justice for our lost loved ones.

You failed us again.

You heard your beleaguered, misunderstood colleagues begging for mercy.

You provided.

You left us brokenhearted, emotionally devastated and in search of peace and comfort

Your coldness and disinterest are glaring reminders of what corrupt miscreants you are

Your lack of ethics and moral compass will be exposed in a new book, soon to be released

Your lack of compassion and ineptitude will become well-known

The Jig Is Up!...DEAL WITH IT!

Scott Fine

ACKNOWLEDGEMENTS

1. Joey's Legacy's team of attorneys, who deal with an incredibly challenging area of law and consistently deliver successful results for our members.

2. Joey's Legacy's team of veterinary experts, who exhibit the courage and wisdom to confront their colleagues when veterinary negligence causes the permanent injury or death of the family members of our members.

3. Attorney Tiffany Bolling, one of Joey's Legacy's attorneys, who has worked tirelessly for animal advocacy and has provided countless pro-bono hours toward many of our projects.

4. David Anderson, admin of the Facebook group "Vets, Vets Now and RCVS Complaints", who is a contributor to this book and who deals with the same immorality and sleaze that we deal with in our vet mal group.

CPSIA information can be obtained
at www.ICGtesting.com
Printed in the USA
LVHW082047110321
681300LV00001B/1

9 781513 678795